Expression in the Performing Arts

Expression in the Performing Arts

Edited by

Inma Álvarez, Héctor J. Pérez and Francisca Pérez-Carreño

CAMBRIDGE
SCHOLARS

PUBLISHING

Expression in the Performing Arts,
Edited by Inma Álvarez, Héctor J. Pérez and Francisca Pérez-Carreño

This book first published 2010

Cambridge Scholars Publishing

12 Back Chapman Street, Newcastle upon Tyne, NE6 2XX, UK

British Library Cataloguing in Publication Data
A catalogue record for this book is available from the British Library

ISBN (10): 1-4438-1953-0, ISBN (13): 978-1-4438-1953-4

TABLE OF CONTENTS

List of Figures ix

Preface xi

Introduction 1

Part I: Theatre

Chapter One 16
Performer Subjectivity and Expression in Theatrical Performance
James R. Hamilton

Chapter Two 28
Performing and Rehearsing
Susan L. Feagin

Chapter Three 35
The Performer in the Empty Space
Sven Kristersson

Part II: Music

Chapter Four 50
Subjectivity Unhinged: *Elektra* in Zurich
David Levin

Chapter Five 66
Musical Expression and the Second Person Perspective
Antoni Gomila

Chapter Six 86
The Cognitive Value of Emotions in Musical Understanding
María José Alcaraz

Chapter Seven... 102
Expression and Expressing Oneself in Music:
An Approach towards the Expression of Subjectivity
in the Arts through the Artist Novel
Miguel Corella

Part III: Dance

Chapter Eight... 118
Dance, Dancers and Subjectivity: Some Questions about Subjectivity
and the Performing Arts
Graham McFee

Chapter Nine.. 151
Is a Word Dead When It Is Said?: Relationship Between Text
and Performance in Martha Graham's *Letter to the World*
Rosella Simonari

Chapter Ten 167
Café Reason's *Orpheus*: An Ethnographic Performative Investigation
of Butoh Dance in the United Kingdom
Paola Esposito

Part IV: Cinema

Chapter Eleven 182
Subjectivity, the Emotions, and the Movies
Noël Carroll

Chapter Twelve 203
How Do Documentaries Raise Emotions?
Salvador Rubio

Part V: On Performance

Chapter Thirteen 218
Aesthetic Distance in the Performing Arts
Alessandro Bertinetto

Chapter Fourteen 235
Witnessing the Pain of Others: How Performance Art Is Perceived
Doris Kolesch

Chapter Fifteen 247
The Silent Utopia: An Approach to Light and Colour in the Work
of Robert Wilson
Antonio García and Francisco Guillén

Chapter Sixteen 262
Queer Subjectivities: Practices of Embodiment, Politics
of Experimentation and Contact Pedagogies through Performance
Judit Vidiella

Contributors.. 277

Index.. 281

LIST OF FIGURES

Figure 3-1 Performance of *Gilgamesh* by Sven Kristersson.
Photo by Jean Hermanson.. 37
Figure 9-1 Sections in Martha Graham's *Letter to the World.* 152
Figure 10-1 Rehearsal of *Orpheus*, 2008. Photo by Dariusz Dziala...... 169
Figure 10-2 Rehearsal of *Orpheus*, 2008. Photo by Dariusz Dziala..... 170
Figure 10-3 Rehearsal of *Orpheus*, 2008. Photo by Dariusz Dziala...... 175
Figure 12-1 Luis Buñuel, *Las Hurdes*, 1932... 209
Figure 12-2 Luis Buñuel, *Las Hurdes*, 1932... 210
Figure 12-3 Luis Buñuel, *Las Hurdes*, 1932... 210
Figure 15-1 Robert Wilson, *Portrait, Still life, Landscape*, 1993.
Boymans-van Beuningen Museum, Exhibit Room 8, Rotterdam.
Photo by Jannes Linders 254
Figure 16-1 Lecture-performance at "The Expression of Subjectivity
in the Performing Arts" Conference, November 26th, 2008,
Valencia 266
Figure 16-2 Body-crossing workshop on the re-de-construction
of identities. Festival Las Otras Caras del Planeta [The Other Faces
of the Planet Festival] (LOCP), April 21st–29th, 2006, Gijón. Photo
by Judit Vidiella.. 271

PREFACE

This volume is a selection of papers that were presented at an international conference, 'The Expression of Subjectivity in the Performing Arts' held at the Polytechnic University of Valencia (Spain), in November 2008. The editors of this book were the conference organisers and the editors of the online proceedings.

One of the main reasons for the conference was the major conceptual reorientation of postgraduate academic studies of performative disciplines at several universities. Theatre, music, dance, and even film studies, had been approached almost exclusively from theoretical perspectives, i.e. rarely were artistic practices included in the core research work of a doctoral dissertation. However, especially in the last decade, doctoral projects on theatre, cinema, music and dance have given way to new forms of doctoral theses in which performative art practice itself has become central to these projects and various research strategies. The performing arts are forcing us to rethink the current models of investigation, as it happened previously from the influence of other disciplines such as anthropology. Today, academic institutions such as the Sibelius Academy, the Orpheus Instituut or the Polytechnic University of Valencia, in the field of music, or the Institute for Theaterwissenschaft of the Freie Universität in Berlin in theatre and the University of Wales and University of South Australia in the performing arts curriculum are consolidating their strategies in performative research through a variety of options and academic formulas that are still fairly experiential and open. At the conference we did not encourage attention to methodological aspects of research, but to issues arising for researchers devoted to the performative phenomena, primarily through aesthetic reflection. The conference brought together established academics, research students and artists from a range of disciplines to debate current issues around various kinds of performative events. Therefore, contributions to this volume reflect academic discourses but also some performative discourses emanating from the field of artistic practice.

The book is divided into five parts corresponding to the different performing arts discussed at the conference: theatre, music (including opera), dance, cinema as well as other general issues relating to performance. The papers explore the characteristics and particular challenges of aesthetic engagement with various kinds of performances. They focus in particular on how subjectivity emerges in the theory and practice of the performing arts, and on how recent discussion on different fields, can help to articulate new ways of understanding our experience of artworks. The introduction to these parts offers an overview of some past and present philosophical concerns regarding the performing arts as well as a summary of the points addressed by the different authors. Readers are presented with similar issues to contemporary debates on art as well as unique issues to the performing arts, such as identification of authorship, technical realization, ontological status, fictionality, or spectators' role.

The purpose of the book is to capture current ongoing thinking on the performing arts that can give insights to philosophers, art historians, art critics and artists. It is hoped that this collection will stimulate further reflection on key issues around expression in the performing arts and contribute to continuing the construction of new knowledge on aspects of these arts and our experiences of them.

The editors would like to thank Michele Cometa, Kari Kurkela, Derek Matravers, Christoph Menke, Vicente Ponce, José Pavía Cogollos, Julie Van Camp and Gerard Vilar for their invaluable assistance in selecting the original papers that were presented at the conference, many of which have made possible the present volume. We would like to acknowledge that the conference would not have been possible without the support of the Ministerio de Educación in Spain (project funds FFI2008-00750 and FFI2008-01705-E/FILO). Finally, our gratitude also goes to Stephen P. Hasler for his careful reading and editing of some parts of the book.

INTRODUCTION

The complex nature of the performing arts demands multiple levels of philosophical attention. It requires the study of their objects, that is, of both specific works and their particular instances realised in performative events; reflection on the processes of creation, performance, and reception; as well as consideration of the roles of the relevant agents involved—author, performer, and spectator.

A dominant view of the performing arts is that performances are tokens of a type, in other words, instances of works of art. Performances are generally considered the outcome of the reading, interpretation or realisation of a work which exists independently of its multiple instances. This conception assumes an identity correlation between works and types, as held by Richard Wollheim (1981). Probably, our understanding of the nature of performative arts is related to other shared ideas about art *tout court*. Among these ideas figure prominently the notion of a work of art as the finished product of an artist's—composer, painter, choreographer, writer, etc.—creativity. Every realisation of the original work is understood to entail an interpretation of that work which is put usually on the stage for an audience. The intentions of the author determine the identity of the work, thus good performances or tokens of a piece are the result of the correct interpretation of the author's intentions, which are in most cases recovered through the reading of the instructions specified by the artist in a script or notation. Particularly, expressive intentions determine expressive properties of the work and its instances, and therefore provoke affective responses from the public. For example, some kinds of written musical works seem to fit this model well; every performance being an instance of a previously established work, so the conductor of an orchestra and the musicians join forces to realise a composer's piece.

This understanding, however, is not without problems. First of all, a performative work of art is portrayed as an artefact whose properties are to be identified in an experience of it. In the performing arts the properties of the work—notoriously their aesthetic and expressive properties—are known through their performances. If we take also into consideration the acquaintance principle—by which an artwork, as artwork, is not known unless one has had a direct experience of it—then, in any understanding of the performing arts, performances are as necessary to works as works to performances. So, it seems we are caught in a loop when referring to the properties of the performing arts, since there is no way to experience them without a performance, and a performance is said to be of a work if it realises some properties the work essentially possesses.

In most artistic traditions there are author's written indications about what properties the performance should have (with the exception of dance, where documentation of works' specifications has been rare). In addition to prescribing to a greater or lesser extent how the performance should look, sound and feel, there are conventions and traditions about the properties relevant to different artworks. However, it is only when the properties are displayed in the performance that we experience the work as art, get to know it, enjoy it and are able to appreciate and evaluate it fully. More to the point, it is not that a property exists as something just by prescription of a creator artist, but rather that the property of the work is identified in the experience of the performance, hence in the experience of the work. It may be enlightening to refer here also to Wollheim's (1980) account of painting, where representational or expressive properties of the work could not be accesible to the author prior to the activity of painting itself, since it is only artists' *fulfilled intentions* that determine the representational or expressive content of the work. In the same sense, it can be argued that only when the performance takes place does it makes sense to speak about properties of the work. With respect to this point, Graham McFee (Chapter 8) distinguishes between artistic appreciation of the properties of a dancework and the distinctive contribution of the dancers whose particular characteristics might not belong to the work they are performing.

There is a wide variety of positions regarding the relation between the properties of the performance and the properties of the work. They range from those holding a more empirical stance, like James Hamilton's (2007) claim that theatrical performances are works of art, to more conceptual ones, like Graham McFee's (1992) view that performances are instances of works. In any case, what is commonly agreed is that every performance is a specific object of artistic and aesthetic experience and judgement, whether or not it is an ontological type on its own, and this is precisely what is of relevance to the topic of the present collection.

Despite its centrality for the performing arts, the general debate between works and their instances is not directly entertained in the chapters of this book but it certainly figures in the background of all. Every work of art is an artifact created to be perceived, interpreted, and taken into consideration in different ways at different times by different kinds of spectators. What is specific to the performing arts is that the work is previously conceived, and usually rehearsed, in order to repeatedly take place later on in front of an audience. In addition, it is characteristic that performers share space and time with the spectators of the piece. The aim of this book is to analyse issues surrounding how expression occurs in the performing arts from the point of view of their particular nature.

Two contributions share an interest in expression, with a reflection and exploration of the general response to and the aesthetic experience of the performing arts. Alessandro Bertinetto (Chapter 13) focuses on the nature of performance, addressing the nature of performing arts from the point of view of the experience they call for. He criticizes Erika Fischer-Lichte's claim (2004) that distance and disinterestedness cannot characterize performing arts, and that, contrary to the rest of the arts, the performing arts are events, actions really performed by the actors, singers, etc. in the presence of a public; therefore, there is no difference between meaning and action, fiction or illusion and reality, work and public, and the rest of dichotomies in play when dealing with disinterestedness. Since the avant-garde, performance art exploited what was always part of the nature of the performing arts: an artist may be a performer; improvisation is a form of creation; and the public can interact and affect the work. Since the audience is also participant, it makes no sense to call for distance. Bertinetto criticizes the idea that performances do not represent or express anything but themselves, the idea that improvisation precludes the existence of a previous work, and more to the core, the idea that performances cannot be experienced with detachment, that is, aesthetically. He maintains that participation does not preclude the spectator to having a disinterested experience of what is happening, that is to say, considering it for its own sake, and not functionally. However, Bertinetto argues for a logical and not psychological version of disinterestedness which entails considering works of art out of the stream of life, in the sense of appealing to imagination and the play of faculties, instead of action or instrumental reasoning. Radically Bertinetto claims that it is possible to aesthetically contemplate any objects and events, but getting rid of your aesthetic attitude in your experience of them leads to the concealing of their artistic character.

Susan Feagin (Chapter 2) also refers to the nature of performances exploring the differences between performance and Peter Kivy's claim in *The Performance of Reading: An Essay in the Philosophy of Literature* that a silent reading to oneself of a novel or a short story is a performance. She criticizes Kivy's idea, and comments on her own experience as spectator of a theatrical rehearsal with puppets. For her, performance is informed by several substrates of activities that are internalized by performers, while Kivy asserts that the performance appears in the first reading. Feagin concedes to Kivy that reading is not different from many other actions we perform, but in the sense that philosophers are wont to describe any action as an action one performs. Differences are argued with respect to the goal of the agents involved: the goal of a performer is a presentation, while the goal of the appreciator of the work is understanding and appreciating it. The most striking differences between reading and performance however are the diverse processes to which a rehearsal serves for the preparation of a performance. Feagin argues that the material of a work requires a lot of "starting and stopping, trying out and reconsidering" during rehearsals, a pretty different process from the continuity of reading.

The process of rehearsal is precisely the focus of Paola Esposito's study of butoh dance (Chapter 10). Esposito highlights the importance of attending to the production process during the creation of a work for our understanding of the performing arts. She follows Dwight Conquergood's (2002) suggestions on researching with proximity, i.e. closing the gap between analysis and action, rather than with distance. With this in mind, she offers a personal account of how she used participant observation during the rehearsals of the piece *Orpheus* by the butoh dance theatre company Café Reason. Esposito parallels commonalities between doing ethnography and the making of a performance as processes that involve difficult dialogues and share a sense of the unexpected, the unfamiliar, danger, curiosity, commitment and trust. Using ethnographic methods, she investigates the relationship between the peculiar use of language and the body in training (Butoh-fu), concluding that the different roles or modalities of participation among performers intersect to create the subjective paradigm of Butoh dance and of performance.

Before we continue, readers should know that we have included the practice of film making as a performative activity; although some of the characteristics of the performing arts mentioned at the beginning of this introduction are very different from those of films. Films are artistic objects that contain drama, live music, dancing, but, nevertheless, they have not been systematically considered as performative artistic practices. There are differences in the creative conception of the pieces (scriptwriter, filmmaker, producer), the mechanic reproduction of the work instances, and the actual experience of it since film actors never share time or space with the espectators during its artistic development. In addition, the living dimension of the representation is replaced by the projection of a film. There are however some important reasons for deeming cinema as a performing art. Since the earlier debates about the artistic nature of cinema, cinema was compared to theatre (Benjamin 1934). After all, cinema is mostly practised as a narrative artform, in which the representation of the events is realized by acting. Moreover, as a relevant consequence, movies, unlike literature or paintings, use the human body as their main vehicle of expression. In this sense, cinema becomes very close to the performing arts. Cinematic practices are clearly at the borders of this category, becoming an interesting case for reflection on performative events that complements and enriches the debate, even when our perspective is focused on the most cinematic aspects of it.

One of the topics explored by several authors in this collection is the specific contribution of the agents involved in the processes of the performing arts. We have mentioned already the artistic merit attributed to the author of the works. An example of this is when a composer writes down a score, gives instructions over its executions, assumes many implicit conventions and envisages, to some extent, how it will be received and interpreted by the listener. Acknowledging that performing works of art are to be performed does not imply that the authority, and responsibility, of the creator with respect to her work disappears. Indeed, McFee (Chapter 8) establishes a distinction between responsibilities of artists as creators of the work and dancers as interpreters, and contends that dancers are not artists, as they are not—in most cases—makers of the artwork.

A central theme related to authorship in the performing arts revolves around authors' intentions. Several ideas have been advanced. An author cannot properly have intentions about every property of the performance, hence of the work. Authors do not control wholly how their work will be executed, how it will look or sound every time it is performed, on this stage or concert hall, and with this public. Even when the work has been recorded with precision, performative texts have been subject to interpretation, to a reproductive cycle that has allowed the intervention of improvisation and imagination to a greater or lesser degree throughout history. Thus, original creative intentions might be more or less respected, more or less fulfilled in performance. On the other hand, it may be said that it is obviously true for every work of art that the author's intentions do not determine completely the aspect of the work, works of a unique token included. But there is something more illustrative about intentionality in general and the social character of it in the performing arts. The author's main intentions assume that the work will be performed, hence that others are to direct the piece, act the roles, design the costumes, attend the spectacle, and so on. Normally the production process is a cooperative enterprise in which all individuals involved contribute to the completion of a work. The responsibilities of these agents inevitably exceed the loyalty to the author's intentions in that every performance will be judged for itself. The expressive and aesthetic properties of a performance can be critically appraised independently of the original properties assigned to the piece; therefore artistic or aesthetic value is then attributed to agents beyond the author. The important point here is that the intentionality of the work is one to which all contribute, with bigger or smaller responsibility, and which is imposed to all of them. And clearly the main intention is expressive.

In addition to the collaborative authority of performing works of art, it has been pointed out that there is a characteristic interaction between performers—acting, representing or executing a work—and the audience—appreciating and enjoying a work. On the one hand, performers act in front of and for an audience, intending to grasp their attention, to be understood, and to arouse emotional and other responses. On the other hand, observers react to the presence and actions of the performers which may affect the performance. How the audience is addressed, how the audience responds, and how the work is affected by the response is central to the very nature of the performing arts. There is a general recognition of the fact that the roles of author, performer and spectator sometimes overlap. For instance, in music, when there is a chance for the performer to create, as defended by Alessandro Bertinetto (Chapter 11), in the practice of musical improvisation, or when the audience has a chance to participate in the work and become a performer, as suggested by Miguel Corella (Chapter 7). It could also be that a single person controls the whole process of production, for instance, a composer of music, who writes the piece and conducts the orchestra, or better, writes a solo and plays it, becoming creator and performer at the same time.

Turning now to expressive intentions, this collection of essays reflects very specifically on the way expressions of subjectivity are to be understood in the context of the performing arts. Expression through performances is analized in relation to the way the work is conceived, the work as presented to the audience, and the affective responses the work elicits in the audience. The expressive conception of a work is exemplified in Rosella Simonari's essay on dance (Chapter 9). She examines the interaction of Emily Dickinson's poetry with the dancing in a choreographic piece by Martha Graham. Simonari produces an account on how the spoken lines are in many cases used to portray and highlight the mood changes of the different characters. Expressivity in performance is discussed by James Hamilton (Chapter 1) and Francisco Guillén and Antonio García (Chapter 15). However, while Hamilton searches for expression in the basic performative components of theatre, in the actors, Guillén and García focus on the expressive role of illumination and chromatism. Hamilton presents a series of intuitions about this issue. The first intuition he comments on is that actors in narrative performances convey (rather than express) the feelings and moods of their characters. Another is that spectators and performers may differ about the moods and feelings of given moments in a performance. A third one concerns the fact that when an actor varies his physical orientation to the audience, what he says will have a different impact on the way spectators experience the mood and feeling of the moment. The fourth intuition is that recognizing the role of causal inducements in theatrical performances is connected to the physicality of performances. Hamilton states finally that the recognition of at least some of the foregoing is required for an appreciative response to any particular performance. In contrast with this point of view, Guillén and García dissolve the primacy of the performer and his word in the theatrical narrative and open up its meanings. They analyse in particular the role light and colour play in the work of Robert Wilson. Their proposal is that these elements liberate individual spectators' visual thoughts into a contemplative emotional state whether it is a dance, theatre or cinematic event.

A historical approach to the origin of the expressed emotions in performance is offered here by Miguel Corella (Chapter 7). Corella starts by considering different manifestations of Expressionism critical to the developments of the avant-garde, to go on examining Romantic music, as presented in different literary visions. Corella explains how artist novels contrast the subjectivity of the creator with the objectivity of the work, its autonomy from its author. He points out a paradoxical situation in the expression of subjectivity: it appears to be "a process of disindividualisation" where one's own subjectivity is partly recognised through the appropriation of performative structures or patterns. The expressive gesture might come from a conductor or a soloist but also, in some popular instances, from each of the spectators who are compelled to become performers themselves by singing and dancing along. He illustrates this by reminding us of the tradition initiated by Plato's theory of poetic inspiration where the artist is presented as a vehicle of expression of a divine or demonic force. In the literary tradition the artist appears as a creator of original and subjective forms that seem to obey a necessity and are able to be immediately recognised as rules.

Nöel Carroll (Chapter 11) contributes to this discussion with a critical account of the history of the theory of motion pictures, showing how the discourse of subjectivity entered cinema studies as a concept employed by Althusserian-Lacanians. After tracing certain cognitivist approaches to different levels of the engagement of affect by motion pictures, Carroll defends, against Marxist-psychoanalists, a cognitive account of the role of emotion in film. He explains his concept of criterial prefocusing which specifies that for the elicitation of a certain emotion from the audience, a movie maker must provide scenes and sequences with the right properties as salient. Carroll's concerns about radical cognitivism are echoed by Salvador Rubio (Chapter 12) who explores the complementary side of the fiction paradox related to documentaries. Carroll concludes with a discussion of the ways in which recent psychological approaches to the moral emotions can enrich research into the emotional shaping of subjectivity by the moving picture media. Carroll completes this cognitive account with a reference to moral emotions, in order to provide further insight into the subjectivity of the viewers. A programme for future investigation should attend to developments in moral psychology. An account of our moral emotional responses should contemplate them as evaluative judgements of certain situation without necessarily involving rational deliberation.

Until now, the issue of responses to moral emotions has been mostly discussed in relation to performance art, probably since the corporeality of the theatre brings a different dimension to the experience, opening up wider possibilities of transgression during performance. Doris Kolesch's contribution to this volume (Chapter 14) looks precisely at the moral emotions prompted by the representation of pain. Herbet Blau has pointed out that "the bodily sacrifice of the subject" (1992, 125) is not a new phenomenon of the avant-garde but one that links contemporary performances with ancient theatre. In a compelling account of pain in performative events, Kolesch investigates how responses to the presentation of pain in performance art—in which performers are effectively suffering pain—differs form the representation of pain by other means, pictorial or cinematographic. Kolesch argues that in observing these events, spectators not only perceive, but also sense and get affected by pain. Compassion, indignation and the like are inevitable responses when perceiving the suffering of others. But, as Blau had suggested, the aestheticized violence in the theatre might also lead to desensitizing and even to transforming a passive audience into a participating one which becomes the inflictor of pain. Kolesch acknowledges the fact that the public is not mere spectator but witness and participant. However, she is more interested in those cases in which response turns into responsibility rather than real action.

The relation between reality and fiction is another topic mentioned with respect to different performing arts. Doris Kolesch (Chapter 14) emphasises the non-fictional character of performance art. Paola Esposito (Chapter 10) refers to the influences between the real and fictional activities of performers. Salvador Rubio (Chapter 12) holds that documentary films, though assertive in character, prompt in the spectator responses not dissimilar to those caused by fictional cinema. In fact, he defends that rhetorical mechanisms in documentary films are basically the same as those used by fictional works in order to arouse emotional responses in the viewer. On the part of the viewer, he argues that imagination plays the same role, even if it is beliefs and not merely non-asserted thoughts which are set in motion to understand and emotionally experience the work.

Music has been, without doubt, the artistic field that has led to the most nuanced reflection on the aspects of expression. For centuries there has been a strong tension between advocates of musical formalist purity, exemplified by instrumental music, and those who regarded it as the most expressive art considering the example of vocal music. For the vast majority of musicians, expression is fundamentally a difficult goal, only reached when all the technical resources of the instruments are fully mastered. For thinkers, this concept is also difficult to address, without falling into reductionism (and here the non-representational character of the music has been a serious problem.) One of the greatest contributions to the evolution of theories of musical expression has been based on some consensus about the expressive nature of music. This has led to suggestive reflections, from those about the role of the imagination to the interesting hypothesis of the similarities between music and the world as the origin of experiencing expression.

Three contributions to this volume connect directly with some discussions in this context. David Levin (Chapter 4) turns to some recent thinking about presence and mediation in our engagement with operatic performance to answer this question. Antoni Gomila (Chapter 5) and María J. Alcaraz (Chapter 6) defend the value of music in the capacity of the performances to arouse emotions in the listeners. Gomila explains musical expression in terms of an expressing agent, actual or imagined; implying an interpretative activity on the audience's part that fails to explain the more immediate and non-reflective experience of expression in music. He argues that the second-person point of view permits the attribution of expressive intentions in interactive situations, in which there isn't an interpretation in terms of a third person or a deduction from the behaviour of the expressing subject, but a spontaneous reaction on the part of the second person to certain perceptible features in the situation. Gomila defends that the second person is not reducible to a first person point of view, as it is not always necessary or sufficient to identify with the expresser in order to understand expression. The listener is ready to be emotionally affected by the way the music sounds, that is, to recognize intentional expressive attitudes in it. What count as the ground of musical expressivity is that music affects us emotionally; there is no further necessity of logical or analogical justifications. Since music is a human activity musicians intend to ostensibly express through it, looking for the acknowledgment of their intention. The audience reciprocally perceives music as the product of an agent, and respond to it spontaneously. Even atonal expressionist music can be explained within this interactive framework as music that seeks to express the experience of crisis, and revolt against the Bourgeois art and world.

Alcaraz clarifies the issue of emotional experiences in music by suggesting that to be moved by music does not entail that the music is expressing some inner state. Furthermore she admits, as formalists do since Hanslick, that absolute music—not having representational character—is not capable of expressing mental conditions. So we respond emotionally to certain properties of music as we sometimes respond emotionally to other abstract arts, and here she mentions dance, but painting could also be a case in point. Even in representational arts as literature or cinema, emotional responses cannot be completely warranted by propositional or representational content. Alcaraz finds Peter Kivy's suggestion about the syntactic relevance of expressive properties of music to be insufficient for an account of how emotions are related to music. The expressive character some pieces of music exhibit may only be acknowledged when we respond emotionally and properly to their qualities. As in literature, emotional responses help to organise the content, to fix attention on some character or other, or to provoke expectations about the story. Finally, in responding emotionally to music we may be in a better position to wholly understand and appreciate it.

Two further articles by Sven Kristersson (Chapter 3) and Judit Vidiella (Chapter 16) present a very singular view of performance and text. Kristersson's ideas relate to a performance where he shows the structure of a research developed in and through performance. The author, a professional singer, puts forward subjectivity as a narrative choice in the exposition of his own work, an artistic research process included in a doctoral thesis. Kristersson explains the project, developed around the *Gilgamesh* epic in collaboration with Karim Rashid, an stage director based in Malmö. Using Shakespearean traditions as described in Peter Brook´s *The Empty Space*, where scenic communication is established using verbal imagery rather than a stage set and props, Kristersson embarks on the embodiment of a series of performances and a subsequent "reflective interpretation of the interpretations." For this, he makes use of artistic methods related to various musical, theatrical and literary traditions as well as the myth of Orpheus as analytical tools. Similarly unique, in her discourse, Vidiella argues that as performers, we dis/un-cover ourselves by putting our own selves at risk and into play, manifesting the power relations between spectators and actors. She maintains that, as spectators, we attend a performance in order to inhabit zones of alternative subjectivities, which we put into play in and outside of the act. Vidiella concludes that this allows us to confront macropolitical and micropolitical subjectivities in a concrete time and space.

The contributions in this book are arranged in five parts which reflect writers' interests on particular performing arts. As we have tried to articulate here, many of the issues discussed within each part clearly present relevant comments to other parts of the book, so readers will be able to make many connections between them.

Part I offers three chapters with a focus on the theatre. In the opening chapter, "Performer subjectivity and expression in theatrical performance," James R. Hamilton looks at the role of the physicality of performers in the inducement of moods and feelings in theatre audiences. Susan Feagin's essay "Performing and rehearsing" considers differences between theatrical performances and rehearsals. This first part ends with a more practical study "The performer in the empty space" by Sven Kristersson on how to communicate historical songs and poetry to contemporary audiences.

The four essays in Part II direct the attention to the world of music. David Levin's initial essay, "Subjectivity unhinged. *Elektra* in Zurich," bridges the discussion between expressing in theatre and music as it is focused on the expression of subjectivity in opera. He examines in particular in Martin Kusej's contemporary production of *Elektra,* asking about how we might delineate and theorize the distinctions between textual, performative, and mediated subjectivities. In Chapter Five, Antoni Gomila points to the interactive character of expression in music with his essay "Musical expression and the second person perspective." He acknowledges the complexity of the expression of emotions in this medium and articulates extrinsic and intrinsic aspects of them. In the text that follows, "The cognitive value of emotions in musical understanding," María J. Alcaraz continues the discussion focusing on listeners' emotional stimulation by musical works. She provides an explanation of how emotional responses may have a role in the understanding of music. This part of the book closes with an essay by Miguel Corella, "Expression and expressing oneself in music." He, however, approaches the expression of subjectivity in the arts from artist novels, in particular those featuring musicians (performers and composers.)

Part III is dedicated to dance, a performing art that encompasses multiple arts. Graham McFee's chapter, "Dance, dancers and subjectivity" describes danceworks as "performables" which differ in ways relevant to expressiveness or appreciation. He focuses on the distinction between artistic appreciation of danceworks, which involves attention to the features or properties of the work itself, and the distinctive contribution of the dancers who instantiate them. The other two chapters on dance are dedicated to analysing expression in specific works. In her article "Is it a word dead when it is said?" Rosella Simonari analyses the relationship between text and performance in Martha Graham's dance piece *Letter to the World*. Utilising ethnographic methodology, in "Café Reason's *Orpheus*" Paola Esposito looks for evidence of whether the production of a Japanese Butoh dance affects the participants' notions of self and body identities.

In Part IV, Noël Carroll's text "Subjectivity, emotions and the movies" opens up considerations of expression from the point of view of the theory of motion pictures. He argues that emotions are, compared to processes of rational deliberation, very fast decision-making routines. A second text in this part by Salvador Rubio proposes a questioning essay "How do documentaries raise emotions?" in order to explore the complementary side of the fiction paradox related to documentaries. Rubio's work focuses on the film *Las Hurdes. Tierra sin pan,* by Luis Buñuel, and shows how the viewer becomes caught at times in conflicting emotions which converge to give a feeling of discomfort.

The final part of this volume concentrates four final essays that consider, in diverse ways, how expression occurs in the performing arts. Alessandro Bertinetto addresses the nature of these arts from the point of view of the involvement of the audience with "Aesthetic distance in the performing arts". However, Bertinetto still defends the relevance of the concept of aesthetic distance in the experience of the performing arts with a logical rather than psychological version of disinterestedness. In the following chapter, "Witnessing the pain of others," Doris Kolesch invites us to reflect more specifically on audiences' experiences of and reactions to the depiction and demonstration of pain in performance art. Chapter fifteen, "The silent utopia" by Antonio García and Francisco Guillén, offers readers yet another focus on significative aspects of production processes in theatrical performances commenting on the role of illumination and chromatism in the work of Robert Wilson. The book ends with a truly performative script, "Queer subjectivities," by Judit Vidiella where she indicates the adoption of different roles of gender stereotypes and rhetoric in order to reveal how everyday discourse and behaviour are subjected to performative conventions.

Works cited

Blau, Herbet. 1992. *To All Appearances: Ideology and Performance*, New York: Routledge.

Benjamin, Walter. 2008 [1935]. *The Work of Art in the Age of Mechanical Reproduction*. London: Penguin.

Hamilton, James. 2007. *The Art of Theater*, Malden & London: Blackwell.

McFee, Graham. 1992. *Understanding dance*. London: Routledge.

Wollheim, Richard. 1980. *Art and its Objects*. 2nd. ed. Cambridge: Cambridge University Press.

PART I:

THEATRE

CHAPTER ONE

PERFORMER SUBJECTIVITY AND EXPRESSION IN THEATRICAL PERFORMANCE

JAMES R. HAMILTON

In this chapter, I focus primarily on theatrical performances of narratives. The contents of such performances are stories. Stories are the representations of sequences of actions put in motion by agents. This narrowness of focus is put in place in order to help get us started. But the view I propose has more general application.

The problem I will address is how theatrical performances generate moods and feelings apart from those moods and feelings that are generated by the grasp of the contents in a performance. For example, a spectator may feel sad for a character's plight and even at the resolution of the plot but still think the overall mood of the performance is light-hearted. And she may not be able to point to anything particular in the content of the performance that would justify her overall characterization. The inability fully to explain felt reactions to whole performances is fairly common. And, it seems, it has more to do with facts about performances themselves than with facts about the contents of performances.

Here, I offer an explanation of this phenomenon by emphasizing the role that the physicality of performers plays in the inducement of moods and feelings in spectators.

What seems obvious

Expression of emotion is central to theatrical performances of narratives in some way. Here are five widely believed claims about the relation between expression and performance.

Actors in narrative performances convey the feelings and moods of their characters.

It is appropriate to describe theatrical performances using emotion and mood terms.

What actors do to convey characters' feelings and moods is connected to what justifies spectators' ascription of emotion and mood terms to theatrical performances.

The physicality of the relation between performers and spectators has something to do both with how character feeling and mood is conveyed and with what justifies spectators' ascriptions of feelings and moods to performances.

Recognition of at least some of the foregoing is required for an appreciative response to any particular performance.

In this chapter, I will consider only the first four of these claims. The fifth takes us beyond the current topic.

I will regard these claims as intuitions. By calling them "intuitions," I mean they are claims many of us are prepared to believe before we engage in critical reflection. They can be wrong, the results of mere prejudice. But they often afford a place from which to start a discussion. And, of course, they are often right; which helps explain why they afford such a place. In the next section, I will discuss each of the first four claims in greater detail.

Four intuitions in more detail

1. Why should we use the term "convey" in (1) rather than "express" when talking about actors? Doesn't the latter make better sense? The idea that actors "convey" their characters' moods and emotions sounds flat. And good acting, in particular, seems correctly characterized as involving the *expression* of emotions, not their mere conveyance.

However, substituting "express" for "convey" in (1) is a mistake. If to express a mood or feeling requires actually being in that mood or having that feeling, then puppets do not express them. Yet spectators sense emotions and moods when observing puppets. Moreover, in narrative performances it is characters who express emotions and suffer moods. And the fact that characters express emotions or suffer moods does not entail that actors express emotions or suffer moods. But, what about *good* acting? It might help here to think for a moment about one species of bad acting. Actors sometimes talk about something they call "committing to the action." The difference between performing an action in that manner and failing to do so can be demonstrated, but it is best explained by reference to several reasons for which actors may fail to be committed to an action. They may fail because they are nervous about what they are supposed to do. They may fail because they do not actually understand what they are doing and why. But, generally, they fail when they are self-conscious for some reason.

The self-consciousness of which I write here is not to be confused with self-awareness. For example, if the style of performance calls for it, an actor can be self-aware and aware of her relation to spectators without being self-conscious. Moreover, self-consciousness can undermine a deliberately self-aware performance as easily as it can undermine acting/performance in any other kind of style. All it takes is for the performer to be uncomfortable acknowledging her relationship to spectators.

This species of acting failure is often obvious to spectators. When an actor is self-conscious about what she is doing, her unguarded mannerisms reveal her sense of discomfort. This is why a fair amount of actor-training involves learning how not to be self-conscious in the performance of those actions that will become the routine developed in rehearsals and performed in front of others. "Committing to the action" is one way in which actors overcome self-consciousness.

It is also a way to infuse the doing of any action or set of actions with the kind of focused energy that enables the actor to make the actions convincing, that is, to make them convincing examples of actions done with certain feelings and moods. This observation applies to acting training that insists the actors must feel the same things as their characters feel in order to portray those feelings, in the manner of "The Method", perhaps. It also applies to actor training that insists such same-feeling is not necessary at all, in the manner suggested by Diderot. So, all things considered, it seems to me we should stick with the word "convey" in (1) and not substitute the word "express."

2. Spectators ascribe feelings and moods to whole performances. And it seems right to say that a performance may be correctly described as, for example, dark and cynical. But beyond this observation, we seem to be pulled in different directions by other facts about emotion ascription to performances.

I have hesitated to write that performances *express* moods and feelings. Sets, costumes, props, lighting, sound, and other technical elements contribute in some way to whatever moods and feelings spectators experience. On a standard conception of expression, as requiring a subject who expresses, this would make no sense. More importantly, it is unlikely that these elements make their contribution as the result of spectator recognition of them. Instead, it is more likely these elements causally induce spectators to have particular experiences that are related in some way to their sense of what is going on in the content of the performance.

I have also hesitated to write that the moods and feelings ascribable to performances are the same moods and feelings that spectators *experience*. This is because, while moods and feelings induced in performances *are* experienced by spectators, it is not clear what the relationship is between such induced experiences and the ascriptions of mood and feeling that spectators make of performances.

Another point about ascriptions of feelings and moods to performances is this: there is logical space for differences in ascription. For example, I may think the production is dark and cynical, you may think it is merely hostile and adolescent. And it is unclear whether these differences are resolvable or whether they even need to be resolved.

Note however that the range across which differences in reception occur appears to be small. It would take unusual circumstances for me to find a performance dark and cynical that you found light-hearted and optimistic. Moreover, there is not much difference between judging a performance to be cynical and judging it to be adolescent, even though one of these judgments is likely to support a positive evaluation and the other to support a negative evaluation.

Yet another general point is this: spectators and performers may differ about the moods and feelings of given moments in a performance. Moreover, it is possible for spectators to be right about what feelings and moods to ascribe to a performance, and performers mistaken about the moods and feelings they have presented in the performance. It is a fairly common, especially but not only in amateur productions, for performers to induce moods that are quite different from those they imagine they are presenting.

All these facts seem to pull us in different directions. So, they will be of central concern in this chapter. We need an explanation that renders this set of facts coherent or shows us which ones are genuine facts and which ones are only putative, merely reflecting some of the prejudices we bring to the study of theater.

3. Consider the following open sentence. Imagine the result of filling in its blanks with either the term "recognition" or the term "experience."

The _____ of the feelings of characters contributes to or is a constituent of the _____ of the mood and feeling of a performance.

There are only four possible combinations. If the term "recognition" (or one of its cognates) appears in both slots, this will be a fully cognitivist view. If the term "experience" (or one of its cognates) appears in both slots, this will be a fully experientialist view. I suspect most of us would be drawn to some sort of mixed view. But which one we should adopt as most plausible is not at all obvious.

It is tempting to suppose this canvasses the only available explanations of both the connection between the feelings and moods performers convey in portraying characters and the moods and feelings spectators ascribe to performances.

In contrast, however, I will present a view that is quasi-recognitional and generally cognitivist but that is not the result of arguing for a particular way of filling in this open sentence. As we have already seen, any solution must allow for causal inducements of moods and feelings. An actor may say a line in much the same intonation but with different physical orientation to the audience or to other characters, and the line will have a very different impact on the sense spectators have of the mood and feeling of the moment.

In a recent performance of *Gilgamesh—the Man Who Refused to Die*,[1] spectators observed Gilgamesh confronting various gods and human beings, bowing and saying this line:

> My name is Gilgamesh
> and I come from Uruk
> where I am King.
> Enkidu, my friend, is dead
> and I'm grieving.[2]

In the performance referred to, the line was always delivered in profile. If that line had been delivered directly towards the spectators, even once, the effect would have been decidedly different, even assuming the line was delivered exactly the same way each time, in the manner of a formula.[3] Similarly, as Doris Kolesch has written,[4] uses of the voice in theater affect the acoustics of the physical spaces in which performances take place in a number of ways; and one such effect is that of inducing or creating the physical sense of theater spaces.

The view I favor acknowledges these causal facts about performances. Recognition of these facts, I believe, forces us to a more sophisticated and nuanced position than is represented by the tempting strategy of restricting the available explanations by filling in the blanks in the open sentence given above.

4. Recognizing the role of causal inducements in theatrical performances is connected to the physicality of performances. This might already be evident. But two points about it bear special mention.

First, the kinds of moods and feelings that can be induced by the physicality of performances are typically not those that are generated by spectator understanding of the content delivered in a performance. Instead they contribute to spectators' grasp of that content. Nevertheless, they also may reinforce, reveal, or challenge that content.

Consider, for example, the related fact that performers create physical images on stage. These images may illustrate, illuminate, or undermine the content presented by other theatrical means. For the images to work—whether to induce moods doxastically or sub-doxastically—performers must do things that focus spectators' attention on some aspects of their bodies and voices and to focus attention away from other aspects of their bodies and voices. Whether what is to be seen is the way the performers are arranged relative to each other, the way they stand relative to the spectators, or some pattern in the way they sound and deliver lines (and so on), the result is almost always achieved by groups of performers and is also almost always achieved by physical aspects of performers rather than by features of the content of the performance.

Although not directly concerned with inducing emotions or moods, the *Gilgamesh* example given above demonstrates how the physicality of what performers do may help spectators grasp the content of a performance.[5]

Second, the fact that actors induce certain moods and feelings by means of the physicality of their own features has been considered the source of a serious worry about theatrical performance. The worry is most often expressed as a concern about the features of actors and the characteristics of characters. The worry, sometimes referred to as the problem of the "subjectivity of the performer," has to do with the dual aspect of performers; they are themselves and they appear to be fictional characters as well.

Note that, while the fictionality of characters is illustrative, it is not crucial. If this is a genuine worry, it will affect even the representation of non-fictional characters in non-fictional narratives. Indeed it will infect anything the performers represent, even or perhaps especially, when they aspire to represent themselves.

Some resources

Think first about how performers construct performances. Three basic issues must be addressed in the generation of any theatrical performance:
1. who utters what (including words, gestures, and so on) and how each utterance sounds or appears;
2. what each performer is doing at each moment in the performance and how she is doing it; and
3. where attention is to be directed at each moment and how that direction of attention is to be achieved (Hamilton 2007, 153-154).

Describing a set of responses to this list of performers' basic issues, which we may call "the basic performers' questions," does not fully explain how a complete performance is shaped, nor does it distinguish between choices that are the result of whim or accident and choices made in the service of some further ends. Generally, performers also try to do two further things with the answers they provide to the basic questions.

First, when answering the performers' basic questions, companies seek to arrive at weakly coherent collections of means for displaying features in ordered sequences that constitute one way, among other possible and differently weighted ways, they could create the characteristics of the developed object in the performance (Hamilton, 155). We may define *theatrical conventions* as just such weakly coherent sets of features chosen for display and having different affect-inducing capacities, or "weight."

Second, when making choices companies seek to arrive at similar conventions throughout an entire performance, governed and connected by some conception or aims for the performance as a whole (Hamilton, 157). We may define *theatrical styles* as sets of conventions that are governed in this way. Styles are important for theater because reference to them is required for explaining what, finally and ultimately, is going on in a theatrical performance by way of an achievement. An important aspect of style attribution is that, in order to grasp them, spectators have to formulate hypotheses about the deliberative process of companies of performers.[6] This hypothesis-formation looks a lot like what many philosophers of art have called "interpretation." And that is how I shall refer to it below.

Consider second how spectators grasp what is presented to them. Whatever explanation we give is constrained by the fact it must account for how spectators with very limited knowledge of what they are about to see still manage to understand it.

Clearly most people who go to theater at all do so fairly frequently; so we can assume that most of them come with considerable background knowledge. But even they had to start somewhere. They had to gain that knowledge. So they were at one time very much like the completely novice spectator and will still be confronted with forms of theater that are unfamiliar.

The latter point explains why the account must also cover non-narrative and non-representational forms of theater. To be sure, narrative theater is widespread in every culture. But many cultures have other forms of theater and the avant-garde traditions in the West are now replete with such forms of theater. These forms of theater may be new to some spectators, but even so they do still seem to grasp what is going on, at least at a basic level. Accordingly, I propose we adopt the following as a reasonable, minimal, and quite general standard of evidence that a spectator has understood what she has seen.

A spectator has basic understanding of a theatrical performance if she (1) can describe the object that was presented over the course of the performance, (2) reacts physically in the right ways to what is happening in the performance as those things happen, or (3) adopts the moods responsive to what is happening in the performance as those things happen (Hamilton 2007, 74).

The importance of reactions and moods cannot be overstressed. Spectators often demonstrate their understanding of a performance by their reactions and moods. And these reactions are often contagious. Spectators exhibit "flocking behaviour" in response to physical aspects of what they hear, see, and sometimes smell.

This statement of a minimal standard of evidence for basic theatrical understanding is disjunctive. It allows us to acknowledge discursive evidence of understanding, represented by a spectator describing what she saw. And it allows for non-discursive evidence of understanding, represented by either her physical reactions or her adoption of[7] moods. Either will do.

It might be objected we need a stronger standard because some reactions spectators have are not evidence of understanding but are, rather, merely idiosyncratic or momentary, like spasms (Woodruff 1991). I am relying here on what Paul Woodruff has called the "principle of cognitive uniformity." The idea, as I employ it, is this: if a description or reaction is evidence of understanding, then others are likely to offer the same description or have the same reaction. There may be situations in which only one person understands something, but—if the person has genuinely understood—then the same perspective is logically open to others. *Purely* idiosyncratic descriptions and reactions, in short, do not count as instances of understanding.

Consider just some of the differences that can exist among spectators of the same performance. One of us may have just had a wonderful lunch. Another may have just flown in from an eighteen-hour journey. A third may have only recently gone through a horrible and devastating divorce. Surely then, even if we have reason to suppose most spectators will grasp mostly the same things—and will, accordingly, react in pretty much the same ways—there can be no guarantee that will happen.[8]

So, we need a test for when a reaction or the adoption of a mood counts as evidence a spectator has understood a moment or sequence in a performance and when it does not. Conveniently, there is such a test. Spectators, even when induced into relatively passive acceptance of what they see, still do think about what they see. Among other things, they think about how to square their reactions with what they think they are observing. A cogent test, then, employs the discursive evidence any spectator thinks she has in common with other spectators as the benchmark against which to determine whether her sense of the moods and feelings of a character in a moment or sequence is in fact consistent with what she understands to have taken place in the content of that moment or sequence. Most of the time, spectators' reactions are consistent with what they would describe were they to give a description of what had happened. But a spectator could find herself experiencing moods and feelings that are inconsistent with what all of the spectators understand is happening. When that is so, that mood or feeling is aberrant, and there is no sign she has comprehended the moment or sequence.[9] It could, of course, be valuable to her for some other reason; but it will not be valuable as evidence of understanding.

An important entailment of acknowledging how spectators think is a consciousness principle about the reception of theatrical performances. This is: Spectator recognition of what is happening at moments or in sequences of a performance is sometimes is not a conscious process at all and it is rarely an entirely conscious process.

This consciousness principle is true even though the test for the reliability of that which is grasped by physical inducement, sub-doxastically, crucially involves reference to the discursive evidence regarding the moment or sequence. Recognizing what is going on in any moment or sequence, then, is both like and unlike recognizing a tune. The demonstration one has understood a bit of a tune is not linguistic—one does this by humming or whistling (or playing) the bit. Similarly, it is frequently the case that one shows one has understood a bit of a theatrical performance only by the way one reacts. The difference is that, in the case of a theatrical performance, one can often provide the discursive evidence as well; and that evidence serves as crucial assistance to spectators when they find they must sort the reactions that are reliable from those that are not. But a spectator may only demonstrate understanding by her physical reactions or the moods she has adopted. She may never have occasion to provide the discursive evidence and she may never discursively articulate her understanding of a moment or sequence at all. Feeling may not be all; but it is often enough.

Moods and feelings of whole performances

I have said I will present a view that is quasi-recognitional and generally cognitivist; and I have said that the view I favor acknowledges causal facts about performances.

The importance of reactions and moods is crucial to spectator uptake of performances. Reactions and moods are, as already noted, contagious; and spectators exhibit "flocking behaviour" in response to physical aspects of what they see. Think again about how a listener demonstrates she has recognized a tune. She does this by humming or whistling or playing a few bars. In the case of a theatrical performance she may only react, and demonstrate her comprehension by her non-linguistic behavior. Or she may be called upon to talk about what she saw and, in response, provide the discursive evidence as well.

All of this accounts for the cognitive dimension of what is felt in a performance. What is left over in any performance, however, is a feeling of the sheer physicality of it. That is, even if a spectator has assured herself – assuming a case in which she needs to – that she has understood what she is seeing, she has still had an intense physical experience that remains as a kind of residue of the performance. This residue of feeling and mood—while consistent with her understanding of the content of the performance—may linger as relatively free-floating feelings and moods that she does not connect to particular moments in performances but rather to the performance in its entirety.

Suppose, as is common among spectators, that she wants these feelings and moods to be explained. She might seek to explain these "leftover" feelings and moods in the same way she tested her moment-to-moment feelings and moods, by reference to what she understood in the performance. But if we conceive of spectators thinking this through, we immediately see they cannot proceed in this manner. For, they have already explained whatever can be explained in this way. The scope of their thinking can change, from a focus on particular moments to a focus on whole performances.

That is, what spectators can do with greater success is appeal to the larger intentional environment to provide an assessment of their lingering feelings and moods. Spectators may appeal to the thought that the performers have induced such feelings and moods for some reason. They may then reflect on how all of the intentional apparatus of an entire performance—the lighting, costumes, props, positioning, voice, acoustics, and blocking – have fed into their reception of the piece. They may speculate about what the performers' intentions might have been.

If so, then clearly the scope of spectator reflection has changed, from trying to figure out a moment or a sequence of moments to trying to figure out the performance. In short, they have begun to think about style. They have begun to interpret the piece.

To be sure, not every spectator does attempt to think these things through. And, for those spectators, such moods and feelings just linger in their imaginations and in what we may call the "felt-afterlife" of the piece.

What then about the worry about the dual aspect of performers? The worry stems from the fact they are themselves and they appear to be fictional characters as well. As I noted earlier, if this is a genuine problem at all, it is also more general. For it affects the representation of non-fictional characters in non-fictional narratives, the aspirations of performers to represent themselves, and attempts by performers just to speak for themselves. But, as the foregoing has suggested, this is only part of an even more general phenomenon. That is, there really is no special problem about the physicality of particular performers and the features of the characters they portray, at least not if it is thought of as connected to the emotional quality of performance and the emotional qualities of a character.

Features of performers give rise to feelings and moods of spectators. Insofar as those feelings and moods contribute to the understanding of whatever aspects of character or events in the performance, they are playing a strictly cognitive role in the thinking of spectators. Insofar as they are distractions—and, notoriously, they may be—they come either to be ignored by spectators or, if they cannot be ignored, they interfere with spectator comprehension of the performance. And, finally, insofar as they linger in the felt reactions and moods of spectators, they may be cited as bits of material in support of an interpretation of the performance as a whole. For many spectators, however, such moods and feelings may just be allowed to linger in the mind.

Notes

[1] Performed by Sven Kristersson, with percussion and vocals by Tina Quartey, directed by Karim Rashid, based on a translation of the *Gilgamesh Epic* from Swedish by Alan Crozier, with lyrics by Sven Kristersson and music by Sven Kristersson and Fredrik Myhr. Mr. Crozier's translation into English is based on the Swedish translation from Akkadian by Lennart Marrings and Taina Kantola.

[2] This English line was provided to me by Sven Kristersson, personal communication.

[3] In the performance referred to here, each of the three times the line was

delivered, Mr. Kristersson employed the same intonation and stood, bowed, in the same posture, with the same gestures. The example assumes this would not change, only the direction of address.

[4] See Chapter 14 in this volume in which Kolesch illustrates and expands on a very similar claim.

[5] One could think of it this way: it is now generally recognized that pragmatic concerns determine communicative content in two ways. One needs to know the context of an utterance to determine what is conversationally implicated by what is uttered, whether it is ironic, and so on. But one also needs to know the context in order to disambiguate words, or to fix the referents of any indexicals contained in the utterance. The former involves ties between what is said and what follows from it by reference to context; the latter involves employing knowledge of the context of utterance in order to determine what *is* uttered. What I am focusing upon is analogous to the latter of these tasks, but without the requirement that the context must be recognized, or known, in order to play the relevant content-fixing role.

[6] This may take the form of attributing decisions to directors, individual performers, or to the collective company. Nothing I write here turns on the difference.

[7] "Adoption" may suggest that moods are acquired by spectators by conscious decision. That is not the view I am proposing. But I know of no better word here.

[8] In Chapter 6 of *The Art of Theater*, I argue that we *do* have reason to believe this. I do not rehearse that argument here.

[9] The appeal to discursive evidence of what is understood as the test against which spectators then understand what has been experienced is what gives the view I favor its cognitivist structure.

Works Cited

Diderot, Denis. 2007 [1769]. *The Paradox of Acting*. Translated by Walter H. Pollock. London: Kessinger Publishing.

Hamilton, James R. 2007. *The Art of Theater*. London: Blackwell.

Krasner, David, ed. 2000. *Method Acting Reconsidered: Theory, Practice, Future*. New York: Palgrave.

Woodruff, Paul. 1991. "Understanding Theater." In *Philosophy and Art,* ed. Daniel Dahlsrom, Studies in Philosophy and the History of Philosophy 23, 11-30. Washington, DC: Catholic University of America Press.

CHAPTER TWO

PERFORMING AND REHEARSING

SUSAN L. FEAGIN

I recently had the opportunity to attend a rehearsal for a play in production by the local puppet theater. Serious puppet theaters are rare in the United States, so this was an opportunity not only to see the creative process at work in an under-appreciated form of art. The play was *Animal Farm*, an adaptation of the novel by George Orwell. It was in the early stage of production, only the second day of rehearsal, and it was not expected that the actors would know all of their lines. The main goal of this rehearsal was to block out the movements of the actors in relation to each other and to the audience in one short scene.

One result of observing the rehearsal that was especially striking to me, though not particularly deep, was the realization of how complicated a performance is with respect to layers of decisions that need to be made, decisions that need to be worked out serially. For example: how an individual character will move; how to ensure the actor can move like that when in costume (and, in this case, holding a puppet); how the actors move in relation to one another; how to avoid having the actors facing a wall when they speak so they can be heard; the inflection in speaking their lines; how long to take for a particular exchange and for a given scene as a whole; how to make sure the moving and speaking fits into the chosen time frame; how each scene fits into the progress of the play through time; and so on. As is to be expected, there was a lot of starting and stopping, try things one way or another, and going again. Actors stopped in the middle of a speech and asked for a line, asked where to stand, how to cross the stage when another actor is in the way, where to look and what direction to face, and so on.

These features of the rehearsal prompted me to think of Peter Kivy's claim in *The Performance of Reading: An Essay in the Philosophy of Literature* that a first-time, silent reading to oneself of a novel or short story is a performance, or, as he puts it with reference to Plato's early dialogue *Ion*, we are all "silent Ions" (2006, 63). In this paper, I begin with

Kivy's claim that readers are "silent Ions," and then raise some objections to his claim that reading is a performance, objections grounded in differences between theatrical performances and rehearsals. Though I use Kivy as a target, my objective in this paper is less to argue against his view than it is to try to reveal something of interest about theatrical performance.

A slippery slope

Kivy recognizes that his claim that silent reading to oneself is a performance is counterintuitive, and he attempts to alleviate some of its counterintuitive character by looking at the history of reading practices. This history, he alleges, constitutes a kind of slippery slope, so that if we are willing to take each step down that slope with him, we will find ourselves assimilating silent reading to oneself to Ion's performance. The slope goes something like this. For most of the history of human beings, only a small percentage were able to read, so that the main mode of access to poetry and stories was aural, that is, through listening to them being read, recited, or told. It was the "job" of people like Ion to give performances, so that people could hear and hence appreciate the poetry and the prose. As literacy became more widespread, one didn't have to depend on others for access to the stories, but, even so, not everyone who was able to read could read silently to oneself. As Kivy points out, a simple orthographic development in writing greatly facilitated the development of the ability to read silently: putting spaces between words.[1] If we want to block Kivy's assimilation of silent reading to oneself to performing, one thing we need to do is to explain which step or steps down this slippery slope to block.

One objection blocks the initial characterization of readers as "silent Ions," on the grounds that it is highly unlikely that Ion and his ilk would have been reading "their lines," and it is also unlikely that they would have been able to read. This distinction is often glossed over in English. What we call a "lecture" may or may not be read. In my conversational Spanish class, however, the teacher has pointed out that I gave "*una lectura*" only if I literally read the paper I had written; otherwise, it could be a "*charla*" or "*presentación*." In many quarters, one is encouraged to give a talk rather than to read a paper precisely because it encourages a little more animation and expression and (at least the appearance of) spontaneity in one's delivery, so as to engage the live audience, as in theatrical performances. Reading out loud not merely binds one's words but also one's movements, and it changes the way one achieves expressiveness. Some people are better able to achieve expressiveness as speakers and others as readers. The distinction between those who have memorized their lines and those who read them is far from trivial from the perspective of performance. Memorization allows one to do more as an actor and changes the dynamic of a performance. Naturally, then, it changes an audience's expectations with respect to what they will see and hear.

A second objection to readers being "silent Ions" addresses the fact that Kivy's claim is intended to apply to first-time readers, which, he plausibly claims, constitute the bulk of silent readers, a point that is rather crucial to his case. Even if the Ions of the ancient world were able to read, and even if, what seems contrary to fact, they would have given readings, "*lecturas*," their performances would not have been first-time readings. Thus, whether or not first-time silent readers (to oneself) of a novel or short story should be described as performing or not, they are, nevertheless, not "silent Ions."

Being complicated

I mentioned that one especially striking aspect of the rehearsal I observed was how complicated it was, in the sense that it requires having made decisions that need to be worked out serially. One implication of this fact for the subjective experience of performers is that they cannot think about every meaningful aspect of their performance at a given time. Much of what a performer does, if not all, has to be internalized or semi-automatic. So, as with giving a lecture, "*una lectura*" in the Spanish sense, part of the challenge is to "stick to the script" and to the agreed "movements," but without appearing to be doing so simply by rote. One may also note that philosophers tend to use "perform" rather promiscuously—we "perform" actions in our everyday life, where they are sometimes described as performances. James Hamilton notes we may praise an action as a performance because of its improvisatory achievement, but we may also praise an action as "quite a performance" when it involves saying the same thing that we have previously said over and over again (Hamilton 2007, 6-7). These two different achievements point to an important distinction in kinds of performances, about which I'll say a bit more below.

That different aspects of a performance (or production) need to be worked through serially came through clearly after the rehearsal when the director spoke with those of us who were guests at the rehearsal. Some guests complained that they couldn't hear the actors when they spoke their lines. The director explained (repeatedly) that making sure that was not on the agenda for the day and that they would work on delivery later, when they would also make a final decision about the extent to which the animals would have British accents. (Should the pigs sound snooty? Should the horse have a cockney accent?). He also emphasized (again, repeatedly) that what we saw was not a performance but a rehearsal, and that we were not members of an audience at a performance, but guests at a rehearsal.

Though I didn't realize it until I saw the actual performance, watching the rehearsal was a bit like watching a movie being filmed. The scene I watched being rehearsed for an hour and a half was just a few minutes long in the final production. In addition, little of the way it took form in that particular rehearsal remained. Indeed, the scene was almost unrecognizable. Clearly, decisions were made later in the development of the production that affected the provisional conclusions that were reached that day about how to stage that scene. Even the script itself was changed, with some lines excised and others added. Rehearsals often have a creative dimension that informs the production, and hence the performances of that production. One might think that a director would or should be able to work this out in his or her head. I shall not address this point, except to point out that relying only on what one can work out ahead of time can result in insensitivity to the strengths and limitations of individual actors, and to their group chemistry.

A second type of preparation for a performance is practicing what one already knows needs to be done, such as practicing an English accent, or a particular gesture of nonchalance, and so on. (This may involve employing what is sometimes called "technique," that is, a method for delivering a consistent performance night after night.) And a third type of preparation involves learning relevant things about the content of the material being performed, what I shall call "research". This may involve, for example, reading other plays by the same author; or seeing other productions by the same director; or reading about the time and place in which the play is set, or about the character types in the play. It may also involve listening to what the director says about how he or she views the various scenes and the play as a whole.

All three types of preparation would seem to be well within the norm for performances, but only the third is possible for reading silently to oneself. I may read up on the Indian myths and stories and history that Salman Rushdie draws on in *Midnight's Children* or *The Enchantress of Florence*. Or I might read some criticism and analysis of a Brecht play. But it is not the norm for readers to rehearse or practice reading a short story or novel. I may start to read and discover, five pages in, that I had misunderstood where and when the action took place, or thought it was ironic when it wasn't, or for some other reason, decide to start over. But it does not follow that, in reading the first five pages, I was practicing or rehearsing.

Kivy may defend against this line of attack by pointing to the fact that his claim is that first-time readers are performers, so that he is not concerned with cases where one might rehearse or practice for the performance. He says he wants to make the case for first-time readings being performances because, for the most part, people read novels only once, and readers are able to acquire a fairly high level of understanding and appreciation during that first reading. But the limitation to first-time readers does not salvage Kivy's view, because the point is that practicing and the creative aspect of rehearsing are not activities one engages in to prepare for silent reading to oneself, whether it is the second, third, or whatever time around. They are not ruled out just in the case of first-time readings, but are not within the norms of preparation for any reading.

Kivy contrasts the ability to read a novel for the first time with a reasonably high level of comprehension with the ability to "hear" a musical work when reading a score for the first time. The latter, he points out, is an exceedingly rare ability, even among musicians, and hence it does not provide a suitable model for the far more common ability to read. People exhibit different kinds of virtuosity, some of which are more rare than others and many of which are admired precisely because they are a kind of rare virtuosity. First-time reading of a score is one of the very rare ones. Another is the ability to come up with a pun or witty remark, no matter what the topic of conversation. These are examples of types of first-time performances that we admire.

I agree that this is not the model to which we should assimilate first-time readings of novels, but Kivy's concerns seem oddly pragmatic: we don't generally have time to read novels more than once, so we should not read as if we will get another crack at it. No rehearsals; no practice reads: just go for it. But reading, in this respect, is no different from many other actions we perform, and, in this sense alone, is a "performance," that is, in the sense that philosophers are wont to describe any action as an action one performs.

We are simultaneously granting both too much and too little to our accomplishments in first-time readings, if we think of them as performances. Too much, as I have just claimed, because they are insufficiently differentiated from genuine virtuosities, and too little because of the lack of recognition that what silent reading does, once one is able to do it well, that performing does not do. I pursue this idea in the next section.

Starting and stopping

In addition to the complicatedness of performing, and hence a need to work out various aspects or layers of it serially, I mentioned above also the fact that there was a great deal of starting and stopping, trying out, and reconsidering of how to perform the material. One doesn't do all this starting and stopping in a performance: one is supposed to keep on going through to the end. If you muff a line, you don't back up and try it again, the way you might in a rehearsal. Or if different performers in the same scene have different beliefs about where they are in the script, you can't just stop and decide where to pick up again. One may, of course, set various tasks for rehearsals, including not stopping, just as if it were a performance. But this is optional in rehearsals; it is not optional in performances. In contrast, when reading a novel, one can start and stop all one likes. One may linger over a phrase or a sentence, or double-check what a character previously said, and so on. It would serve readers well not to stop and start too much, of course, because it might break the flow of the story or the rhythm of the narrative, but these are constraints on readers because their goal is appreciation, which does not require that one read through to the end without ever backing up or double-checking. In contrast, there are constraints on performers, because of the goal or function of performances, that do not constrain appreciators.

Thus, there are different norms for performers and readers because they have different goals. Roughly, the goal of a performer is presentation, whereas the goal of an appreciator is understanding or appreciation. Performers and readers have different "jobs" or functions, and what is needed for the one will sometimes conflict with what is needed for the other. Audience members, since they do not have to perform, are freed up to understand the work better.

The distinction between performer and appreciator does not entail or even imply that audience members ultimately will appreciate a play (the production of the play, or the particular performance) better than the performers. Whether any individual audience member would be a better appreciator depends on contingent matters, including the appreciative skills of audience members and the intelligence and technique best suited to any given performer. It is an old question: one inevitably thinks of Plato's view that Ion would not necessarily be the best appreciator of the works he performs. Plato notably proposed that what enabled performers to be effective is not some body of knowledge, but a talent or knack that can be developed and improved through practice, and not through the acquisition of a systematic understanding of the means to achieve the relevant ends. We still wonder about the extent to which such things can be taught, in the sense that one's abilities can be increased through understanding a theory, and the extent to which they are increased through something more like an apprenticeship, observing and doing under the guidance of one or more masters.

This debate, however, points in the wrong direction. For the question here is not whether performers are or need to be appreciators, but whether appreciators are or need to be, in some significant sense, performers. One of the advantages of reading silently to oneself is that one can make one's way through a novel much more quickly than one could reading aloud or even if just mouthing the words as you go. Once the skill becomes relatively common, the products (such as novels) evolve to make use of those new abilities, with the result that readers engulf large quantities of narratives, even with all the starting and stopping, in a way we couldn't if we had access to them only through oral performances. In this way, we attribute too little to our abilities as first-time silent readers to ourselves if we do not recognize what they can do that, in performing, one does not do.

To sum up, I have argued that, first, silent reading to oneself is not to act as a "silent Ion," since the oral Ions would not have been reading, a fact that furthermore changes profoundly the character of the actions they perform when performing. Second, I proposed that the complicatedness of the central cases of theatrical performance makes creative rehearsal and practice important preparations for it, preparations that have no analogue for reading. And, third, I argued that performers and appreciators have different functional roles, roughly, respectively, to present a work to an audience and to appreciate that work.

Notes

---

[1] In addition, various kinds of punctuation also facilitate silent reading to oneself, and to this day there are debates over the use of, for example, certain kinds of commas. There are those who defend the use of commas to indicate where one would take a breath or where one would pause, if reading aloud; and there are those who argue for using commas only for, let us say, conceptual reasons, such as to mark off nonrestrictive clauses.

Works Cited

Hamilton, James R. 2007. *The Art of Theater*. Malden, MA: Blackwell.
Kivy, Peter. 2006. *The Performance of Reading: An Essay in the Philosophy of Literature*. Malden, MA: Blackwell.

CHAPTER THREE

THE PERFORMER IN THE EMPTY SPACE

SVEN KRISTERSSON

To whom do I want my classical singing to matter? This was the question that I asked myself in the middle of the eighties. Having thought for a while I realized I wanted my singing to matter, at least to my friends. But they did not understand neither German nor French. Many of them did not like classical singing—some did not even like classical music. So, when I wanted it to communicate what I considered were the deep existential and artistic truths embodied in the *lieder* of Hugo Wolf or in the *mélodies* of Francis Poulenc, I failed. I was not able to communicate the songs that I loved that I loved to the people I loved. Having also been involved in highly communicative action like telling musical stories to children and singing my own cabaret songs, the problem of not being able to convey this classical heritage grew increasingly frustrating.

In 1999, by coincidence, I met with a young director, Jesper Hall. Together we decided to stage a stand up tragedy version of Schubert´s song-cycle *Winterreise*. I translated the songs and wrote the script. Singing the songs in Swedish and giving the audience a story to follow, I felt that I at least could communicate the Schubert songs in a way that I was satisfied with myself, even if there were other voices: "I was deeply moved, but I did not like it," said one of my former singing teachers. What I was trying to do was in fact to sing the Schubert *lieder* more like an actor or a singer-songwriter.

This performance combined with a written reflection became my Masters thesis within artistic research at the Academy of Music and Drama in Gothenburg. Reflecting brought to light and made conscious what traditions we had used, consciously and half-consciously in the performance, like the combination of the *lieder-abend* and the theatrical storytelling of Dario Fo. Another thing which may seem self-apparent, but which was important to me, was that I discovered that the empty concert stage had very much in common with the theatrical "empty space", a term coined by the director Peter Brook in the sixties (Brook 1968). Brook referred to the Shakespearean tradition, which does not use much stage decoration, but where the visual moments of the performance actually are created by the images in the poetry of the text, thus making the spectator realize the visual moments of the story in her own fantasy. I also realized that this particular artistic field, located between music, literature and theatre was not yet much explored, neither artistically nor scholarly. Of course a lot had been written about lieder, theatre and storytelling, but not so much about what happened when these traditions were combined. But how could this be understood and described?

Having brought my use or abuse of different artistic traditions to a conscious level became important when I fell upon my next performance, which was to become the first part of my doctoral project: another musical monologue, directed by Karin Parrot. This monologue, however, I conceived in blank verse around the songs of John Dowland, playing the protagonist myself. The fictional location is the castle of Greenwich outside London, where Dowland makes an inauguration speech as he finally, at the age of fifty, takes up his duties as a composer and lute-player at the royal court. The stage is very simple: a chair and a table. And of course my two co-musicians: a guitar player and a clarinet player. All together this constituted a space which I would call empty enough to qualify as an "empty space". And the learned aristocracy, played by the audience, has gathered, since the aristocracy of that time were participating practically in cultural life. Dowland could expect the audience to understand him when he was talking about "the wisdom of the ear" and "the knowledge of the hand." I actually made Dowland reflect on what we today would call "tacit knowledge" and "knowing-in-action."

But I would not call this performance in itself artistic research, though. The Dutch scholar Henk Borgdorff gives four requirements for research: having *research questions*, a *research context* which in our case is the artistic society and the world of *artistic research*, some kind of *method* of investigation and finally a *documentation and dissemination* of the work (2006, 10).

These points are by no means unproblematic. In my own practice, I do not start an artistic project because of a research question like: how can we use blank verse in a contemporary way? and then try to find out. Some artists may do this, but to me it is like putting the cart before the horse. To me, the reasons for starting a particular project has much more to do with finding the right material, the right circumstances and the right collaborators, and of course there has to be some spark of ignition, an inspiration that is able to start a process and then to feed the work through the stages of conception, rehearsals and performances.

If there are questions, these are primarily *artistic* ones: How do I communicate the songs of John Dowland to an audience of today? Not to mention practical and financial issues: How and where are we to perform it? From where do we get the money?

This does not mean that I am not interested in investigating form and experimenting with different means of expression. So when I stumbled upon the next part of my doctoral project, the *Gilgamesh* epic, one of the sparks of ignition was my curiosity to see what could be done in with this epic poetry, by trying different ways of singing and musical declamation. (*Gilgamesheposet*, 2001)

By coincidence an Iraqui director,   Karim Rashed, living in Malmö also wanted to do something with this pre-biblical story, written around 1300 B.C., but with its roots further back in Sumerian times, some thousand years earlier, in the region which today is Iraq. Rashed had been brought up with the epic, and knew it very well, which of course I did not. We found it extremely interesting working with something which East and West had in common: the *Gilgamesh* epic is a source both for the Bible and the Koran, both for the works of Homer and for a *One Thousand and One Nights*. Having applied for funding our project, we ended up with our minimum cast for making a performance at all: me and a drummer (fig. 3-1).

Figure 3-1 Performance of *Gilgamesh* by Sven Kristersson, 2009. Photo by Jean Hermanson.

In order to make the epic usable as a story on stage I completely rewrote the newly made Swedish translation. The translator, Lennart Warring, had no objections, on the contrary he helped us immensely. Then, together with the drummer Fredrik Myhr I set my text to music, using rhyming and rhythmical speech, inspired by different poetical and musical traditions like rap-music Arnold Schönberg's *Sprechgesang*, jazz and Turkish music.

I have up to this point discussed artistic research in relation to my performances, which are two interpretations of the songs of John Dowland and of the *Gilgamesh* epic respectively. These performances represent two thirds of the artistic part of my doctoral project. I will create one more performance though, an interpretation of the life of my grandmother, who was a very ordinary Swedish working class woman. This performance will be is a class-and-gender-oriented reply to my earlier performances, which were all about the doings and beings of men. I will impersonate my grandmother on stage. Since I have inherited her eyes, in a way she will now face the audience herself.

The second part of my project is a DVD documentation, which is yet to be made. It will be filmed by the Swedish maker Lars Westman, and it will include commented excerpts from my performances. It will also include a critical interview with me, made by Astrid Kvalbein, a Norwegian singer and musical journalist who is a doctoral student within artistic research at the Musical Academy of Oslo.

The third part of my doctoral project will be written reflection which I would call an interpretation of the two interpretations. This is where research questions really need to be posed: How did you make the performances? How do they relate to what other artists are doing? Are there any patterns that can be discerned that can contribute to the understanding of your artistic territory?

We have already stated that art in itself, even if it is knowledge, is not research. And even if working with art in itself includes research of certain types, we also have to clarify in what way the art we are creating is knowledge. Artistic research "is about articulating knowledge and understandings as embodied in artworks and creative processes," says Henk Borgdorff (2007, 17). But what kind of knowledge are we talking about here? In fact, the *Gilgamesh* epic can already in itself be seen as a project of knowledge in several ways. From an epistemological view, the Gilgamesh figure works as an example: we follow his struggles, but if we try to put in a formula what we have learned from his struggles, we find that we have reduced our knowledge to just part of what the story tells.

And how does the practical knowledge that I as an interpreter put into play, relate to the knowledge already inherent in the epic?

Just having touched on the questions of knowledge and epistemology briefly, let us move on to method. The questions of method are obviously in the centre of artistic research, and they are there tightly connected with the epistemological questions.

For articulating artistic knowledge within my project I use three methods, of which the first one is descriptive, with the purpose of describing the artistic territory within which I work, located between music, theatre and literature. In this description I will discuss what artistic methods I have used in the performances: In the Dowland performance I used theatrical and literary traditions and methods to communicate songs. In the performance of the *Gilgamesh* epic, theatrical and musical methods and traditions were used to communicate poetry.

The second method of my reflection is comparative, and I make two different comparative studies: one about The Dowland performance, and one about the *Gilgamesh* epic. The comparative study of the Dowland performance was made possible through my being artistic director of a one-day, huge manifestation of lieder singing. This gave me the opportunity to invite artists, all Swedish, who are working within the same artistic field as myself, communicating songs in the lieder tradition by linking them with a story or using some other dramatic concept. All the productions had few participants, and were situated well within the genre of classical singing, all of them trying to brake away from the tradition of *lieder-abend*, but also, paradoxically, maintaining their links to it. So I compare seven performances of my colleagues with my Dowland performance, using certain criteria: where did the idea originally come from? Who wrote the manuscript? Were the songs translated, and if, by whom?

This gives, I believe, together with my descriptive study, quite a good picture of where my Dowland performance is located within my this particular artistic area the way it looks in Sweden today.

My version of the *Gilgamesh* epic is, on the other hand, located in another part of the artistic territory than the Dowland performance. It has much more to do with theatre, and therefore I will compare it to a Palestinian theatre performance of the epic, which also uses two participants on stage. This comparison is made possible through a cultural exchange between Sweden and Palestine, which meant that we performed our *Gilgamesh* in Palestine and the famous Al-Hakawati theatre came to Sweden. I think that the Palestinian performance in itself will supply sufficient material for making a relevant comparison, since the performances, though dealing with the same material, are very different. In connection with both the Dowland and the *Gilgamesh* performances, we also make an evaluation of the productions. The evaluation will be based on the views of me, the director and the other musicians. What the press has written will also be taken into account.

Except for the descriptive and the comparative methods in my written reflection, I will use a third method. This means a self-understanding examination of my role as a composing and writing singer, using the Orpheus myth as a tool.

The Orpheus myth as an analytical instrument

Many opera patrons are well-acquainted with the myth of Orpheus, the Thracian poet who so moved the rulers of the kingdom of Death with his singing that he was allowed to bring his Eurydice back to earthly life again. Orpheus had to face one stern condition, though: he was not allowed to meet her glance while ascending to the realm of the living. However, Orpheus could not resist her prayers for him to look at her, and so she was transported back to Hades. Chrushed with grief, Orpheus let himself be torn apart by the furious *menads*. His limbs were then thrown into a river and carried out into the Aegean Sea, where his head was still singing its mournful songs. This is, in brief, the story as it is told by Ovid and Virgil, the principal sources used by opera composers from the Renaissance onwards.

The myth has been used not only by composers; painters and authors have also contributed in various ways to the widespread fame of Orpheus. During the twentieth century the myth was used and reused by poets (Rainer Maria Rilke, *Die Sonette an Orpheus*) filmmakers (Marcel Camus, *Orfeu Negro*), novelists (Thomas Pynchon, *Gravity's Rainbow*) dramatists (Jean Cocteau, Tennessee Williams) and rock poets (U2, Nick Cave), just to mention a few of those who have found the Orpheus myth relevant for their artistic purposes. In most of these cases the myth has been used as a base upon which a narrative architecture has been constructed. The main features of the myth have been kept, and a story of a similar but modernized kind has been modelled upon the basic pattern of the myth.

Sometimes, but not very often, scholars have also used the Orphic myth as an analytical tool. By this I mean using the myth or parts of it as a means to shed light upon different fields of knowledge, like literature, music making, religion, and natural history. The myth contains many archetypical features: the power of music and words, descent into the land of the dead, love as motivation for courageous deeds, the price that has to be paid for art, and much more. In the following I will give a few examples of how different scholars have used the myth as an analytical instrument. I will then give some suggestions of how the myth can be used as a tool of reflection in relation to performances of poetical-musical monologues of my own creation.

A highly challenging work that uses the myth in defence of poetry as being able to articulate knowledge and truth is Elizabeth Sewell's *The Orphic Voice* (1971). One could imagine that a work with this title would deal with subjects within the realms of poetry or music, but Sewell has a wider purpose than this. Departing from the picture of Orpheus moving humans, animals, and even rocks with his song, Sewell sets out to investigate the power of language, exploring how a scientific approach to natural history can be unified with a poetic perspective. This may sound like a dangerously wide task, but already in the first pages of her book, Sewell deals with the haziness and ambiguities of myth in general:

> Mythological statements lead to questions. Then follows something rather strange, for to these questions only the story itself can make an answer. The myth turns back upon itself because it is a question that figures its own reply, and it is that inner movement or dynamic which makes it feel obscure. This kind of unclearness is not muddle or mystification, however, but an indication of method. The myth of Orpheus is statement, question, and method, at one and the same time. This is true of every myth. (Sewell 1971, 20)

Sewell is worried about the increasing chasm and contradiction between what she calls "language-as-mathematics " and "language-as-poetry" when it comes to interpreting and describing different phenomena. Instead, with the help of historical thinkers and scientists, she wants to bridge the present gap between science and poetry by sketching a more unified (and unifying) perspective: "The human organism, that body which has the gift of thought, does not have the choice of two kinds of thinking. It has only one, in which the organism as a whole is engaged all along the line." Having drawn the conclusion that "science cannot absorb myth" she suggests that we should

> try the other way around, taking myth as a nearer model of the activities we want to explore... Discovery, in science and poetry, is a mythological situation in which the mind unites with a figure of its own devising as a means toward understanding the world. That figure always takes on some kind of language, and that is why we have to go more deeply into language instead of trying to escape from it. Discovery is always under Orpheus'

patronage, so to speak; something that the good poets have always known. (ibid. 20)

She then sets out on a journey where we meet poets, philosophers and scientists. One of them is Francis Bacon, the early seventeenth century philosopher, who in the view of Elizabeth Sewell is highly "Orphic" since many of his thoughts seem derived not from philosophy but from poetry: "It is not that he was a poet who thought himself being a philosopher, as his version of Orpheus at first sight suggests. He was a poet who did not trust poetry." Deploring Bacon´s lack of trust in his own poetical talent, Sewell moves on to Shakespeare,

> who picks up precisely what Bacon wants to reject—poetry, dreams, and shadows—with an immense respect for each, and presents through them a vision of *his* method, a mythological vision of the relationship between man's mind and the natural universe. It is not an abdication from rationality but a widening of it to include the world of dreams as well. (ibid. 120)

Sewell coins a special expression for characterizing the Orphic mind, calling it "postlogic". By this she seems to mean a poetic mind that includes science. In Novalis, the German philospher and poet, Sewell finds "an Orphic poet asserting poetry and technology as kindred disciplines". She notes that Novalis also has an interesting way of looking upon fairy tales and myths as knowledge and she quotes a part of one of his significant poems:

> And recognize in tale and verse
> True histories of the universe.
> (My translation).[1]

The Orphic Voice was first published in 1960. Sewell worries about the scientific and literary world´s disbelief in language-as-poetry:

> To reject language-as-poetry or to bewail its loss of power is to affirm language-as-science. There has been wholesale withdrawal from mythological or metaphoric or poetic thought, now relegated to the emotive, the imprecise, symbolical, metaphysical-nonsensical. Neither linguistic philosophers nor critics nor, a far more serious matter, poets, trust language-as-poetry any more... One result has been the general tendency in modern poetry toward the dry, ironic, self-deprecating conversational tone, the deliberate ascetical abdication from that power which language-as-poetry wields, a tendency broken only by occasional

despairing incursions of language-as-poetry into the world of magic. (ibid.
8)

This way of refraining from high Orphic claims has been observed
used the Swedish literary scholar Ingemar Algulin in his study *Den orfiska
reträtten* [*The Orphic Retreat*] (1977), in his quest to "trace some
important patterns common to the work of the Swedish lyric poets whose
breakthrough came in the 1940s". Algulin uses the expression "orphic
retreat" (borrowed from a poem by the Swedish poet Sven Alfons) to
describe how the poets after the romantic era gradually have descended
from their prophetic tribunes to more modest positions, characterized by a
reduction of the use of highly euphonic language and traditional symbols
(which are replaced by "low valued concepts like ruins, ashes silence
etc."). The more visionary "singing" of traditionally Orphic poets is
replaced by a poetry which distrusts the traditional values of symbols,
reduces the pretensions concerning what is possible to say about life and
descends from the poetical heights. The poet is no more a singing prophet
and a seer, but rather a sceptical poetical clerk. It is notable that Algulin
uses the poet's expressive term "Orphic retreat" instead of a more
intellectual definition. This title is in itself a Sewellian example of how
poetry sometimes is more informative and precise than a more formal
language. One interesting aspect of Algulin's concept is also that he uses
the Orphic myth in an entirely "negative" way, analyzing poetry by saying
what it is not instead of using traditional or newly-invented scholarly
terminology for his project. As a result we see *both* the Swedish poets of
the forties and their Orphic predecessors in a new light.

To make his points clear Algulin, like Sewell, uses the term "Orphic"
not only referring to the ancient myth, but to the "entire Orpheus-tradition
within Western culture". This way of proceeding is implemented in a
comparative study where the Orphic myth and how it has been used
through the centuries throws light upon the Swedish poets of the forties.

The total opposite to Algulin´s approach can be seen—but should
rather be heard—in the English lute-player Anthony Rooley's:
Performance—Revealing the Orpheus Within (1990). Rooley uses, as was
common during the Renaissance period, Orpheus as a symbol for the inner
creative powers of the musical performer. What then, is the essential
Orphic quality, ascribed to composers/performers like Francesco da
Milano or John Dowland? Rooley says:

> Simply put, it was recognized by men of their own age that these men
> carried the fabled power of Orpheus to communicate, fairly directly, the
> divine inspiration which had been symbolically granted to Orpheus.

Is it possible to teach and learn these qualities? How can you possibly talk about things like "divine inspiration" without being incomprehensibly abstract? Relating to Baldassare Castiglione's *Il Cortegiano* [*The Book of the Courtier*], Rooley first explains the term "*decoro*," which refers to

> all that the student (of life or of the performing arts) can control and study, develop and refine. Included here is a sense of duty and dedication, a care in preparation and an ever-refining sense of what is appropriate. All things relating to practise come under this heading. Finally *decoro* embodies all that is understood by tradition, the laws or rules which holds right conduct in place. (Rooley 1990, 11)

The second principle which must be observed by a true student of Orphic matters is *sprezzatura*. This is explained as "a love of improvisation, a kind of calculated carelessness…a sort of buffoonery that has wisdom". *Decoro* contains the rules and the limitations while *sprezzatura* represents "the ability to embrace the unknown". These two ways of relating to music (and to reality as well) have to balance each other: *decoro* alone results in a conventional, dull performance, using only *sprezzatura* would lead to bad discipline and negligence. However, there is one more principle, to which *decoro* and *sprezzatura* have to "bow down to in submission". This is *grazia* which

> is not quite the same as the Christian concept of Grace—it is that, but with a touch of pagan magic about it as well.… The first thing to learn of *grazia* according to Castiglione is that it is a gift, belonging to no one but its source of emanation… It is, writers agree, a state of bliss. (ibid. 13)

Rooley uses the priniples of *decoro*, *sprezzatura* and *grazia* to talk about performance in our time. To find a term to include the audience and the performing space (the stage och room) in the Orphic experience, Rooley turns to a term from ancient Greece:

> As Orpheus steps forward a new quality, or dimension, takes the stage, which feels like stepping into another reality. This, in my experience, is witnessed as much by the audience as the performer. The new space is *temenos*, an ancient Greek word for an ancient concept—a sacred space, often in the enclosure of a temple, in which sacred acts are performed with dignity and appropriate ritual… Sound qualities change, so that there is a limpid clarity to the voice and the music. Time takes a different pace, as though every detail might take a delightful eternity. These are all signs that *temenos* has been marked out. (ibid. 88)

Of course these different principles or states of mind can never be proven scientifically. Neither can they be explained, merely understood: one has to experience the "Orphic" presence, either as a performer or as a listener, to get a glimpse of what it means. Trying to explain *grazia* to someone who has never had any experience of it, is close to the efforts of making a believer out of an atheist, Rooley says. A book can never replace the living contact between teacher and student, frequent performing in front of an audience, and the constant self-evaluation made by the musician or singer herself.

The Orpheus myth as an embodiment of "knowing-in-action"

I have now presented three examples of how the Orphic myth can be used for different ends: Elizabeth Sewell has in *The Orphic Voice* used the myth to compare poetry and natural science; Ingemar Algulin has used the expression *The Orphic Retreat* to "trace certain literary patterns" common to the work of Swedish lyric poets of the 1940s; Rooley in *Performance— Revealing the Orpheus Within* has suggested a renaissance for a Renaissance method of teaching. Of these three methods, the one I find most useful in my own case is Rooley'sway of both describing and teaching stage presence.

As we have seen there is not one Orpheus, there are several. One which I find particularly useful for my own purposes is the Orpheus that we meet in the *Argonautica* of Apollonios Rhodios, written around 200 B.C. In this work, Orpheus is a far more powerful figure than in the more melancholy version of Virgil and Ovid. The action of the *Argonautica* takes place in the time before the *Iliad* and the *Odyssey*, and describes the lengthy voyage of the ship Argos, and Iasons capture of the Golden Fleece.

Of all the members of the crew, Orpheus is chosen first because of his artistic, social, historical and religious skills: with his lyre he beats the time for the rowing of the oarsmen, his singing creates peace among the men when there are quarrels, he leads the crew in prayers and services of the gods, his playing protects the crew from the sirens´ perilous singing, and his singing teaches the crew about how the world was created. This is also the Orpheus that the early 18th century Italian Giambattista Vico refers to in his *New Science* when he sees civilization brought to Greece by Orpheus with his lyre: "to the accompaniment of which, singing to them the force of the gods in the auspices, he reduced the beasts of Greece to humanity" (2001, 219).

This Orpheus puts knowledge into action. The Orpheus of the Argo never gathers knowledge for its own sake, instead he puts it to work in a context which has to do with exploring, education, group dynamics and – yes, entertainment and celebration: at the wedding of Iason and Medeia the crew gathers in a wedding song:

> And the heroes in their hands wielded their spears for war, lest first a host of foes should burst on them for battle unawares, and, their heads enwreathed with leafy sprays, all in harmony, while Orpheus' harp rang clear, sang the marriage song at the entrance to the bridal chamber. (Apollonios, Book 3)

Having said this, it seems reasonable to regard Orpheus – especially as we meet him on the Argos and in the renaissance pedagogics of Anthony Rooley –as an embodiment of what the scholar Donald Schön (1983) calls "knowing-in-action" and "reflection-in-action." Therefore it by no means seem improbable to use these sides of Orpheus figure as a means of self-understanding, exploring the artistic territory of my performances.

I also think that the connection between mythology and "knowing-in-action" might open up new fields of within artistic research: in the world of myth, not only Orpheus himself embodies artistic knowledge. His mother, the muse Calliope, represents the power that gives all epic poets their ideas and inspiration. She also has eight sisters, all of which represent different fields of knowledge within the arts and sciences. It is also interesting to reflect upon the identity of their parents: their father is Zeus, but who is the mother of all ideas? The answer is: *Mnemosyne*, Memory. This means that Orpheus and his mythical surrounding actually is an expression of an epistemology of practical, artistic knowledge, with a background in history. Thus myth tells us that our ideas are genealogically linked with memory and the past. As artists and scholars, can we learn anything from this insight?

Notes

---

[1] "Und man in Märchen und Gedichten/ Erkennt die wahre Weltgeschichten."

Works cited

Algulin, Ingemar. 1977. *Den orfiska reträtten—studier i svensk 40-talslyrik och dess litterära bakgrund.* Stockholm: Almqvist & Wixell International.
Borgdorff, Henk. 2007. Artistic Research and Pasteur´s Quadrant. *GRAY*

Magazine, issue 3 (special: Artistic Research): 12-17.
—. 2006. The Debate on Research in the Arts. *Dutch Journal of Music Theory* 12, 1: 1-17.
Brook, Peter. 1968. *The Empty Space*. London: Penguin Classics.
Gilgamesheposet. 2001. Translated by Lennart Warring and Taina Kantola. Stockholm: Natur&Kultur.
Rhodios, Apollonios. *Argonautica*, Book 3, *The Gold Scales* http://oaks.nvg.org/sa4ra16.html#tres (accessed December 2008)
Rooley, Anthony. 1990. *Performance – Revealing the Orpheus within*. Worcester: Element Books.
Schön, Donald. 1983. *The Reflective Practitioner: How Professionals Think in Action*. New York: Basic Books.
Sewell, Elizabeth. 1971. *The Orphic Voice*. New York: Harper and Row.
Vico, Giambattista. 2001 [1725]. *New Science*. London: Penguin Classics.

PART II:

MUSIC

CHAPTER FOUR

SUBJECTIVITY UNHINGED:
ELEKTRA IN ZURICH

DAVID LEVIN

The following paper is in two parts. I begin with a brief and
speculative section on the expression of subjectivity in opera; in the
second section, I move on to a consideration of an exceedingly
provocative production of Richard Strauss and Hugo von Hofmannsthal's
Elektra.

"Where opera was, there psychoanalysis shall be?" Opera, psychoanalysis, and the expression of subjectivity

Opera doesn't merely warrant a discussion of the expression of
subjectivity in the arts, it begs for it: just consider the number of characters
who fall to their knees and implore heaven, who weep copiously and
lament piously, who fight valiantly and die heroically, let alone those
villains who sententiously defy God, betraying friends and family —it
would appear that the hyperbolization of experience and perception is
nowhere more voluptuously overwrought than in opera—except, perhaps,
in professional wrestling.[1] Opera's familiar affinity for grandiloquent
pathos marks it as a generic soapbox for the expression of overwrought
subjective states. And the generic norm according to which multiple
characters on stage can launch into musical expression at the same time
suggests that opera affords the simultaneous expression of a multiplicity of
subjectivities under a rubric that leads, in opera's classical form, to their
harmonization. Opera, we might say, enables the expression of difference
with the assumption that in the course of expression, difference dissipates,
tending towards resolution.

But in the modern period, opera's ability to resolve its diegetic (and
formal) differences begins to buckle: differences become increasingly
intractable; in the course of the 20th century, some of the grandest and

most ambitious works, once launched, are left incomplete (think, for example, of Puccini's incapacity to complete work on *Turandot*; Schönberg's inability to complete *Moses und Aron*, and Berg's unfinished *Lulu*); the primacy of classical harmony (and with it the transparency of resolution) famously comes under siege; the dramaturgical-compositional umbrella under which different voices can be gathered and their differences comfortably accommodated begins to fray.[2]

This historical development would seem to be directly at odds with another, related development. That is, the dissolution of opera's affinity to set *out* and in turn reign *in* the expression of difference at the outset of the 20th century, its stalling out as a vehicle that not only transports the emotions but in so doing, brings them to a place where those expressed differences can be resolved; in short, opera's decline as a forum for the expression and resolution of difference coincides with the emergence of another, related practice that takes on just this challenge—I am thinking, here, of the emerging practice of psychoanalysis.

At the outset of the 20th century, psychoanalysis takes over opera's identity as the privileged forum for the expression and resolution of suffering. In so doing, it hardly shuts down the voice; rather, it shifts the voice's mode and address, privatizing the enactment and expression of woe, and distilling the generic terms of expression. In lieu of the grand public resolution formulated through the dictates of music and spectacle, comes the individuated focus of the analytic scene. I am tempted to say that the operatic voice is abducted by psychoanalysis, its impulse to a totalizing expression (as well as the imperative of resolution) is transposed to a different (analytic) scene; opera's singing voice is refunctionalized for the talking cure.

The work that I propose to explore in this chapter sits at the crossroads I have just sketched here, the place and time when opera at once resumes its origins and prospectively figures its own impending obsolescence. Richard Strauss and Hugo von Hofmannsthal's *Elektra* is arguably the first work (but by no means the last) in which opera brings the enormity of its resources to bear on a clinical case study. The piece is about to celebrate its 100th birthday: it premiered in Dresden in 1909.[3]

As many of you know, Strauss and Hofmannsthal located *Elektra*'s world on the border between ancient Mycenae and contemporary Vienna, conjoining the terms of Attic tragedy with the emerging vocabulary of Freudian psychology.[4] In their nascent clinical practice, Sigmund Freud and Joseph Breuer sought to demonstrate the efficacy of what they famously termed the "talking cure"; that is, the sense that repressed traumatic events could be resolved in the course of their narrativization.

And indeed, the logic of the talking cure bears affinities to Aristotle's familiar argument regarding the efficacy of Greek tragedy, where the conjunction of dramatic enactment and spectatorial identification produces the salient effects that follow from catharsis. As any number of commentators have observed, these effects are both communal and individual—modeling collective narratives as well as collective and individual norms of spectatorial engagement.

But what would it mean to understand opera as ceding its privileged claim on the capacity to formulate and resolve hyperbolized difference to the analytic scene? And what would it mean for *Elektra* to occupy a place that conjoins attic tragedy with Freud and Breuer's *Studies in Hysteria*? And most important, what will any of this mean on stage? With these questions, we have arrived at the second section of my article.

Elektra in Zürich – subjectivity unhinged

According to the literary scholar and musicologist Lawrence Kramer, Strauss and Hofmannsthal's one-act piece is not so much an opera, as "an enormous *Lied* expressing Elektra's subjectivity. The shifting expressive focus basic to opera as a genre is arrested; what we hear is the musical equivalent of obsessional thinking, half by Elektra, half about her" (Kramer 2004, 194). In Kramer's view (and I think he is right on this important point), Elektra is far removed from an ideal moment, according to which the work would lend expression to multiple subjectivities; instead, the opera fixes on a single subjectivity, deploying it as a symptom. Rather than a means to the consolidation or reconstitution of community, the work offers up a disfunctional community, a community in disarray. The character Elektra, rather than emerging from or returning to a community, is and remains removed, isolated—*allein* [alone] as she puts it in her first words in the opera, *ganz allein* [all alone.]

And the piece goes about elaborating the terms of her radical isolation. In that (diegetic) sense, it's interesting to note that Elektra remains isolated; this radical isolation is hardly redeemed. Thus, at the conclusion of the work, she may be vindicated in her determination to exact revenge, but she is hardly reintegrated. In her dance, and in her collapse, at the work's conclusion, she remains, as it were, *ganz allein*. The piece lends lush and expansive expression to this radical subjectivization in notable and noticed ways: the moment, near the conclusion of the work, where Elektra claims that the piece's music emanates from herself (a moment we will see, hear, and have occasion to think about) is as powerful and cogent a statement of radical solipsism as any in opera. But what are its implications?

It has, historically, been difficult to specify this piece's place in the dramaturgical landscape, to determine its proper register: is *Elektra* a piece about a young woman's psychological interiority? about a daughter's undying (if ultimately fatal) fidelity to her father's memory?[5] or perhaps it is a piece about the title character's inability to let go? or is *Elektra* perhaps best understood as a cipher for familial and social conditions gone awry? an embodiment of principled integrity in the face of opportunism and corruption? To all of these questions, the answer, I suppose, is "yes"—yes, it's a piece about Elektra's radical interiority, about her radical estrangement from extant social relations, about her radical fidelity to her father's memory, about her radical defiance of her mother's decision to marry Aegisthus. In short, this is a piece that offers expression to multiple subjectivities that are, however, fixed in (or indeed, unhinged in, ricocheting through) a single character. (Of course, there are other characters in this piece, but their function is remarkably subordinate to the expressive space afforded and assumed by Elektra.) To return to Kramer's formulation, "what we *hear* in Elektra is the musical equivalent of obsessive thinking"—half by her, half about her.

Kramer's enormously suggestive observation alerts us, then, to the music's account of obsessional thinking, and its monological form. And what do we see? That is, if, as Kramer puts it, the music offers an account of obsessional thinking, what happens on stage? This is not just an academic question, but the most immediate interpretive question facing any production team entrusted with a new staging of the work.

In 2003, the Zurich Opera put the question to the Austrian stage director Martin Kusej. The resulting production featured Eva Johansson as Elektra; Marjana Lipovsek as Klytemnestra, Melanie Diener as Chrysothemis, Rudolf Schasching as Aegisth, and Alfred Muff as Orestes. Christoph von Dohnányi conducted; the sets were by Rolf Glittenberg, Heidi Hackl designed the costumes. In 2005 the production was recorded for release on DVD; I think the results are quite extraordinary—and deserving of our attention here.

I do so out of a sense that we should be attending to the interpretive achievements of operas in performance—in this case, operas in performance on DVD. Put otherwise, my sense is that the opera house provides a compelling forum in which to explore and revise our understanding of a given piece.

In recent years, the opera houses of the world have come to serve as interpretive laboratories. In the 1980s this was a phenomenon largely restricted to certain houses in Europe—mostly in Germany. But in the course of the 1990's, the phenomenon, now dubbed "director's opera," spread across Europe and to the US. With it came a new forum, if you will, for the expression of subjectivity, namely, the subjectivity of the director, or, more broadly conceived, the expressive subjectivity of mise-en-scene.[6]

Over the past decade, the results of this newfound culture of interpretive contestation have become commercially available. When it comes to the opera house, we might say that the aesthetic revolution has been televised, and the results are being distributed, worldwide, on DVD. To some extent, they are even being broadcast into movie theaters—but that is a topic for another paper.

The dissemination of theatrical experiment on DVD and in movie theaters has real implications for our conceptualization of opera's medial status as well. When I envisioned the study of *Elektra*, I thought I would explore the implicit analogy of this production's medial situation on DVD (which renders it portable, reproducible, and in some sense personal) and the diegetic scene of mediation (since Elektra is first and foremost a character who bears within her the memory of her father, whose fate she channels and whose mandate she bears). I will have a bit more to say about this constellation as we make our way through this production.[7] But the more I thought about this material, and its relation to the topic of this gathering, the more fascinated I became by the status of subjectivity in this production. That is, the Zurich production offers an account of subjectivity that is at once compelling and confounding.

When rehearsals began in Zurich, Martin Kusej had been directing opera for seven years, having made a name for himself with a host of exceedingly provocative productions of quite varied repertoire in Stuttgart, followed by a very controversial set of Mozart productions in Salzburg under Nicholas Harnoncourt, including *Don Giovanni* in 2002 and *La Clemenza di Tito* in 2003. From his early days in Graz doing experimental theater, Kusej had distinguished himself as having a keen eye for women's lingerie and the apocalypse; the trappings of intimacy and the inevitability of catastrophe. His productions are almost invariably populated by a pervasive, bureaucratic coldness combined with or sometimes in the form of anonymous, utterly depersonalized kinkiness. Sleek bodies, often in some form of undress, have tended to form a backdrop for the failed intimacies of his protagonists. By the time Kusej got to Salzburg to prepare his production of *Don Giovanni*, his reputation preceded him. His production (featuring Thomas Hampson as the Don and Anna Netrebko, discovered here by the international press as Donna Anna) was co-sponsored by Palmers, a German haute-lingerie company.[8] Kusej's sensibilities, then, arguably matched up well with Strauss and Hofmannsthal's *Elektra*, which is as preoccupied with the exigencies of intimacy as it is with the inevitability of the apocalypse.

I propose to talk about a series of scenes from the production in order to account for what they are up to. I do so in part because the piece is so interesting for a discussion of the expression of subjectivity in the arts. But also because it strikes me that this sort of production—one that is marked by a strong interpretive hand—is, as I have suggested, becoming ever more common in Europe and even in the United States, and it behoves us to develop a vocabulary with which to engage them—ideally, a vocabulary that is somewhat more nuanced than mere denunciation or celebration. In that, I suppose, I am proposing a model for a different register of the expression of subjectivity in the arts: in this case, on the level of reception (how we talk about the works we experience) rather than just the level of production.

Let's begin at the beginning. According to the libretto, it is evening in a courtyard at the royal court of Mycenae: five maidservants and various overseers are congregating at the well, under the watchful eye of overseers; Elektra is the focus of their gossip—this, after all, is the appointed hour when, every evening, she bemoans the loss of her father, Agamemnon.

There are lots of things deserving of our attention in this excerpt: the setting is one, the lighting, another; and of course, there is the transformation of the maidservants at the well, into maidservants preparing to serve at—and perhaps as?—the evening's festivities in the castle, of which this space is an "inner courtyard". I'd like to ask you to consider something else, something related, namely the radical isolation of Elektra here, her inflection as an outsider at the center of a circle of derision and contempt.[9] The question that comes to mind is not just *who* she is, but *where* she is—and where stage events are in relation to her.

In the dramaturgy of the piece, Elektra is an absent presence in this scene. Spoken and sung about, she is seen but unheard. This embodied remove will become a central concern for this production, which will formulate a series of questions—"where is she? and where, precisely, are these events taking place?—in ever more urgent, creative, and confounding ways. To gain a clearer sense of this, I would like us to take a brief look at the outset and the conclusion of Elektra's monologue, which follows the scene of the maid-servants. It is delivered here with characteristic gusto by the Danish soprano Eva Johansson.[10]

Later I will want to explore with you the scene and status of Elektra's isolation, her status, to quote her, as *ganz allein*. But in order to undertake such an exploration—one that I think this production inflects in exceedingly interesting, suggestive ways—we need to gain a clearer sense of Elektra's social world as it is constructed in the Zurich production. And in order to do that, I want to describe to you the final part of Elektra's monologue, as she imagines the scene of celebration and triumph when the king and queen will be deposed and slaughtered. At that moment, she muses, she herself will dance a dance of triumph and celebration that will be transparent to one and all—even to those, as she puts it, who are so far away that they can only see her shadow. The orchestra samples this dance music as Elektra imagines her exultation.

The dance that she and the orchestra imagine here will return, in idiom and in fact, as a waltz at the work's conclusion. In the meantime, Kusej is particularly attentive to a fact of social relations in this piece. Those relations are exceedingly cold, exceedingly impersonal – there is no exchange between Elektra and the courtiers in the piece, from the start, she is a spectacle of suffering (and of course, we are implicitly aligned with the ogling maidservants, who would attend to her suffering; and with the amalgam of hipsters who gather here, at the conclusion of her monologue, to see Elektra gyrate to the fantasy of her father's presence and her mother and stepfather's demise. As such, she is indeed *ganz allein*, even—or indeed, especially—when she is in the presence of the courtiers. Her reveries—if that's what they are—are interrupted by the arrival of her conventional little sister, Chrysothemis, whom Kusej and his costume designer deck out, quite conventionally, in a virginal white dress.

The increasingly fractious exchange between the sisters is, in turn, interrupted by the sound of preparations in the palace: Klytemnestra is up and about, and she has been having nightmares. The exact nature of the preparations instigated on the queen's behalf remains unspecified in the score, although the text hints broadly that a sacrifice is called for. Kusej's account of the scene, according to Hofmannsthal's stage directions, commences with the unseen but heard sound of a whip cracking. There are a few additional and evocative stage directions:

> A hurried procession clatters and shuffles by the harshly-lighted windows. It is a pulling, a dragging of animals, a subdued scolding, a quickly stifled outcry, the whistling of a whip, a regrouping, a staggering onwards. Clytemnestra appears in the large window. (trans. Susan Webb; Met Libretto, 34)[11]

Let me also clarify one thing. Towards the end of the scene, a massive figure decked out in furs, wields a gun. It is Aegisthus, on the prowl for a sacrificial lamb. One of the spooky things about Martin Kusej's production is the difficulty one has in locating it. Not just in the sense of what continent we might be on, or what country, but what space we are in: is this a projected space? In Rolf Glittenberg's sets for the Zurich production, the "interior" of the castle to which assigns the action emerges as quite another interior than the one conventionally associated with the piece.

The Zurich/Kusej interior is pronouncedly difficult to locate, since it arguably operates on a physical and psychological level: that is, the scene here represents two interiorities—the physical interior of the castle as envisioned it; as well as a psychological interior—in this case, a fantastmatic or psychological vision, one of Elektra's making—or of ours. In the Zurich production, the chorus bears the weight of this interpretive conundrum. The world depicted here is nightmarish—but it is unclear whose nightmare is occupying the stage. Let me sketch some possible interpretations; you may well have your own.

Taken as an account of political realities, this harried scene—the to and fro, the frenetic undress, the general confusion—could be an expressionistic account of the nightmare that is life at the court of Klytemnestra and Aegisthus: a perverse sacrifice at a court that is not averse to perversions (after all, the last king, Elektra's father, was slaughtered in the bathtub upon his return home from the Trojan war). Alternately, and by diegetic right, we might ascribe the scene to Clytemnestra: after all, she is the one who has been having bad dreams. Or indeed, the scene might embody the detritus of Elektra's imagination.

The multivalence of this scene, the variety of ways in which we might understand it, instantiates the difficulty in specifying location that I have been trying to grasp—its unhinging from any obvious mimetic referent. Let me put the problem somewhat differently. I think this production gains tremendous mileage from Hofmannsthal's assignment of the setting to the castle's interior recesses. As I've been suggesting, the set on the Zurich stage appears to comprehend this interiority in a variety of ways—as a space of mental projection; or, more literally, and more obviously, as a space of Elektra's isolation; then again, somewhat more abstractly, we implicitly understand this space as exceptional. In Hofmannsthal's account, the stage picture is defined by what it is not; that is, it is presented as an exceptional space, at a physical remove from the surrounding structure. The Zurich production lends form to that exceptionalism with those multiple doors on either side of the stage, with the uniform, cold, white, padded exterior.

I will have more to say about this multiplication of plausible locations a bit later. For the moment, I want to examine some further evidence for the problem I have in mind. And since this production is astonishingly cogent in its expressive means, more evidence is close to hand. I will skip over the ensuing scene of the opera, the astonishing confrontation between Elektra and her mother Klytemnestra; a scene in which the daughter's contempt for her mother is lent a truly breathtaking force of expression— vocal, scenic, and orchestral.[12] The mother-daughter tête-à-tête climaxes in a grisly turn, when Elektra suggests that her mother's nightmares will end only when the queen has been sacrificed—or indeed, butchered, just as she, Klytemnestra, in turn, butchered Agamemnon. A messenger interrupts the conversation, and in the course of the scene, Clytemnestra's horror is slowly transformed to a perverse delight: Orestes, the missing brother on whom Elektra has pinned her hopes of salvation, is dead.

The entrance of the queen's messenger and confidante is accompanied here by the very crowd that we last encountered in the dreamscape of the sacrifice; and indeed, the confidante who enters here is the sacrificial lamb upon which Aegisthus set his sights, the doe that he bagged. She enters, of course, foretelling death; and the bodies that enter with her appear to be an errant pack of corpses that litter the ground, a corporealized anticipation of the messenger's message. This represents a different, and differently temporalized inflection of the subjective interiority we noted earlier: their entrance, we might say, pre-figures the news to come.[13]

This is not the last glimpse we will have of this bunch; they will return at the piece's conclusion; when the tables turn yet again. But before we turn to their final appearance I want to linger for a moment on the notion of subjective interiority that I think the production engages. So far, I have been relating that interiority to a detail on the level of Hofmannsthal's ideas for the set design; but in fact, it has an exceedingly important correlative in the piece's dramaturgy, one that demands our consideration. I am thinking here of the utterly confounding moment, towards the very end of the piece, when Chrysothemis enters to announce Orestes' return and the death of Klytemnestra and Aegisthus. Chrysothemis asks her sister whether she hears the general jubilation that has spontaneously erupted, to which Elektra famously replies, "*ob ich sie höre? Ob ich die Musik höre? Sie stammt doch aus mir!*." [Whether I can't hear? Whether I can't hear the music? The music comes from me.]

Here, then, at this very late moment in the production, we have a much richer statement of the paradox of interiority that has been occupying the piece—and this production: a moment where the piece ascribes its own emergence to an interior recess of its own making. Elektra, at this moment, lays claim to the piece's expressive origins, to its "site of enunciation" to use a rather bulky term. Put otherwise, we have, in this statement, a condensed and quite radical claim to art as the expression of subjectivity, a claim registered from within the confines of the work, from its interior recesses, we might say.

Before we consider Kusej's account of this moment, and the opera's conclusion, I want to cite Hofmannsthal's stage directions for the dance that concludes the work. This is the dance that Elektra has been anticipating since we first encountered her—the dance that marks her brother's return, her mother and stepfather's overthrow, and her father's redemption. The stage directions for Elektra's dance are as follows:

> Chrysothemis runs off. Elektra strides down from the threshold. She has her head thrown back like a Maenad. She tosses her knees, she stretches out her arms; it is a nameless dance, in which she strides forward. Chrysothemis appears again in the doorway. Behind her torches, crowd, faces of men and women.
> Chrysothemis: "Elektra!"
> …
> Elektra manages to take a few more steps of the most intense triumph and collapses. Chrysothemis goes to her. Electra lies rigid. Chrysothemis runs to the door of the house, beats on it.
> Chrysothemis: "Orest! Orest!"
> *Silence. Curtain.* (Met libretto, 92/93, 94/95.) [14]

In the last scene of the piece, Orestes, it turns out, was not dead at all; and Elektra's sister Chrysothemis enters amid the confusion at court—confusion caused by Orestes' murder of his mother and stepfather. Let me begin at the end, with the first—hallucinogenic, surreal—version of Elektra's dance. Conventionally, it is rendered as a "maenadic" dance, a kind of corporealized peripeteia, an embodiment of Elektra's transport into transgression and pleasure. In the Zurich production, Elektra's movements are in a weird kind of dialogue with those of the Brazilian Samba troupe—she does not dance with them, and yet, her movements roughly correspond to them, are oddly in sync with them. This raises, once again, the question of subjectivity, interiority and reference. On the one hand, the samba troupe materializes the utter weirdness of the moment: we might say that at the moment of its arrival, the Samba troupe evinces in a surreal register what Hofmannsthal characterizes as the "namelessness" of the dance. But to pose the very same question again (since, after all, the production keeps posing it), where do we locate this dance? Is it, like the crowd, conceivably a materialization of Elektra's internal mindscape? But then, what of the crowd? Which is to say, what are we to make of its sudden transformation into the inmates of a lunatic asylum (assuming, of course, that this is what has transpired)?

In a sense, their transformation is more readily anticipated, since the padding on the exterior of the doors leading to the castle had been visible enough—and legible enough—to anticipate this turn. On the one hand, this turn for the literal comes as something of a disappointment, recalling the framing coup-de-cinema in *The Cabinet of Doctor Caligari*, that ur-expressionist war-horse directed by Robert Wiene and released in 1920. In *The Cabinet of Doctor Caligari*, the protagonist Francis's account of a world gone awry emerges as fully delusional, and the characters who have populated his narrative emerge as inmates in an asylum in which he too is confined. The frame in Doctor Caligari, imposed by the film's producers over the objections of the screenwriters, is rather neat and straightforward—it recasts as delusional and subjective the narrator's account of events—which the audience had presumed to be objective and true.

The Zurich production suggests a different and less schematic turn. There is at least an implicit analogy to Dr. Caligari here—the sense, namely, that Elektra, like Francis in Wiene's film, is indeed mad, and that the entire diegetic account has been delusional, a product of her lunatic musings. But it strikes me that this particular incarnation of the crowd functions less as a final revelation than as merely the next step in a series of re-incarnations of the chorus, a series that we have explored here today. In that sense, my impression is that Kusej deploys the chorus as a principle of visual and dramaturgical composition—a point of reference, amplification, and contrast—that offers a means of contrast to and distanceation from diegetic events. In each of their appearances, the chorus stands in juxtaposition to Elektra—they enable her to stand out, and in so doing, singularize her, isolate her. As you will recall, they mock and denounce her in the opening scene, serve as dispassionate observers to her initial rehearsal of her celebratory dance; then they reappear as figures in an increasingly frantic nightmare scene, culminating in Aegisth's capture of his prize sacrificial object; then they enter as heaps of bodies, initially immobilized, and then resuscitated; and finally, here, they emerge as inmates in an asylum. In this sense, the chorus embodies a dissociation that recurs in the piece—a dissociation from Elektra, but also, more generally, from local dramatic events. The conundrum is that in thus standing apart from Elektra, they marginalize her.

Let me conclude with a proposal for how we might account for the interpretive achievement of the Kusej/Zurich production. In order to do so, I want to turn to and extend an idea left uncharacteristically unexplored in Carolyn Abbate's wonderfully suggestive reading of *Elektra* from the late 1980s entitled "Elektra's Voice: Music and Language in Strauss's Opera." In her essay, Abbate is interested in freeing up our understanding of the musical dramaturgy of Strauss's work. Thus, she is interested in interrogating and revising the sense that the music means in any strictly referential sense. Abbate begins by observing the extent to which characters talk about hearing, both in Hofmannsthal's 1903 play and in the subsequent libretto he prepared for Strauss's opera. The epigram for her article is the exchange:

Chrysothemis: "Hörst du nicht, so hörst du denn nicht?"
Elektra: "Ob ich nicht höre? ob ich die Musik nicht höre? sie kommt doch aus mir."[15]

Abbate's gloss on the exchange is as evocative as it is apt: "What we hear at the end of the opera," she writes, "is music Elektra not only hears... it is music she has created, a sonorous world which is her thought, loosed upon us" (Abbate 1989, 109). The polemical force of Abbate's claim involves a couple of methodological disputes that have receded since the time she published the essay: she is intent on freeing up our conceptualization of the referentiality of operatic music, unshackling it from univocal meanings, its ascription to individual characters, and enabling it instead to refer and express in a manner that Bakhtin will famously characterize as "dialogical." Here is how Abbate puts it:

Elektra's words—'the music comes from me'—confirm her status as true hero and protagonist of the opera, a status sometimes denied by what can only be called formidably masculine readings of the opera. But beyond this, the words also hint at a richer hearing of Strauss's music, not as the stolid, monolithic utterance of the composer [a position famously associated with Edward Cone], but as music whose tonal language, vocabulary, degree of fusion with words, may shift fluidly to accommodate many different voices. (Abbate 1989, 110)

What are the implications of this fungibility for the piece's scenic realization? There is an easy answer to this question—one encapsulated in the formulaic claim that Elektra is a hysteric, fixated on her father. This, we might say, demonstrates the problem of lay analysis on the operatic stage: it strikes me as insufficient to the piece's referential complexity.[16] I think the Kusej production offers a more confounding and compelling answer to this question. In its account of the play of interior and exterior worlds and the undecidability, the instability of what we might call the 'referential truth value' of its account of either, the production offers a properly dialogical mise-en-scene, one in which the dialogue extends beyond a mimetic consensus, such that we in the audience consume the conventional signifiers of a naturalized reality (say, the reality of life in the castle) and the equally conventional signifiers of an exceptional hysteria (say, the hysteria of Elektra's ecstasy). Instead, what the Kusej production offers is a mimesis that corresponds to neither a conventionally interior world (say, of Elektra's fevered imaginings) nor a conventionally exterior world (in which Elektra would stand out, say, as an hysteric). Rather, it offers a doubled or what we might (somewhat willfully) term a "bi-mimetic" account, legible not just as either interior or exterior, but also as both exterior and interior.[17] That is, my sense is that the production functions as a properly dialogical object, one that posits Elektra (as a character and a piece) not as paradoxical, but as multiply legible—a wavering between interior and exterior voices, between hysteria and psychosis, between perversion and dementia, in its individual and social forms. Thus, it is not clear whether the social world depicted here is a function of projection, with Elektra, glowering, stumbling, dancing, at its center, as its 'author' (such that the visual and social world, like the music—or indeed, as an extension or materialization of that music, emanates emphatically from her[18]), or whether she occupies a nightmarish position of radical exception, *ganz allein* in the face of a generalized social and political perversion, a lone voice whose music cannot and will not harmonize with the prevailing discourse of power emanating from the castle—a discourse that expresses in the social and political realm the king and queen's perversion.

My sense is that the Zurich production raises these questions—is it one? is it the other? is it both? is it neither?—as questions, without resolving them—suggesting that the piece traffics in ciphers of psychic and social derangement, but where the undecidability of the specific terms of derangement add to the pervading sense of anxiety that they figure.

Notes

[1] See Roland Barthes 1972.

[2] In this respect, Bernd Alois Zimmerman's *Die Soldaten*, is especially interesting as a piece that offers vocal simultaneity absent ist formal (harmonic or dramatic) reconsolidation.

[3] Hofmannsthal refashioned the opera's libretto from his own play of the same name that he wrote in 1903 for the Berlin theater director Max Reinhardt and the actress Gertrud Eysoldt. When it premiered in Dresden in 1909, Strauss and Hofmannsthal's operatic *Elektra* represented the second straight scandal to greet a Strauss opera: the character of Elektra, many critics felt, was a fitting, (which is to say, a fittingly debauched) cousin to Salome, whom Strauss had brought to the operatic stage in Dresden four years earlier. (In fact, the scandal died down in the immediate wake of *Elektra*; according to a standard account of compositional history, with *Elektra*, Strauss took a turn away from the bad-boy identity he had

forged for himself in the world of opera, opting instead for a mode of ironic sentimentalization in *Der Rosenkavalier* and subsequent works that lent him a popularity that was surely shot through in part by relief—these works weren't just sentimental, or indeed, they weren't just ironically sentimental; they were also *not scandalous* in their ironic sentimentality.)

[4] The tragic derivation was drawn largely from the dramatizations by Aeschylus and Sophocles. On the conjunction of tragedy and psychoanalysis see Heinz Politzer 1973. See also Karen Forsyth 1989.

[5] But if that is the case, then what is the nature of that memory: and where does her sacrificed sister Iphigenia fit into the equation? See, on this point, Catherine Clement's comments on *Elektra* in *Opera, or the Undoing of Women*, as well as Julia Kristeva's "On Chinese Women." Is Elektra's recently-sacrificed sister Iphigenia to her what Medea's murdered brother is to her?

[6] For those who have an acute sense of theater history, we would have to say: that forum didn't so much emerge as it re-emerged, having played an enormously important role in the theatrical landscape of the 19-teens and 20's.

[7] Elektra as a character is, of course, a privileged sort of bearer of the mediated memory of her father. She channels him. Agamemnon, we might say (and in doing so, we merely echo Elektra's own claim), Agamemnon lives on in his daughter's will to commune with him. She bears his memory and invokes it—daily, in song. So on the one hand we have a rather conventional scene, in which the daughter's stolid and ethical commitment to commemoration is opposed by the pressures of everyday life at the court—in this case, accommodation with the new familial order, that precipitated the murder in the first place; and the desire to escape the confines of the palace, which can only happen once the state of siege has been lifted; and *that* can only happen once the ongoing protests have been suspended. So: she channels him at her peril; and everyone would just as well she would get over it. Of course, the piece channels her channeling him; and the DVD in turn channels the channeling of the channeling. The move to mediation: here, subjectivity comes to us on DVD; in that sense, or at least, insofar as it is portable, it is materially, technologically subjectivized. Relationship to liveness? One possible line of argument: that the piece rehearses its medial status – from the co-presence of 'liveness' to the solipsism of DVD? Central to the piece is the notion that Elektra bears Agamemnon's memory within, that she reserves and cultivates it. Her subjectivity, then, as one of private communion.

[8] When he wasn't otherwise occupied—and often when he was--the Don walked across a cold, antisceptic landscape, all Richard Meyer white steel lines and imposing glass, populated (in a surreal gesture that has since become a signature of his style) by women of all ages, shapes and sizes, each of them decked out (if that's the phrase) in white lingerie. Here, then, Leporello's famous catalogue aria itemizing the Don's insane history of bedroom conquests—1003 of them altogether; mille e tre!—struck one not only as comical, but as immediately plausible, disquietingly compulsive and ultimately (and surprisingly!) tedious.

[9] A topic I am not exploring here, but that demands consideration: On Agamemnon and/as the Name of the Father: Put otherwise: this is a piece that doesn't merely

evoke but goes so far as to *stage* the burden of bearing a paternal mandate—and it does so from the very outset, when the orchestra intones those sententious initial chords, commonly referred to as the Agamemnon motive. The piece, we might say, invokes and explores the literal and figurative resonances of the Name of the Father, Jacques Lacan's famous term to designate the fantasmatic origin of phallic authority, the guarantor of symbolization and the site of the paternal mandate.

[10] In the libretto as in the Zurich production, one of the maids is denounced and dragged off for doing speaking up for Elektra. A few minutes into Elektra's monologue, delivered here by Eva Johannsen, one of the maidservants will reappear to clean off fingerprints from the door-handle through which she and her colleagues exited to beat the upstart in their midst. There is one further interruption. As Elektra invokes and communes with her dead father, two additional figures appear, passing through, at the very rear of the stage: Clytemnestra and Aegisth, who appear to be in a hurry, but pause long enough to register their disgust at Elektra's nightly ritual.

[11] "An den grell erleuchteten Fenstern klirrt und schlürft ein hastiger Zug vorüber: es ist ein Zerren, ein Schleppen von Tieren, ein gedämpftes Keifen, ein schnell ersticktes Aufschrein, das Niedersausen einer Peitsche, ein Aufraffen, ein Weitertaumeln. In dem breiten Fenster erscheint Klytämnestra."

[12] This, then, is the ur-scene of what Carl Jung will term the "Elektra complex," a female correlative to the dynamics of the Oedipus complex.

[13] We might also note that the crowd here enters into the interior space, from the outside; that is, presumably, from the castle. As such, it arguably makes sense that they are in a state of undress: they come to us, presumably, from the party in the castle, the one that followed the sacrifice. Aegisthus' sacrifice party.

[14] "Chrysothemis läuft hinaus. Elektra schreitet von der Schwelle herunter. Sie hat den Kopf zurückgeworfen wie eine Mänade. Sie wirft die Knie, sie reckt die Arme aus; es ist ein namenloser Tanz, in welchem sie nach vorwärts schreitet. Chrysothemis erscheint wieder an der Tür, hinter ihr Fackeln, Gedräng, Gesichter von Männern und Frauen. And then: Sie tut noch einige Schritte des angespanntesten Triumphes und stürzt zusammen. Chrysothemis, zu ihr, Elektra liegt starr. Chrysothemis läuft an die Tür des Hauses, schlägt daran: ‚Orest! Orest!' /Stille. Vorhang."

[15] Chrysothemis: "Can't you hear? So then can't you hear?"
Elektra: "Whether I can't hear? Whether I can't hear the music? The music comes from me."

[16] I think it holds better for other pieces—say, for Schnitzler's *Fräulein Else*, where I think it's adequate to say that the protagonist is a hysteric. But that is also why I think Schnitzler's short story is ultimately unsatisfying—the question at its heart is too thin, the solution too simple.

[17] My argument intersects with thoughts presented in Lawrence Kramer's "Fin-de-Siecle Fantasies: Elektra and the Culture of Supremacism": "The power of Strauss's opera, including its power to survive the cultural myths on which it rests, lies in its location of intellectual and ethical power in the same Elektra who is the locus of contamination. It is as if Elektra were at one and the same time a figure of

atavistic regression and a figure of the ethical consciousness that separates the civilized and the primitive in fin-de-siecle thought. This is the nub of what I call Strauss's *double (or double-plus)* reading of her" (Kramer 2004, 203) my emphasis.

[18] I wonder whether there is much to be gained, in this regard, from Elektra's fleeting companion claim, a few bars later: "Seht ihr denn mein Gesicht? Seht ihr das Licht, das von mir ausgeht?" [So you see my face then? Do you see the light that emanates from me?] (1916/1943 Boosey & Hawkes Studienpartitur, at rehearsal marking 244a, pg. 350; also Met libretto, 92-93.)

Works cited

Abbate, Carolyn. 1989. "Elektra's Voice: Music and Language in Strauss's Opera." In *Richard Strauss: Elektra*, ed. Derrick Puffett, 107-127. Cambridge: Cambridge University Press.

Barthes, Roland. 1972 [1957]. "The World of Wrestling." In *Mythologies*. 15-25. Farrar: Straus and Giroux.

Clement, Catherine. 1988. *Opera, or the Undoing of Women*. Minneapolis, MN: The University of Minnesota Press.

Kramer, Lawrence. 2004. "Fin-de-siecle Fantasies: Elektra and the Culture of Supremacism." In *Opera in Modern Culture: Wagner and Strauss*. 190-220. Berkeley: University of California Press.

Kristeva, Julia. 2000. *About Chinese Women*. London: Marion Boyers Publishers.

Politzer, Heinz. 1973. Hugo von Hofmannsthals "Elektra": Geburt der Tragödie aus dem Geiste der Psychopathologie. *Deutsche Vierteljahresschrift für Literaturwissenschaft und Geistesgeschichte* 47.1, 95-127.

Forsyth, Karen. 1989. "Hofmannsthal's *Elektra*: from Sophocles to Strauss." In *Richard Strauss: Elektra*, ed. Derrik Puffett, 17-32. Cambridge: Cambridge University Press.

Puffett, Derrick, ed. 1989. *Richard Strauss: Elektra*. Cambridge: Cambridge University Press.

CHAPTER FIVE

MUSICAL EXPRESSION AND THE SECOND PERSON PERSPECTIVE

ANTONI GOMILA

Introduction

Music and emotion are related in many different ways. Some of their ways of relating maybe common to other art forms, while others have been thought to be unique to the musical experience (Juslin & Sloboda, 2001). Thus, for instance, from the perspective of art creation, it is not strange that artists place in a particular emotional experience the origin of a particular work ("I composed that out of the rage felt at what I saw", or "I wanted to celebrate my falling in love with her"). From an audience perspective, the music may be exciting, relaxing, or boring. It can also enlighten memories of past times, with a strength and vividness that seems distinctive of music, something that gives music-therapy its bite. It can also give rise to apparently basic psychophysiological responses, such as thrills (and yawns also). It makes most people move, rhythmically also. More exceptionally, highly intellectualized emotional responses can also occur, as when an expert wonders at the subtle aesthetic value of a minor detail in a work, in contrast with the precedent tradition. Finally, the perspective of the performer can also be considered, suggesting new ways to relate music and emotion; thus, a performer may fall into trance, or feel absorbed, or in a state of flow; she may also be affected by the scenic nervousness, or by an emotion produced by some event, that may affect her performance.

In all these cases, though, the connection between music and emotion is extrinsic. Emotions appear as causes, or effects, or as accompanying the musical experience, but they are in principle detachable from that experience. In other words, all those possible links are not required for the musical experience to take place, and are irrelevant to the aesthetic value of the music. As a matter of fact, these are elements that may go with any kind of musical activity, be it popular, electronic, mechanical, collective, in different ways at each time, but as independent of the music. Musical experience can take place without any of those multifaceted emotional events.

On the contrary, there is one aspect of the musical experience that seems intrinsically connected to emotion: its expressive dimension, through which we perceive expressive qualities in the music: as sad, nostalgic, indignant, rebellious, loving... This is intrinsic in the sense that expressiveness cannot be detached from the music itself –just as we hear meaningful speech, not acoustic waves from which we infer meaning. The analogy with language is useful also in making clear that this ability for expressive perception is something to be acquired, and that is made possible by subpersonal processes that work automatically and quickly. However, from a phenomenic point of view, the experience of expression, as that of meaning, is perceptively direct, not inferential, not relying on imaginative elaboration or projection.

However, in contrast with the language analogy, the expressive experience of music seems to be somehow anomalous, or misplaced. Given standard knowledge of the emotions, they are complex psychological states involving, at least, four levels: psychophysiological arousal (that involves changes in skin conductancy, heart rate, hormonal blood levels), qualitative sensation (feeling good or bad), appraisal (the assessment of a particular event in terms of the subject motivational set-up), and expressive (through face, gesture, voice, bodily posture). In the case of the expressive perception of music, we attribute the last *expressive* level to an event that is ontologically unable to exhibit the other three. So, the question arises as to how to make sense of such an experience. This is the problem I will focus on. Note, though, that the challenge is to explain such an experience, not to explain it away, for the experience is undeniable.

Expression has been a central theme in contemporary aesthetics, at least since Romanticism, when expressive content substituted for mimesis as the source of aesthetic value for artworks. This move helped in placing music center-stage. After the mimetic theory of art , music was problematic in that it lacked representational content. Romanticism, though, viewed in music a paradigm medium for subjective expression. Initially, though, expression was accommodated within the mimetic approach, thus suggesting that, contrary to the previous stance, music could be considered a representational art, whose content, however, does not imitate external nature, but rather subjective emotional states. It is this view that Hanslick's formalism opposed. Subsequently, the Expressionist movement went further to claim that indeed music is not representational, but expressive in itself, thus radicalizing the idea of the subject's activity, and so stressing the subjective character of music.

In the second half of the last century, the problem was reformulated, like all philosophical problems along the linguistic turn, as the problem of the truth conditions of the sentences that attribute psychological predicates to musical events (Goodman 1976). The transformation had the side-effect of splitting the question of expressive perception from that of aesthetic value, but it is easy to realize that the former hangs on the second: a non-formalist aesthetics for music only makes sense when an account of musical expressive perception is put forward satisfactorily.

In order to motivate a positive proposal in this regard, I will start by reviewing summarily the main theoretical strategies currently offered, and their general difficulties. What most of them have in common is a surprising feature, the split of expression from expressiveness; that is to say, they try to account for expressive perception while renouncing the consideration of music as expressing emotions. Expressive perception is ironically accounted for in terms of mimesis, of resemblance between aspects of genuine emotional expression and aspects of music, thus coming a full circle. While I will also pay attention to some such correspondences, I will do so from a socio-pragmatic approach, that attends to the communicative function of emotional expression in intersubjective interaction. From this standpoint, rather than resemblance between stimuli, similar effects produced by music and emotion account for how we come to perceive music as expressive of attitudes. The expressive qualities we perceive in the music are rightly so perceived when they are there because the composer found out that they have similar effects in the audience as those elicited by natural emotional expression. In this way, the connection between expression and expressivity will be restored.

Such a view will be developed with the help of Jenefer Robinson's important book *Deeper than Reason*, one of the few dissenters from the predominant formalist consensus. She proposes a neo-Romantic theory of expressivist bent, according to which music is properly viewed as the expression of emotions, in acordance with her general account of expression in the arts (also visual and narrative ones). This is because, she contends, music can also appeal to the central expressive resource for emotional expression in art, viz., presenting a point of view (some works may present more than one), which the spectator can occupy, thus grasping the emotions corresponding to that point of view. Music, according to Robinson, is also able to articulate at least an "implied author" point of view.

I will resort to Robinson's theory as a pump to articulate my proposal. In previous work I have defended the idea that intersubjective interaction cannot be properly understood in terms of standard "first-person" or "third-person" perspectives, but that a distinctive second-personal perspective needs to be acknowledged as more basic and foundational (from which first and third personal stances develop). I will summarize the proposal and elaborate it in the context of musical experience. I will contend that expressive perception, when it is justified, involves, not just finding superficial parallels between the music and the emotional experience, but viewing such analogies as intentionally worked out. It is not the emotion felt by the composer which grounds the emotional content of the music, but rather the communicative intention that she tried to convey by resorting to the musical medium. This will mean recovering the distinction between basic expression and ostensive expression (Wollheim, 1974; Green, 2007).

I will conclude with the examination of the conditions required for such sort of communication to go through. There is no expression in the void. To be understood, to get her communicative intentions properly recognized, the musician has to take stock of the audience's capabilities; in particular, the already given shared background of communicative practices (just as a blush is a neffective way to indicate embarrassment or shame because it can be properly recognize as such). This may develop into conventional expressive codes, but also the will to avoid clichés, well-practiced formulas, when the intention arises to express new experiences, to convey a novel human awareness. I will examine this dialectics in connection with the appearance of the first atonalism in the early twentieth century.

Contemporary theories of expression

It is generally agreed in contemporary debate that those different relationships between music and emotion, which we went through at the beginning, and that could be related to traditional views, are hopeless. Neither a biographical nor an evocative, theory of expression can work. Neither the emotional state of the composer at the moment of creation nor the emotional reaction of the audience can ground the expressive content of a work (for an exception, see Matravers 1998). Both aspects, as already asserted, are extrinsic to the music. Beethoven composed the *Ninth Symphony* at the end of his life in a state of infelicity and enragement, while the first movement of that work epitomizes challenge and optimism. In addition, emotional feelings are dynamic, just as the composition takes time; but from there it does not follow that the work parallels the effective succession of emotional states in the composer during the composition. In the same vein, the symphony expresses confidence, not because it makes the audience feel confident, but because it is perceived as an expression of confidence. For somebody that happened to hear that piece of music after the death of a beloved parent, it may always be a reminder of the sad event. But this associated element does not transfer to the perceived expression. On the other hand, listening to happy music may make us feel happy, by some sort of empathic, or contagious, response, but in such a case we need to account for the expressive perception in the first place; to account for what it is to perceive the music as happy.

This is not to say that the author's intentions do not have a role to play in understanding her work. Creating music is an intentional activity, which requires the composer to occupy also the role of audience to make sure that she succeeds in what she intends. But those intentions are to be revealed, and detected, in the work, not by means of biographical research or by autobiographical confession. As a matter of fact, the author may follow intuitions, or unconscious intentions, and hence, her words may turn out to be a biased, or misleading, guide as to what is in the work. Sometimes, as it happens, these intentions may consist in that the music expresses some emotion or experience. In this regard, it is important to keep in mind that expression has, at least, two relevant senses in this context: on the one hand, expression means that dimension of an emotional state that makes it public through changes in face, voice, gesturing...; on the other hand, expression can also be an intentional action of directing the public's attention to those changes. The second case involves an ostensive element of making apparent the presence of such an emotional expression. It is in this sense that we can talk of a more or less expressive gesture, according to how effective it is in making what it expresses graspable; in the same vein, we may say that some expression seems inexpressive. It is this second sense that is relevant in connection to music and to aesthetic expression in general. Expression is to be conceived as a form of intentional communication, whose success depends upon its audience's recognition. Musical expression, therefore, is to be properly understood in the context of intentional interaction between composer and audience.

However, in contemporary debates, the rejection of the traditional ways of conceiving of the link between music and emotion has gone through a predominance of musical formalism. From this point of view, music cannot really express emotions, expression is no longer key to aesthetic value, and the phenomenon of expressive perception is conceived as a sort of perceptive illusion, something that the spectator hears in the music because of the similarities with the genuine expression of emotion , not because of any indication of such an attitude. The main explanation of the phenomenon of expressive perception is in terms of resemblance (Langer 1942; Kivy 1980; Davies 1994; Budd 1995): some features of the music resemble some features of emotional expression. Cadence, intonation, phrasing, timbre, tessitura, are aspects of music that may happen to share appearances with corresponding aspects in human emotional expression. Resemblance is also found between the dynamic character of music and human movement. The idea is illustrated by examples like the Great Saint Bernard dog: it reminds us of sadness even if its face does not express sadness. To say that we hear sad music is just to say that that music happens to resemble expressions of sadness in some respect, but there is no occurring disgust (obviously, that is the misplacement paradox we started with), nor has sadness anything to do at all with the musical experience (not so obvious). The critical issue is that, while expressive features in emotional expression are somehow intrinsically connected to the emotion they express, current formalism cuts such a link for music: expressive features in music are expressive, not because of a connection with the attitude they might portray, but because they resemble features of human expression. That is why such features may also be found in inert objects, landscapes, trees, or animals that is, in all sorts of entities lacking emotional lives.

A variation of that strategy goes further and denies that music can even express emotions in that sense. On the contrary, what we can perceive in music are just exclusively musical feelings: tension and relaxation, going up and down, acceleration and slowing, resolution and stability (Narmour 1991; Raffman 2003). Resemblance is kept as a more stringent condition. The expressive features, so to say, are taken at face value, not as clues or indications of emotions, as through the previous approach. Expressive perception is just to notice those first-level expressive elements. And these feelings are conceived as serving exclusively the task of musical parsing, of structural understanding of the music.

A simple comparison with poetry, though, is enough to realize the mistake in such positions. In poetry, it makes no sense to say that the poem resembles what it expresses. In the case of music, it is easy to show the short scope of such positions. Take Chopin's *Funeral March* and Brahms' *A Deutsche Requiem*: what are the superficial, apparent, features these works share such that they both express mourning? Resemblance is not an absolute relation, but it is always in some respect or other. And given that resemblance is a transitive relation, the respect which grounds the resemblance relation is to be specified and held constant. And it does not seem feasible for examples such as the former. Kivy could appeal to his notion of expressive codes (Kivy 2001) as an alternative way to account for expressivity in music. In the case in question, maybe the key element is the use of a minor tonality, which is generally associated with sad states, because of the conventions developed during eighteenth century music. What Kivy seems not to realize is that conventions appear as the end product of a previous intentional interaction that takes place in the absence of such conventional—symbolic—resources. It is these previous communicative signals that get conventionalized in the process (thus losing its iconic or deictic character.)

The root of the problem, as anticipated, is the split these theories establish between expression and expressivity: the expressive elements are conceived on their own, as superficial aspects without an intrinsic connection to the construction of the work. Just as the resemblance of the Great Saint Bernard and human facial sadness expression is completely alien to the interests and efforts of these dogs, whatever expressive elements we may find in a musical work–that is, whatever elements happen to resemble aspects of human emotional expression-are thought to be extrinsic to the music and to the composer's intentions in including them. The reason may lie in taking for granted an understanding of expression only in the first sense, as manifestation of an internal state. When the second, ostensive, sense is honoured, though, the link between expression and expressivity may be restored: music can be expressively perceived in so far as the composer took pains to arrange her musical materials so as to give rise to a certain experience. Certainly, as in all intentional communication, the possibility of misunderstanding is open; it may happen that the expressive intention is not well carried out, or not recognized by the audience, or misinterpreted for something else. It may also happen that the audience finds expressive what was not included for that reason. But, as in all intentional communication, all those cases only make sense in contrast to the central case of successful intentional interaction.

The formalist camp, notably Kivy, also resorts to another argument to strengthen its sceptical position. The argument depends on the assumption of a cognitivist theory of the emotions. As stated in the introduction, there is a consensus on the components of emotions; the disagreements turn around the appraisal component. Cognitivist theories contend that the appraisal depends on beliefs and judgements. My envy of my neighbour involves my believing that he is getting more than he deserves and I'm getting less than I deserve. It is these beliefs that elicit the rest of the components of the felt emotion: the qualitative feeling, the motivational disposition, the expressive level. It seems obvious that music is not the proper intentional object for any such beliefs, much less the subject of any such beliefs. Given that music cannot have anything to do with emotions, cognitively understood, it follows that it cannot express them either. However, it should be noticed at this point that the cognitive view of emotion, which has certainly had great predicament in the last decades, is currently in disrepute in the psychological camp. The standard view of emotion is much indebted to Le Doux's work on fear (LeDoux 1996). He distinguishes two appraisal mechanisms, grounded in different neural circuitry; one very fast, non-reflexive, non-propositional, circuit, which goes through the limbic system; and another slower, cortical, propositional, one (Panksepp & Bernatzky 2002). Beliefs intervene later in the process, and are not required for the emotional elicitation, which is thus seen in continuity with moods, but also as involving a dynamic component that extends in time through feedback loops (Lewis 2005). Though this view still makes music emotionally inert in itself, it provides an account of why we react to it as an emotional stimulus, something to be understood as emotionally expressive (Juslin & Västfjäll 2008). Indeed, it is not strange that we feel moved by the music, that it may influence our mood. While this response cannot be simply equated with the expressive content, as previously established, it is relevant in setting the dynamic process of appraisal in emotion, thus driving into the expressive perception of the music, which may or may not coincide with the initial emotional response of the audience, but which makes the intentional attribution required.

In summary, against dominant formalism, I contend that music can be expressive of emotions, that its aesthetic reception involves grasping its expressive content, and that this content depends upon the composer's realized intentions in the music. Expressive content is not due to an occurring emotion during the performance of the music—there is not a person feeling an emotion—, but it is due to music composed to ostensively indicate such an emotion by resorting to those expressive resources which are intrinsically connected to the attitudes expressed. The fact that the composer also occupies the role of audience throughout the creative process, to check for the effectiveness of her work, what I will call its perlocutive dimension, is what turns music into an ostensive way of emotional expression. The question, now, is how we perceive such expression *in* the music. We have already argued that music has the power to give rise to emotional responses, but now the question is how we come to hear the music as expressive of emotions. I have also anticipated that the answer is to be looked for in the context of intentional interaction to get to the composer's communicative intentions. I will turn first to Robinson's theory, in *Deeper than Reason*, as an example of what a non-formalist account may offer.

Robinson's view

In her book, Robinson approaches the issue of expression by considering first how it takes place in visual and narrative arts. The expressive resources in those cases are multiple and diverse, but they all have something in common: the presentation of a point of view. In literature, the point of view may be that of a particular character, who takes the narrative voice; it can also be that of an implied author (which may coincide or not with the real author). In visual arts, in the same vein, the point of view of the depicted characters is presented in the picture, as may also be that of the author towards the scene, through her choice of perspective, composition and style. In those cases, understanding the work requires tracking the different attitudes and psychological states involved, as they are indicated, described, implied or alluded to. Thus, a Pietà can be tragic or sober, compassionate or distanced, according to the expressed author's attitude towards the Virgen's suffering, through the way chosen to depict such suffering. By the same token, a narration may be ironical or sarcastic, for instance, if the text reveals a critical attitude from the narrator towards the facts described. Although Robinson does not appeal to such an example, Expressionism in art emphasized precisely this aspect of artistic creation, through such means as exaggeration, deformation, or abstraction in the representation.

In all these cases, the question of the recognition of the expressive content does not arise, because the representational media allows for expressive resources of the same kind as those of emotional expression. This is clearly so in the visual arts, where we get faces, gestures, and bodily movements depicted. It is also so, according to Robinson, in literature, where elaborated phenomenological descriptions of the subjective experiences of the characters can be provided, or implied by what the characters say or do. More subtle is the question of the implied author, whose attitudes are not directly presented, in image or text, but implied in the way chosen to convey the situation or the story. The attitudes of the (implied) author, then, are not represented, but expressed; they are not said, but revealed in her way to tell or depict. Now, the question for Robinson is whether there exists any equivalent resource in music.

Against resemblance theories, Robinson rejects the idea of musical expression through proper appearances. Music lacks the resources to describe or depict, because music is not a representational art However, music can be heard as expressive of emotions in so far as it is taken to reveal such attitudes of an (implied) author, of an imagined character who would be the subject whose subjectivity is articulated in the music. Remember that we already rejected the autobiographical theory of expression, which determines the emotional content in terms of the author's actual emotions. Robinson concurs, but tries to find a proxy for the author in the point of view revealed in the music. When we perceive anger in the music, so Robinson proposes, we attribute such an emotional state to the subject we imagine responsible for those expressive aspects.

What I find interesting in this proposal is that it places the question of expressive perception in the camp of intersubjective interaction, although in an imaginative and projective way. A work of art that expresses an emotion contributes to articulate that emotional experience, and in so doing invites an interactive stance and elicits an emotional response from the audience. But, in my opinion, such an imaginative projection to an implied author cannot be the default explanation of expressive perception; it imposes a very demanding role for the audience, one that only a minority may be able to carry out. Besides, it is not always required, at least not required in the basic cases of expressive perception, even though it may be always open as a possibility. For me, these considerations are enough to encourage appeal to a more basic, spontaneous, mechanism: the one involved in empathic, intersubjective interaction. I call such mechanism the second person point of view.

The second person point of view

The second person point of view is the canonical mode of intentional attribution in interactive, face to face, interaction with others (Gomila 2001; 2003). Social interaction in general is mediated by reciprocal psychological ascriptions among participants, which take place on line in a dynamical and non-reflexive manner. They are produced as part of mutual sense-making and adjustment processes required for the interaction to be successful. They take into account the context of the interaction (current as well as precedent), as well as the expressive and indicative cues, emotional and intentional, that are directly perceptible. There is no pre-established harmony that guarantees the success of the interaction or precludes the possibility of deceit; though, as already observed, the possibility of those cases relies upon the very existence of successful cases. A prototypical situation of second-personal interaction is joint visual attention: through gaze direction and eye-contact, we can make clear what we are interested in, and grasp what our partner is interested in. Something similar may happen in emotional empathy, where an empathic response may be acknowledged and turn into reciprocal sympathy.

It is not difficult to show that these kinds of attributions are different from first-person and third-person attributions. Self-ascriptions are notoriously authoritative and genuine, while third-person attributions take an objective and distanced approach in order to understand, explain and predict other people's thinking and behaviour, quite apart of our involvement with them. Second-person attributions are interactive and semantically transparent (intentionally de re, not de dicto, in traditional terms). However, the specificity of this stance is not generally recognized, although it is steadily gaining momentum (Darwall 2006; Reddy 2008). Such attributions could be thought as grounded in self-ascriptions, by projecting analogy, or in a more fashionable version, by simulation. Alternatively, they could also be claimed to depend on inference from theoretical knowledge, however modularly organized.

To realize that the first contention cannot go ahead, it is enough to consider that second-person attributions often ascribe an attitude different from what the ascriber may be feeling. This is especially apparent in the case of emotional interaction: I may notice your mourning after the death of a beloved one, and feel corresponding compassion, or great sadness (if I think that I could have done something to avoid it), or happy (if I was looking for revenge). Another example: I see your intention to harm me, even if you failed to carry it out, so I ascribe you a malefic intention towards me. It is awkward to contend that by so doing I have to experience such an intention towards myself in the first place. I may rather mock you, again without a projection of my mocking onto you.

As regards the suggestion that it can be fully accounted for in terms of theoretical ascription, two sorts of considerations make it unlikely. To begin with, from the personal level the ascription is direct and immediate, and it does not even have to be consciously formulated but may be implicit in the social interaction. It does not take place as a theoretical inference from expressive features, but is recognized in those features themselves— it in fact relies on an expressive conception of mentality, according to which we see smiles, not facial configurations out of which we infer an inner state (Wittgenstein 1958; Scheler 1954; for a forceful recent defence, Finkelstein 2003). Just as with any kind of expressive or meaningful perception, such a direct and immediate pattern recognition relies on a process of knowledge acquisition and subpersonal processing; however it is highly contentious that such knowledge is to be conceived as a theory; it is rather practical, know how, knowledge. To see this, compare it with a clear case of theoretical knowledge, as in ascribing an Oedipus complex. Its practical dimension may also be recognized in the context-dependency of the attributions: not just of the situations, but also relative to the past experiences with the subject of the interaction. Besides, the attribution is not guided by an explanatory or predictive interest, but by the online reactive requirements of face to face interaction. In this sense, the kind of knowledge involved can be properly seen as a kind of technical knowledge, as "know how" (Vega 2001). Its expressive dimension is what gives rise to the possibility of fake, of pretending, through the control of its display. To think that such cases might involve some sort of "off-line" processing (as simulation theory contends) turns out as a misplaced idea, for this sort of cases–which is not to say that other cases may require precisely such off-line imaginative processes.

For our present purposes, what is most relevant is that the second-person perspective can also be elicited in non-canonical situations; that is to say, in non face-to-face, real time, intentional interaction. This is perhaps most evident in the emotional involvement of the spectator in cinema; but in general, the phenomenon of identification consists of reacting as if one was really taking part in an interaction which in fact one just witnesses. It sometimes may consist of taking the perspective of a participating agent, but a less participatory stance is also common, as if one was a bystander or secondary character in the situation, and reacting properly. A second personal non-canonical stance is also in operation when we perceive an event as intentional even if no agent is in view, as when I detect an arrow approaching me fast and I assume that somebody is trying to hit me, or I recognize the mourning for an accident death in the bouquet of flowers placed in a certain point of the road. Similarly, we can also understand the expression as intentionally trying to direct our attention to what is expressed. I think this is the case with music.

Second person and musical expression

In expression, we show how we feel, we make perceptible at least one of the dimensions of an emotional state. In ostensive expression, though, an effort is made to make how we feel clearer, that is to say, more communicatively efficient, more easily recognizable by the audience. The ways available for doing so, elucidated in the context of the ethological study of the process of ritualization of signals in animal communication, consist of co-opting part of the behavioural repertoire for this communicative function, making those movements more conspicuous and distinctive and taking them outside their functional context. They also involve a dynamic dimension, in that the expression takes time, and is modulated in time. Similarly, ostensive expression consists of this process of exaggeration and articulation of the emotional experience, so that it can be distinctively recognized by the audience. This recognition of attitudes is a perceptive process involving the second-person perspective. Hence, music manages to express emotions as long as the composer manages to make an emotional experience manifest and articulate in the music, so that the (competent) audience is brought to perceive the music from the second person perspective, that is, as an intentional event, one to be categorized in terms of the attitudes that it expresses. And this is possible in the first place because of the ways music impinges on us, of how it affects us emotionally.

Let's start with this latter element. The idea is that for the music to be able to elicit non-canonically our second-person stance, to perceive it as intentionally expressive, it is first required that the music has an effect on us that is "similar" to the sort of experience we have in canonical intentional interaction. I am not turning to the audience theory to say that the music expresses whatever emotion it elicits in it. I am just saying that for us to perceive the music as ostensively expressive, as expression of a subjective point of view, it is necessary for us to adopt the right sort of stance to so perceive it, and this sort of stance depends upon some power of the music to elicit it so. In a way, what I am proposing is that the "similarity" between music and expression is not to be found in the superficial resemblance between expressive features of emotional expression and expressive features of the music (expressive precisely because of this resemblance), but in their respective perlocutive effects on the audience. It is because the music impinges on us in ways that have similar effects to those that occur when we enter into intentional interactions that our second-personal ability to perceive events in intentional terms gets involved in the musical experience. The effort of the composer has been to look for those effects, by anticipating the audience's experience in the process of composition, and to try to better articulate and make distinguishable what she wants to express (which may turn out to be a certain ambiguous feeling). But similarity of effects does not require (superficial) similarity of causes: just as there are many ways to kill, to travel, or to pick grapes, so there are many ways to make the audience aware of an attitude. Sometimes it may be by the frustration of an expectation, sometimes by colourful timbre, sometimes through ambiguous tonality. Of course, our hearing the music as movement may also be playing a role at this perlocutive level, but not because we turn out to appreciate a superficial resemblance between musical movement and bodily movement, but because we perceive musical movement as intentional. We happen to be similarly affected by intentional interaction and by music, at least in the relevant cases.

Psychological research showed the strength of this phenomenon a long time ago. Early experiments showed that we perceive some movements as intentional, even if it is just inanimate objects being moved (Heider & Simmel 1944). When the movement of the objects do not follow straight paths or react to contact as passive bodies (that is, in terms of cinematic laws of inertia and acceleration), we cannot avoid seeing those movements as animate. It was also shown that we recognize intentional behaviour even in very simple stimuli, as configurations of lights (Johansson 1973): lights were positioned at the joints of a human subject and recorded during different sorts of actions, which were reliably recognizable just from the set of moving lights. Affect can also be perceived through this method (Dittrich *et al.* 1996). Recently, something similar has been done with dancers: abstracting away from the rich visual image to produce stimuli consistent just in bodily contours; the results show that the subjects perceived such stimuli as emotionally expressive (MacFarlane *et al.* 2004). The evidence goes further to establish the precise temporal and spatial constraints for such effects to take place, but the relevant conclusion for our purposes is that our capacity for intentional, expressive, perception is activated also by stimuli that do not consist of humans in action, but that are informationally indicative of that. My contention is that music can also be so perceived, and consequently, be expressively perceived, just as visual images are.

It seems misguided, at this point, to look for a rationale that justifies this power of the music to have this effect upon us. Just as there is no logical connection between sadness and tears, but just a physiological one, no logical grounding is to be found for how we react to music, just a bodily one (Juslin & Västfjall 2008). As a matter of fact, it is not even necessary that the effect be emotional to hear the music as expressive of some emotional experience. It is enough, as in the case of lights in motion, that an intentional pattern is detected.

Formalists could argue at this point that this is not so different from what they defend. We can perceive an intentional pattern in moving dots when there is just moving dots (or in running clouds, when there is no real running), just as we can perceive sadness or melancholy in a dog's face or in a landscape, without there really being any of that. The difference, I contend, is that music is the outcome of human action, and so, adoption of an intentional stance to perceive it cannot be misplaced or a categorical mistake. It is purposive character that requires the connection between expression and expressiveness, to perceive the music as expressive of attitudes, because most music was composed with an expressive intention, and thus organized in order to have a similar effect on the audience, through which such an intention could be recognized in the music. In this regard, expressive music is like ostensive facial expression, of the sort found in theatre or pantomime: of course, it is not required for such an expression be accomplished –communicatively effective- that the actor happens to feel that very emotion at the very moment of its expression (pace Actor's Studio method), nor that he manages to induce that emotion in his audience. The audience just sees the emotion in his face. Much the same, I contend, is how we can best think of musical expression, even if the effect of the music depends on its performance (which makes it possible in principle that different performances of the same work vary in their expressive content, depending on their respective ostensive efficacy). As advanced at the beginning, misunderstanding and inability to so perceive are also possible.

On the other hand, music is particularly well suited to articulating the dynamic aspect of our emotional life. This capacity relies on the former, expressive, one, but it builds upon it to present a forceful unfolding of subjective experience in time. Musical expression is not just in the business of signalling the presence of an emotion, but it rather shows how it is to feel that way, how it takes time to grow—or how it just bursts out—, how it develops into something else… Think of pain, for instance: seeing somebody in pain shows us, not just that it is pain that she feels, but also how it is to feel that way. Similarly for cases like despair, horror or ecstatic pathos an accomplished, ostensive, expression of such attitudes does not just signal its presence, it also makes those experiences shareable, as objective subjectivities, so to say. Against the Cartesian view of the mind as an inner, private, realm of experience, just inferable from the outside at most, the second person view of intentional understanding takes an expressive, pragmatic view of the mental, as grounded in social coordination, as a means for social regulation. Such a view has also had an impact on the psychological study of emotional expression (Fridlund 1995), as it has on the study of the ontogenetic development of such capacities (Reddy 2008). This approach can also shed light on expressive perception of music and musical expression as two sides of the same coin. Music cannot describe the intentional content of the emotion, cannot represent what it is that I feel, but it can have similar effects to those produced by emotional expression, thus engaging the same second-personal, basic mechanism of intentional understanding in the service of intentional interaction.

Expression and shared codes:
The case of expressionist atonalism

One corollary of the interactivist framework put forward to make sense of expressive perception is that it also sheds light upon the communicative tension faced by the composer: on the one hand, the drive to originality and creativity, on the other, the drive to be understood, to get what she wants to express through to the audience. The work has got to be new, but also in a way that still allows the audience to grasp its expressive content. It is this tension that brings about the creation and transformation of expressive codes, but also the effort to overcome them, to avoid the cliché and the common place. Some procedures may be refined, amplified, mixed up, in order to take advantage of the effective communicative resources at hand, but giving them a new twist. This trend may end up creating a conventionalized expressive code. As Kivy (2001) rightly argues, eighteenth and nineteenth century music developed such an expressive code on the basis of progressive tonal harmonies. In analogy with the process of ritualization in animal communication, a code appears when the expressive resources are exaggerated and differentiated, in order to make them easily distinguishable and recognizable, thus losing their initial connection with particular contexts and particularities, but gaining communicative efficacy. However, at some point, this code may be felt as too conventional to be useful to express new experiences and attitudes, and an impulse to overcome it, to introduce new—more "authentic"—resources become pressing.

I think this is the right perspective to understand the introduction of atonalism in early twentieth century music (Gomila, 2008). Atonalism appeared as the musical version of Expressionism in art. Like all expressionist art, its main purpose was revolutionary, not just as an artistic movement, but also politically and culturally. It grew out of a feeling of crisis, which in art was experienced as a crisis of expression: the conviction that the established artistic languages were no longer adequate to convey the sort of experiences the new artists were living (Toulmin, 2001). In music, this experience of crisis was felt most distinctively in the German culture, and focused on tonal harmony, which had become the main expressive element during Romanticism. Wagner had exhausted the code, so to say, in bringing it to its limits, and dissolving its use as the axis of the formal development of melodies in musical form. His ambiguous chords, his oscillations between different tonalities, his use of the motif, were seen by people like Schönberg as the exhaustion of the expressive power of the tonal harmony code. Nothing was left to try in order to express the new vital experiences of the age but to dispose of tonal harmony.

Thus, the first atonalism appears within an expressionist aesthetics. In this regard, to be properly appreciated, atonalism is to be viewed as the corresponding move in music to abstraction in painting. Just as tonal harmony could be considered the kernel of the musical expressive code, figuration was the basics of painting (something which impressionist painters just took for granted). As a matter of fact, both musicians and painters were conceiving their efforts as common. Schönberg, for instance, was linked to the Der Blaue Reiter group, whose leader was Kandinsky, with his project to find in abstraction the grounds for the expression of a new spiritual content (Kandinsky 1912). Under the influence of Wörringer's *Abstraktion und Einfühlung* (Wörringer 1908), a work set to account for the meaningful perception of what was just colours in juxtaposition, they tried to elicit the "empathy" of the spectator—that is to say, their emotional involvement with the artwork, by means of its expressive content, given the lack of a represented content. Abstraction, in suspending the standard objective frame of reference, is thought to induce a subjective grasping of the artwork, as the expression of a subjective world, to which the spectator is expected to empathically resonate. In other words, the formal innovation is developed in the service of an expressive project. Much the same is to be said of atonalism.

However, Kivy (2001) argues that atonalism did not succeed in creating a new expressive code - a code analogous to that of tonal harmony. He considers that this is the reason that explains the lack of success of atonal music in general, and the contemporary return of tonal harmony. To my view, this is the wrong diagnosis. In the first place, I would point to the formalist aesthetics of dodecaphonic atonalism (and the serialism that followed) as the main reason for the lack of success of atonalism: it is formalism that turns atonalism into a closed code, but a code lacking any expressive purpose. As I said, not all music is expressive. That which is not, clearly will have problems to get an audience, given that it is not directed to it in the first place. There is nothing for the music to express. On the other hand, I would insist that it is not atonalism per se that lacks success, but just this formalist atonalism. Expressionist atonalism is in very good health and reaching very big audiences through music for the cinema. It is certainly not the kind of institutional performance conceived for classical music. But remember that Schönberg, for one, also rejected the concert as a "bourgeois" event. The current integration of visual, narrative and musical experience in cinema has a precedent in the kind of performance Skriabin conceived for his later works. But atonalism may recede if it is experienced as an inadequate expressive vehicle. Unfortunately, these art-theoretical considerations are not taken into much account by the hegemonic aesthetic formalism of the day - coherently, but also ironically, given that aesthetic formalists are not much fond of musical formalists.

Works cited

Budd, Malcom. 1995. *Values of Art. Pictures, Poetry and Music*. London: Penguin.

Darwall, Stephen. 2006. *The Second-person Standpoint. Morality, Respect and Accountability*. Cambridge, MA.: Harvard University Press.

Davies, Stephen. 1994. *Musical Meaning and Expression*. Ithaca, NY: Cornell University Press.

Dittrich, W. H., T. Troscianko, S. E. G. Lea, and D. Morgan. 1996. Perception of emotion from dynamic point-light displays represented in dance. *Perception* 25: 727-738.

Finkelstein, David H. 2003. *Expression and the Inner*. Cambridge, MA: Harvard University Press.

Fridlund, Alan. 1995. *Human Facial Expression: an Evolutionary View*. New York: Academic Press.

Gomila, Antoni. 2002. La perspectiva de segunda persona de la atribución mental. *Azafea* 1: 123-138.

—. 2003. "La perspectiva de segunda persona." In *Psicología Cognitiva y Filosofía de la Mente*, eds. E. Rabossi and A. Duarte, 195-218. Buenos Aires: Alianza Editorial.

—. 2008. La expresión emocional en la música desde el expresionismo musical. *Estudios de Psicología* 29 (1): 117-131.

Goodman, Nelson. 1976. *The Languages of Art*. Indianapolis: Hackett Publishing Company.

Green, Mitchell S. 2007. *Self-expression*. Oxford: Oxford University Press.

Heider, Fritz, and Marianne Simmel. 1944. An experimental study of apparent behavior. *American Journal of Psychology* 57 (2): 243-259.

Johansson, Gunnar. 1973. Visual perception of biological motion and a model for its analysis. *Perception and Psychophysics* 14: 201-211.

Juslin, Patrik N., and John A. Sloboda. 2001. *Music and Emotion. Theory and Research*. Oxford: Oxford University Press.

Juslin, Patrik N., and Daniel Västfjäll. 2008. Emotional responses to music: the need to consider underlying mechanism. *Behavioral and Brain Sciences* 31: 559-621.

Kandinsly, Wassily. 1912. *Uber das geistige in der Kunst*. Munich: Piper and co.

Kivy, Peter. 1980. *The Corded Shell. Reflections on Musical Expression*. Princeton: Princeton University Press.

—. 2001. "Making the codes and breaking the codes." In *New Essays on Musical Understanding*, 44-70. Oxford: Oxford University Press.

Langer, Susan. 1942. *Philosophy in a New Key*. Cambridge, MA.: Harvard University Press.

Ledoux, Joseph. 1996. *The Emotional Brain: the Misterious Underpinnings of Emotional Life*. New York: Simon & Schuster.

Levinson, Jerrold. 1982. Music and the negative emotions. *Pacific Philosophical Quarterly* 63: 327-346.

Lewis, Marc D. 2005. Bridging emotion theory and neurobiology through dynamic systems modeling. *Behavioral and Brain Sciences* 28: 169-245.

Macfarlane, Laura, Irena Kulka, and Frank Pollick. 2004. The representation of affect revealed by Butoh dance. *Psychologia* 47 (2): 96-103.

Marks, Lawrence. 1978. *The Unity of the Senses: Interrelations Among the Modalities*. New York: Academic Press.

Matravers, Derek. 1998. *Art and Emotion*. Oxford: Oxford University Press.

Narmour, Eugene. 1991. The top-down and bottom-up systems of musical implication: building on Meyer's theory of emotional syntax. *Music Perception* 9: 1-26.

Panksepp, Jaak , and Günther Bernatzsky. 2002. Emotional sounds and the brain: the neuro-affective foundations of musical appreciation. *Behavioural Processes* 60 (2): 133-155.

Raffman, Diana. 2003. Is twelve-tone music artistically defective? *Midwest Studies in Philosophy* 27: 69-87.

Reddy, Vasudevi. 2008. *How Infants Know Minds*. Cambridge, MA.: Harvard University Press.

Robinson, Jenefer. 2005. *Deeper than Reason. Emotion and its Role in Literature, Music and Art*. Oxford: Oxford University Press.

Scheler, Max. 1954. *The Nature of Sympathy*. Tr. Peter Heath: Routledge & Kegan Paul.

Toulmin, Stephen. 2001. *Return to Reason*. Cambridge: Cambridge University Press.

Wittgenstein, Ludwig. 1958. *Philosophical Investigations*. New York: Macmillan Publishing Company.

Wollheim, Richard. 1974. "Expression." In *On Art and the Mind*. Cambridge, MA.: Harvard University Press.

Worringer, Wilhelm. 1908. *Abstraktion und Einfühlung*. München: Fink.

CHAPTER SIX

THE COGNITIVE VALUE OF EMOTIONS IN MUSICAL UNDERSTANDING

MARÍA JOSÉ ALCARAZ

Introduction

Much theoretical discussion has been devoted to the problem of musical expression; that is, to whether music can be said to express or to be expressive of the garden-variety emotions. The topic I would like to explore in this paper is a related one but it does not directly deal with the issue of musical expressiveness. I am interested not in explaining how music can be expressive of the garden-variety emotions (actually, I believe what I am going to defend is in principle compatible with most of the accounts of musical expressiveness that have been proposed), but on how our response to the music can be, and with a reason, a moved response. My aim is to show that responding to music by experiencing some emotions may not only be a possible musical experience but also a genuine one. In arguing for this, I will mainly discuss Peter Kivy's characterization of musical experience as one where emotion plays no substantial role in music understanding[1].

Let's start with Kivy's view in order to see to what extent the claim I would like to offer here is an alternative to his in this respect. Kivy has not denied one can experience some sort of emotion while listening to music; not even that responding to music with a deep emotional state might be precisely the mark of our understanding the piece and grasping its quality. He denies, however, that we can experience the garden-variety emotions as part of an adequate response to the music; that is, he believes music cannot really make us feel sad or melancholic. In fact, he believes that if it were true that we normally respond in such a way to the music, that sort of response would likely ruin our appreciation of the work. So, he has offered two different strands of arguments in order to reject the claim that experiencing the garden-variety emotions is part of the appreciative experience. On the one hand, he has tried to show that music is not the appropriate object towards which those emotions can be properly directed. On the other, he has claimed that, were these emotions part of the response expressive music aroused in us, we should better repress them, for they will surely distort our appreciation of the work.

In arguing against Kivy's view, I will show that it may be the case that music can arouse emotional states and that experiencing these emotions contributes to our understanding of the musical piece. I need then to respond to Kivy's powerful arguments against this possible understanding of the role of emotion in music appreciation and to provide some positive account about how music can arouse emotional states in the listener. To achieve this I will introduce some qualifications into what is currently considered one of the best views of emotions, i.e., the cognitive view. Secondly, I will borrow some thoughts that have been already developed in the philosophical reflection about narrative arts, where an emotional response is conceived as having a more positive role. Finally, I would like to offer some thoughts defending the claim that the arousal of some emotional response in the listener by the music may be considered as part of its value.

Kivy's arguments for the claim that music cannot arouse the garden-variety emotions

The most powerful argument against the possibility of music arousing emotions such as happiness or sadness relies upon a cognitive view of emotion. According to this view, an emotion is a mental state which has a) an object, b) a belief, and c) some feeling state associated with it. Further elements of this view–although not necessarily derived from the cognitive view as such–are the behavioural and motivational aspects of the emotions. Thus, if I am in a particular emotional state, for example of sadness, there is something I feel sad about (the object), there is a belief about that thing I feel sad about which warrants my sadness (the belief), and, finally, there is some sort of felt state that I experience (some sort of feeling component associated with sadness)

Given the general acceptance of this view, Kivy argues, it seems difficult to explain how music can arouse sadness–or any other sort of emotion–in me, for it is not the appropriate object I could be sad about. What would it be for someone to be sad about a piece of music? Are we referring to the same sort of state when we say one is sad about her friend's misfortune and when one is said to be sad about a musical work?

Moreover, absolute music lacks the representational devices in order to provide a character or situation we could be sad about. In this sense, music distinguishes itself from the representational arts. Hence, despite the very much-disputed problem of the rationality of emotional responses towards fictional characters, one can make some sense of feeling pity or sadness about a character's fate. However, since absolute music has no means to convey a representational content in this sense, it can never provide the sort of object one could have emotional reactions to.

There is a further and similar problem that results from endorsing the cognitive view of emotions. Not only is the object of our emotional reactions to music mysterious, but also the required belief is missing. What do we believe about the music for us to be warranted in feeling sad about it? Again, the question is odd enough to threaten the plausibility of responding truly moved to the music.

The tendency argument

Kivy's second argument acknowledges to some extent it might be possible that music arouses the garden-variety emotions. In examining Colin Radford's view (1991).–but also in discussing some aspects of the views defended by Stephen Davies (1994) and Jerrold Levinson (1990; 1996)–he concedes Radford's point that sad music may arouse sadness in the listener.

Radford's argument for this claim is roughly the following: just as depressive days depress us and happy colours make us feel happy, sad music may make us feel sad and happy tunes may arouse happy states in us. Both depressive days and music have the tendency to depress those who are under their influence. Although Kivy acknowledges that the non-musical examples are very compelling, he still finds his appreciative experience as a listener at odds with Radford's conclusion. Kivy, then, argues against Radford's view as follows: sad music may well have a tendency to make me feel sad but it may also be the case that the conditions under which I experience the music–that is, in the concert hall– are such that that tendency is normally repressed and, hence, sad music never arouses sadness in me. It is perfectly possible that x has the tendency to produce y and also that the tendency never manifests, if the conditions for it to be manifested are never met.

Kivy also notices that sad days, as opposed to sad music, have a more cumulative and enveloping character. Accordingly, it may be easier to be made sad by a sad day (or week) than by a piece of music–which usually never last more than three hours, intervals included.

The behaviour argument

It is a common mark of being under a certain emotional state that one manifests or expresses it through some specific behaviour. If I am sad, I may, for example, bear a long face or cry into my pillow. If I feel happy I will probably smile and move in a lively way. However, none of these expressive features seem to be present when I am supposed to be saddened by sad music. Shall we take this lack of behavioural evidence as a lack of emotion? Kivy thinks that on top of the other two arguments this is another reason not to be persuaded by the idea that sad music can arouse sadness in me. This problem also has an inner link to the first problem mentioned above. Normally, if something makes me feel angry or sad, my emotion–grounded on a certain belief about the object of my emotion–will likely motivate me to pursue some sort of action. However, there is no evidence at all that any such motivation takes place while listening to music. Therefore, the lack of the behavioural and motivational aspects normally linked to our emotional states could be taken as a symptom that what we really experience are not real emotions or fully developed ones.

The negative emotions argument

Another worry that Kivy has expressed towards the idea that music can arouse in the listener the emotions it is expressive of is that we would find it difficult to explain why people intentionally choose to listen to sad music. If sad music saddens me and if equally good but happy music makes me feel happy, how can rational agents choose sad music over equally good but happy music without being masochists? Kivy acknowledges that there might be reasons to engage with works that elicit negative emotions, as the example of tragedy has long established. However, those reasons are not available in the music case, for experiencing the tragic negative emotions is part of a more complex cognitive benefit. However, this cognitive pay-off is not available in music for, as we have already pointed out, music lacks representational abilities and, therefore, it doesn't have the devices to produce a complex cognitive experience, such as the tragic one. So, in the absence of a representational and cognitive justification, the arousal of negative emotions seems to pose a problem for those who also try to defend the value that some sad music may have.

Non-expressive but moving music and expressive but not-moving music

Finally, Kivy has noticed that if there is some experience of being moved by the music this cannot simply rely on my perception of expressive properties. As he points out, many examples of music that cannot be said, properly speaking, to be expressive is however very moving. On the other hand, not all–in fact very few–cases of music expression seem to move the listener. There are many examples of sad music that moves us not at all; in short, not all cases of expressive music moves the audience and non-expressive music sometimes does. How can we accommodate this twofold difficulty within the view that Radford, Davies and Levinson have been defending?

Kivy's view about being moved by music

Kivy doesn't deny that there might be an experience of being deeply moved by music. He is not just defending a cold and stilted way of appreciating it. In fact, he acknowledges he has been moved several times by music, but he thinks this experience is mistakenly characterized by appealing to the garden-variety emotions. What one feels when one is moved by music is not any of these emotions. Rather it is a nameless emotion–or an emotion that can only be identified through its object–about the beauty of the musical piece. What moves us is not jus the perception of some expressive content, but that it is beautifully presented in the music. In fact, music may be moving despite lacking expressive content, for it is the beauty of the music and not its expressive character that moves us.

As a coda, Kivy advances a hypothesis about the role expressive properties do play in our comprehension of the work. He defends the view that they are in fact a source of value; not in virtue of arousing any emotion in the listener–for they, strictly speaking, do not arouse any–but because they contribute to the form of the piece. In short, Kivy's hypothesis is that those expressive properties play some syntactical role that, he hopes, can be further characterized.

The ability of music to arouse emotions in the audience

As it is clear, the defender of an emotional response to music faces a number of problems that may well persuade one to give up. Maybe moved audiences are less common–or more irrational–than it could be thought at first sight. However, I think there can be some ways to accommodate these criticisms as well as to propose a positive role for the emotional response in music understanding. I think these two goals are somehow intertwine and will be developed on a pair.

Two preliminary remarks

I must start by acknowledging that if for an emotion to be aroused we need to pin down all the elements stipulated by the cognitive view then music cannot arouse emotions, in this sense. However, I hope to show there are cases in which we reasonably talk of a particular emotion as being aroused even when some of these components are missing. Maybe this should put some scope-constraint on the kinds of emotions I will be allowed to speak of. However, I still think the mental states that are aroused are–in some paradigmatic cases–emotions and not other mental states.

Secondly, I would like to point that, contrary to the view put forward by Radford, Davies, and Levinson, I will not defend that music can arouse emotions by expressing those emotions. There might be cases in which this is what happens, but music does not have to be expressive in order to move. Hence, music can arouse an emotional state that is identical to the one it expresses, or a different one related to it, or an emotional response towards some non-expressive quality in the music. To that extent, I agree with Kivy that if there is anything like being moved by music this does not seem to have a necessary link with the phenomenon of expression in music. Nevertheless, for some obvious reasons, expressive music may be more capable of arousing emotions in us than non-expressive one.

The view

My departure from the cognitive view can be cashed out as follows: we emotionally respond to our surroundings and to features of them that are not always represented propositionally or that do not belong to what can be cashed out in propositional terms, or not entirely. Sometimes what triggers a particular emotional response is not so much a particular state of affairs as some aspects of it. Consider the following example: I am not disappointed about your intervention at the meeting–actually I shared everything you said–but the attitude you adopted was pretentious and, hence, the way you expressed a view I very much agreed with aroused my disappointment. Thus, aspects of the way something is produced or brought about may ground a particular emotional response[2]. This fact may be even more noticeable in fictional cases: it is precisely the mode of presenting some situation that warrants a particular emotional response. For example, it is the way the criminal is portrayed what grounds and warrants my pity and sympathy for him. Here I think we would say we admire the criminal not so much for his evil behaviour as for other qualities he may possess, and these qualities are conveyed to us through the way the character is presented.

Granted this, the defender of the cognitive approach to emotions can rebut my point as follows: these examples do not prove an emotion can be aroused in the absence of some propositionally expressed content; at most, they show that what warrant a particular emotion is both the intentional object and the way this object is giving to me. Mere non-propositional content cannot arouse emotions. But this is precisely what I would like to defend. How can I do this?

I think that trying to defend the plausibility of non-propositional aspects to be responsible for the arousal of some emotions is more easily achieved in we look at the problem from a broader perspective, one that includes other forms of abstract art.

I take it that the problem of a moved response by absolute music arises for other abstract arts too; and, hence, that if there is room in the appreciation of abstract painting or sculpture for an emotional response, there should be similarly some room for it in the musical case. I think– although this may be due to a matter of current but wrong views about abstract visual arts–that our problem is a much less disputed issue in the pictorial and sculptural cases. After all, no one would be very puzzle if someone said her experience of a Rothko's painting was tinted by a deep emotion. However, mere acknowledging is not explanation, so I need to provide some reason to motivate the claim that non-representational aspects may be the cause and object of an emotion.

Here is what I think. When we learn or acquire the capacities to respond emotionally to situations, people, etc. we not only respond to propositional contents–which is the point I have just made in the previous paragraphs–we also associate certain felt qualities of those contents to the emotions they arouse. Those felt qualities may have a more or less subjective quality for us–as when I associate a particular smell to someone I was always fear of; however, in other cases, these felt qualities may be less linked to our own biography, and our associations between felt qualities, particular contents, and responses may be uniform enough. Now, artists may take these felt aspects of sounds, colours, movements, shapes etc. in order to evoke or arouse some emotional state in the viewer or listener. Moreover, (and this will be the point I would like to develop in the last section) artists may elaborate on those felt aspects and produce a work the apprehension of which may involve the arousal and development of some emotional states linked to the perceived properties of the music.

What is then the relationship between those perceived qualities and my undergoing of some emotion? I would like to show it is not merely a causal one and that, despite its non-propositional character, these felt qualities may ground my emotional response. The composer in responding to the music she is producing becomes aware of the possible responses the audience could have towards the music and partly chooses some sound structure or another by having in mind that effect. Of course, there is more than these felt qualities to take into account, but it seems possible that a musician notices those effects and that she works on them accordingly. Thus, she may intentionally choose some aspects of the composition such that a certain emotional response is warranted and she may try to explore what sorts of expectations and attitudes the music triggers in order to build up a certain overall emotional response. There is a possible worry concerning the idea of a certain feeling to be warranted by the perception of some feature in the music. However, I think there are ways to fix whether a particular emotional response may be warranted insofar as it is grounded in how the music sounds. Sometimes the story that one would need to tell will appeal to the perception of felt aspects of the music as similar to some aspects in daily perception; others the very history of music and its development can provide the sources for disambiguating which emotion might be required. Thus, as well as we respond to felt qualities in life, we respond emotionally to the felt qualities perceived in the music. It is with these aspects—which we find usually difficult to make explicit because of their non-propositional character—that the artists might work in order to provoke some emotional response in the listener. In short, it is possible that perceiving certain non-representational aspects in the music arouses emotional states. I have claimed that non-representational aspects need not be necessarily expressive properties, although they may be so. We sometimes respond emotionally to properties other than expressive ones in the music.

Thus, in listening to a particular piece I may perceive a particular property, or identify certain gesture in it, to which I respond emotionally. I may perceive, for example, the sadness of a piece and respond to it, maybe with sadness or with some other appropriate emotion to the perception of sadness. What is more, the fact that these felt qualities are presented to us without any connection to a representational content may allow the listener to wholly engage with them and to pay attention to the sort of qualities they are. Hence, absolute music allows a sort of engagement with that aspect of our sensibility that representational arts. are less able to provide.

I think what I have in mind may have a strong support from the dance case, but my aim will be to show this might be also the case for music. In abstract dance–where a particular type of object or being is not represented–the perception of the movement is nevertheless linked to, or perceived as, the perception of a human body and hence the connection with gesture and feeling is straightforward. In music the very nature of sounds may render this claim less evident at first. However, I think we listen to certain musical aspects as linked to felt qualities that, in turn, belong to the same world as our emotions do.

The role of emotion in music understanding

Now, I would like to turn to the issue of what contribution do expressive properties and the arousal of emotional states make to the experience of music. Here I also depart from Kivy's view. He believes expressive qualities in the music do play a role that he cashes out in syntactical terms. Expressive qualities may contribute to the sense of closure or suspension within a particular piece. It is the syntactic role played by expressive qualities that bring them a valuable place in music, not the fact that they are presenting musically a particular emotion.

I think a possible worry one could arise against this syntactic role is that it is too narrow. It gives a role to expressive properties that cannot make a difference between our valuing a work precisely because it has a particular emotional character. If expressive properties bear no further value than the value they play in the syntactic relationships of the music, we would not understand someone choosing a work because it is expressive (and maybe moving as well) as opposed to a non-expressive one if the two had the same syntactical worth. But I think we may value a piece of music not only because it is *beautifully* sad, but rather because it is beautifully *sad*. Because in being sad it conveys something about sadness or human reactions towards sad events that we may find worthy and that contributes to the music value.

I think the reason for this is similar to one offered by those who endorse the idea that cognitive and moral values contribute to the aesthetic value of a work of art[3]. It may be true that an immoral work is as good as a good-intentioned one. Maybe its structure is more complex and interesting and the characters are developed in a way the politically correct work has failed to provide. Thus, immoral aspects may not be the last word when it comes to aesthetically assess a work of art. However a fictional work whose moral content is small won't be among our top ten just in virtue of possessing some aesthetic virtues. In narrative arts, the two components go hand in hand, and if it is true that just good morals do not amount to good art, good aesthetics but poor moral content won't make us value a novel as highly as those we usually take to be the paradigms of great literature. Something similar, I think, can be said of expressiveness in music. It is undeniable that a piece of music is not better just because it is expressive; actually there are considerable amounts of musical works that are expressive in a poor way. However, when a piece of music is good in being expressive of some emotion, we tend to consider the emotional content of the music as one of the reasons for valuing it so much. In fact, we usually think the emotional content is presented to us in a particular rich way or with some unusual tones that cannot be explained independently of other features of the music. The beauty and the emotional content are, as it were, of a piece.

If what I have said above about perceived qualities in the music that may ground our emotional responses is cogent, it seems that I could also have a word to say in this context. Where Kivy claimed an emotional response–were it to be aroused by the music–had to be repressed, I would say one's responding emotionally to the expressive content of a musical work may be warranted and part of a genuine appreciative response. Thus, I think there is an alternative to Kivy's syntactical view where our emotional responses are not only genuine, but also part of what constitutes a good understanding of the musical work.

Responding emotionally may contribute to our understanding of a musical piece

Finally I would like to discuss Kivy's claim that if music had the power to arouse emotions in us, we shall better repress them in order to properly grasp the music's qualities.

He thinks this might be twofold motivated, on the one hand, by his syntactical view about the role expressive properties play in our apprehension of the music qualities, and, on the other, by a folk psychology belief about how emotional states may affect our attention and apprehension of what we listen to. I would like to focus now on this second reason for, as I will try to show, it somehow ignores some possible role emotional states may play in our apprehension of the music content that may be worth looking at.

It seems common sense that when one is on the grip of an emotion one's ability to focus and pay due attention to some features of the surrounding may be threatened. If I am really sad or melancholic while listening to a piece of music my perception of the piece may somehow get distorted. Our emotions may tint our perceptual experience and present a particular situation under a light that may be at odds with its particular character. Emotions are said to possess an overriding effect and this might be considered as an obstacle for rightly grasping what it is giving to us in perception.

However, and without denying emotions may have this ability to colour our perception[4], I think that there is also evidence that it is precisely in virtue of this feature of emotions that they may help us to focus upon the right feature, or may organize our perceptual content in such a way that we grasp something about it that could have been missed had we listened to the work in a cold way.

In fact, the view that responding in a moved way to works of literary art as a necessary constituent of a proper appreciation of the work has been long defended by authors such as Susan Feagin (1996) and Noël Carroll (1997) among others. My aim here is to examine whether a similar view could be proposed for music appreciation, and if there is some role for an emotional response within music understanding.

In the literary case it seems easier to defend the reader's emotional response as being warranted by the fictional content. After all, leaving aside the problem of responding emotionally towards something we believe is just fiction, narrative arts typically contain characters who perform actions and who may trigger our emotional responses. Moreover, emotionally responding to them may be part of what constitutes a good grasping of their features, even a necessary component if we are to make sense of some other features of the work. If I do not get anxious about some character's fate I may not see why her ending is so dramatic. Thus, at least in some cases, my emotional response may contribute to my understanding of a work.

However, the problem seems harder when one tries to justify this role in the case of absolute music. The reason why this is so is a familiar one. Music lacks propositional content and, to that extent, it is unable to provide the listener with the materials for her to respond emotionally.

I have tried to motivate the view that music–or any other form of abstract art–does not need to convey propositional content for it to be the sort of thing that may arouse emotional responses. What triggers a particular emotion as a response to the music may be some aspect or aspects that the listener tends to perceive as a form of movement or gesture which warrants that emotion. Moreover, as well as my emotional response may play some role in my understanding of a particular character and her development in a novel, my responding emotionally to the music may contribute to bring different aspects of the music under a common light and to perceive whether those features do fit in such a way. If, as some research on the emotional role in perception has proved, emotions should be regarded as playing an active role in guiding our attention and organizing the information in our surrounding, we may claim that, similarly, emotions may guide our perceptual experience of the music. Where Kivy saw some threat to music understanding, others may see a positive and necessary role.

I mentioned above that artists may even work on this tendency we have to respond emotionally to some aspects to the music in order to build up some expectations that, in turn, guide our sense of fit in the music. It is precisely because we perceive the music under some emotional state that we perceive the climax and the trough in the music. Most of the time emotional states are too fine, subtle and difficult to name; however this lack of precision should not be devastating, as Kivy acknowledges when he contemplates the possibility of music arousing nameless emotions or emotions whose name cannot be but the description of its content.

Responding to Kivy's criticisms

Finally, I would like to say a word about how could this view deal with Kivy's powerful criticisms against those who have defended music can arouse emotional states in the listener.

My answer to the "Uncle Charlie" argument is that emotions may have non-propositional objects. Therefore, the lack of representational qualities in absolute music is not an obstacle for the possibility of experiencing some emotional states as grounded in properties of the music. This response involves some revision of the cognitive view of emotions, but I think its core is preserved. On this view, emotions still have intentional objects; however those objects need not be propositionally expressible. Thus, if one admits this possibility, absolute music, and other forms of abstract art, can arouse emotions.

As for his claim that music may have the tendency to arouse emotions but that that tendency may be systematically repressed, I would oppose the view that allowing that tendency to work may be not only innocuous but desirable too. This does not make one to commit with the idea that the purpose of the arousal of emotions by music is just instrumental. Composers may, while composing, listen to the music so that they may experience the possible emotional responses a potential listener could experience; they may, in turn, work up on those aspects so that the emotions themselves become part of the required response if one is to properly grasp the music work. That sometimes composers do so seems to

be at least confirmed by the amount of music that is produced for cinema–
where it seems clear that there is an intentional work on arousing
emotional states in the listener as a way to prepare her for certain scenes.
Although one could think this is precisely a case in which the tendency to
respond emotionally to music is not at the service of a better understanding
of the music but to the fulfilment of some other purpose, it seems to me
that it still helps to establish that music may arouse some emotional states.

Also, the view I was proposing was slightly different from the one
Kivy discusses. Radford, who may be considered one of the main
contenders in this debate, links the arousal of some emotional state to the
perception of that quality in the music. In his view, sad music has the
tendency to make me sad and happy music the tendency to make me
happy. However, according to the view I have tried to develop, our
emotional responses to he music need not be always aroused by our
perceiving in the music the corresponding emotional property. Features
other than expressive ones may be moving. Thus, I can also accommodate
Kivy's complaint that expressive music sometimes may be not very
moving while non-expressive music may be very moving indeed. One is to
be moved by the music if the composer has elaborated some aspects of the
music that successfully triggers that emotional response.

As we saw, another worry that could support Kivy's denial of the
possibility of absolute music to arouse emotions was that we observe no
behaviour at all that could indicate the listener is experiencing any of these
emotions. I think the best answer to this has been offered by Derek
Matravers (1998) in one of his responses to Kivy's criticism to his view.
As Matravers has pointed out, it is perfectly consistent to hold that a
particular emotion is being felt while acknowledging that there might be
no evidence of it through a manifestation of the emotion in its typical
behaviour. In general, this lack of behaviour has been taken to be a reason
to doubt one feels real emotions towards fiction and works of art.
However, if one is persuaded, as Kivy does, that real emotions may be
aroused in our experience of narrative arts, it seems to me one could
similarly endorse, despite the lack of behavioural evidence, a similar claim
for music. If we think there is room for a truly emotional response in one
case, there should be in the other as well.

Finally, we need to respond to the problem of the arousal of negative
emotions and how one can defend their value within the aesthetic
experience of music. In responding to this possible criticism by Kivy I will
try also to defend the thought that it is precisely in virtue of its capacity to
move the listener–even when the content of the emotion may be
considered as having a negative value–where part of the value we attach to

music experience can be located.

The value of moving music

I have just tried to defend that being moved by the music may not only be less problematic than Kivy thinks, but also that it contributes to our understanding of the piece. It is precisely by responding with an emotional state to the music that our sense of how the music develops becomes precise. As well as one would allegedly miss some important aspects of a novel if one does not respond emotionally as one should, one would not be able to fully grasp the aesthetic value of a piece of music if one rests cold and distanced towards the emotional world opened up for the listener.

So far, everything I have said is compatible with an understanding of our emotional response as one that has a mere syntactical role. Experiencing the emotions the music is supposed to arouse guide our experience of the music such that certain features become salient or organized in a certain way. However, this is still insufficient if one also wants to defend that music's ability to arouse this sort of experience is a source of musical value.

I think my response is again similar to the one usually given in the context of literary appreciation and representational arts in general. There, the emotional engagement with the work is taken to be a source of value because it allows us to explore and to be acquainted with some emotional states that we may have fewer chances to experience in our everyday lifes. Besides, it is said that our emotional engagement with art has a feature our everyday emotional responses lack. We can explore our emotional responses with a sort of awareness not so achievable when pressed by real circumstances. So in responding emotionally to music we not only respond as we should in order to fully grasp a particular work–if the composer has precisely elaborated on those aspects; but also we have the chance to explore particular emotional states with a sort of focus and attention lees available in daily life experience. This sort of experience is a cognitive one, although the cognitive content is again not one that can be grasped propositionally; it is a felt content we become aware of by acquaintance.

Within this understanding of our emotional responses to music it seems lees odd that one could choose music that arouse sadness or any other negative emotion. In responding to the music with sadness we are not merely responding in the right way–if this is what the composer somehow intended in her exploration of the effects her music could have in the listener–but also we value the work precisely for providing us with a particular experience of that emotional state whose character we can explore in a particular and profound way.

Conclusion

I have tried to defend the view that absolute music may arouse emotional states in the listener despite its lack of representational content. This is possible because emotional responses may take non-propositional objects. Thus, the composer may explore the possible emotional responses the audience could have towards some particular sonic structure partly relying in resemblances between the sounds and some felt qualities of our daily experience. In working these aspects out in the music, the composer may aim at arousing some emotional states in the audience, and making them play a role in the overall understanding of the piece. Finally, the composer may use that emotion not only with a syntactic purpose, but also with the intention to explore that emotion through the music, and thus to provide the listener with a work, the appreciation of which involves the acquaintance with a particular emotional state. When this is the case the experience of that emotion not only contributes to the understanding of the piece but also constitutes part of its value.

Notes

---

[1] Kivy's denial of absolute music's ability to arouse emotional states in the listener can be mainly found in Kivy (2001: 71–151) and Kivy (2002: 110–134).

[2] For an extended analysis of this phenomenon in the literary and narrative arts see, Feagin (1996).

[3] See, for example, Berys Gaut (2006), Matthew Kieran (2002) and Eileen John (2000).

[4] One of the more prominent defenders of this view has been Richard Wollheim (1999).

Works cited

Carroll, Noël. 1997. "Art, Narrative, and Emotion." In *Emotions and the Arts*, eds. Mette Hjort and Sue Laver, 190–211. New York: Oxford University Press.

Davies, Stephen. 1994. *Musical Meaning and Expression*. Ithaca: Cornell University Press.

Feagin, Susan. 1996. *Reading with Feeling*. Ithaca: Cornell University Press.

Izard, Carroll E., Jerome Kagan, and Robert Zajonc, eds. 1988. *Emotions, cognition and behaviour*. Cambridge: Cambridge University Press.

Kivy, Peter. 2001. *New Essays on Musical Understanding*. Oxford: Clarendon Press.

—. 2002. *Introduction to a Philosophy of Music*. Oxford: Clarendon Press.

Levinson, Jerrold. 1990. "Music and Negative Emotion." *In Music, Art, and Metaphysics: Essays in Philosophical Aesthetics*. Ithaca: Cornell University Press.

—. 1996. "Musical Expressiveness." In *The Pleasures of Aesthetics: Philosophical Essays*. Ithaca: Cornell University Press.

Matravers, Derek. 1998. *Art and Emotion*. Oxford: Oxford University Press.

Radford, Colin. 1989. Emotions and Music: A Reply to the Cognitivists. *Journal of Aesthetics and Art Criticism* 47 (1): 69-76.

—. 1991. Muddy Waters. *Journal of Aesthetics and Art Criticism* 49 (3): 247-252.

Gaut, Berys. 2006. "Art and Cognition." In *Contemporary Debates in Aesthetics and the Philosophy of Art*, ed. Matthew Kieran, 115–126. Oxford: Blackwell.

Kieran, Matthew. 2002. "Value of art." In *The Routledge Companion to Aesthetics*, 2nd Edition, ed. Berys Gaut and Dominic McIver Lopes, 293–305. London and NY: Routledge.

John, Eileen. 2000. "Art and Knowledge." In *The Routledge Companion to Aesthetics*, 2nd Edition, ed. Berys Gaut and Dominic McIver Lopes, 329–340. London and NY: Routledge.

Wollheim, Richard. 1999. *On the Emotions*. New Haven and London: Yale University Press.

CHAPTER SEVEN

EXPRESSION AND EXPRESSING ONESELF IN MUSIC: AN APPROACH TOWARDS THE EXPRESSION OF SUBJECTIVITY IN THE ARTS THROUGH THE ARTIST NOVEL

MIGUEL CORELLA

Expression

The belief that the arts consist of, or at least allow for, the expression of subjectivity is, probably, the only dogma of Romantic aesthetics that still remains, and with surprising vitality. The idea that art consists of the manifestation of an inner voice or of an undertone that beats under the surface of the objects continues to be adopted by a good part of contemporary artistic practice. This Romantic expressive impulse was sustained and even exacerbated by the historical avant-garde, the first organised movement of which, to be exact, took the name "Expressionism". And Expressionism constitutes the only legacy of the avant-garde that continues to be topical given that, even after various different neo-expressionist waves, an author or a work can still claim to be expressionist, whereas nowadays nobody would say Cubist, Unanimist, Vorticist or even Futurist. The avant-garde aesthetics shapes itself as expressionist poetics in which the spontaneous and naïve gesture is considered the manifestation of inner authenticity, in contrast to the elaborated, secondary and artificial character of conscious and calculated intervention. The gestural and spontaneous component can give rise to automatic or mechanic procedures and can also generate a cult of expressive violence and the twisting of forms, displaying a taste for the deformed and grotesque. On other occasions this exaltation of spontaneity is transformed into the aesthetics of play that aims to return to the innocence of the child and to youthful merriment, but which is perfectly compatible with nostalgic stances as well as with the melancholic delight in the loss. On the other hand, poetic Expressionism has permitted the identification of avant-garde art and progressive values; both supposedly committed to the defence of virtues such as rebelliousness, spontaneity, revolt or inebriation (Clair 1997). Expressionism could thus be considered as the quintessence of the avant-garde.

But, even after the avant-garde impetus seemed to be exhausted and converted into a pose of self-promotion or a perfectly established procedure, the expressionist dogma has resisted the fiercest criticism: not just the diverse "demands of Realism" that, at different historical junctures, opposed the primacy of expression, but even the attempts of conceptual or minimalist artists to eliminate in one fell blow the representation and the expression of subjectivity. Thus, for example, in relation to the pure geometric forms of Minimalist sculpture, it has been argued that in the void of a mute expression the presence of the unconscious beats nonetheless. Even in the attempt to express nothing and to present the object in its pure superficiality, there is something in the object that "looks at us, something which is something else and which imposes an in, a within" (Didi-Huberman 1992). The simple optic plane thus turns into visual power that looks at us, a depth that rises like the tide to the surface. Thus also in the very particular music of John Cage or Karlheim Stockhausen the abandonment of intentionality and the resorting to noises and casual sounds, the renouncing of melodic lineality, of narratory and dramatic quality confers greater prominence on silence; but on a silence that, in Cage for example, is full of spiritual resonances. Hence the surface denies its apparent flat character and refers to a hidden undercurrent that expresses itself in an allusive, veiled or negative way. Completely removed from what is gestural and dramatic this new Expressionism resorts to silence in order to negatively present an absence, since, as Didi-Huberman affirms: what we see (and what we hear) refers to something that sustains it and that is manifested as a "loss". The presence of the object directs our desire and the impulse of the gaze towards what is absent, in the same way that the visible refers us to what is invisible, and music to silence.

In short, Expressionism conceives art as the territory in which it is possible to access an experience that legitimises itself as consisting, in Rancière's words, of "plunging into the original sea" (Rancière 2001). The aesthetic experience is the place in which the subject is quiet in order to look and listen, a space in which something that escapes one's control manifests itself in a veiled way; art which is the "testimony of the action of forces that transcend the subject and pluck it out of itself" (Rancière, 2001). Is it still possible then to continue talking of the expression of subjectivity?

Expression of subjectivity

The fact that Expressionism has linked art to that kind of experience which is beyond the subject has led contemporary aesthetics to pose the idea of an experience without subject or what, in our context, we should call "subjectivity without subject". Is subjectivity that which is expressed in art or is it rather an experience that just escapes or transcends the subject? Martin Jay (2005) has narrated the history of this idea of experience without subject from Nietzsche and Schopenhauer, through Benjamin and Adorno, right up to Foucault, Barthes and Bataille. This is the history of an uncertain sentiment of nostalgia for the loss of a form of accumulative and formative experience that, in the way that the character of a Realist novel is constructed through a vital journey, implies the image of the organic growth of the subject until it forms a self-conscious personality and identity. The division of work, the specialisation and the technification imposed by the bourgeois world may have ruined the possibility of reconstructing this experience that may, at any rate, find refuge in the world of art—the only sphere in which it might be possible to recover the unity and the lost sense. Grosso modo, we may say that in this history Romantic Expressionism represents the first moment of reaction, while avant-garde Expressionism assumes the loss or reduction in experience. The possibility of an Experience with a capital letter having been ruined, the function of art is that of opening routes of access to those other experiences with a small 'e'—experiences without subject. Hence art presents itself as the *via regia* for accessing these forces that transcend the subject and pluck it out of itself. Art as a form of knowledge in which, paradoxically, the contemporary subject, the dismembered subject, the subject of the absence, is only constituted through the loss of the self.

The aesthetics of Lyotard (1979) and his interpretation of the Kantian concept of the sublime is a good example of the attempts to reconstruct what we have defined as the Expressionist aesthetics of the avant-garde. His stance proudly renounces the yearning for an, organic and totalising, experience of the subject, and chooses to persevere in the bid of the avant-garde in favour of constant experimentation. In the face of the demand for organic unity, for closure, security, identity or the reinforcement of the id, and in facing the therapeutic role that is assigned to art from Realist positions, Lyotard sides with fragmentation, opening, insecurity and the constant questioning of the limits of experience. In Lyotard, as in Foucault, Derrida or Barthes, the radical experience that art permits is extreme experience or, we could say, "experience of the abyss".

Between the nostalgia for the loss of full experience and the enthusiastic defence of experimentation to the extreme, Martin Jay believes he has found, in the novel by Walter Benjamin, a solution that is equidistant from both extremes. For Jay the indirect free style that is characteristic of the novel places us in contact with a world of experiences, but from a certain distance, in the same way in which when we retell our dreams we make a "secondary elaboration" that, while it somehow restores the oneiric images that are revealed to us in an isolated and incoherent fashion, introduces the mediation of language and thus orders them into a discourse of certain sense. The indirect free style allows the reader to relive, in the first person, the experience of the character in all his disordered and intense vividness, but at the same time, the voice of the narrator establishes the reflexive distance that makes it possible to integrate the events into the thread of the argument and into the circumstances of the subject. In this way the isolated and intense experiences are set within the core of an accumulative experience; the maximum intensity of the concrete experience does not remain isolated but is integrated into a continuum; the intense experience does not fragment the personality into a series of schizophrenic experiences, but rather turns them into facets of one same identity[1].

The recourse to the novel as a model in which it is possible to overcome the antinomy without solution, which is implied by the thesis of the loss of experience, has been, to my way of thinking, especially fruitful, as is manifested in other approaches. I will only mention that, for Freud, psychoanalytic therapy will manage to re-establish the dominion of the id over that part which has escaped its control only if it is capable of integrating the traumatic memories, the ghosts and delusions in the context of the "family romance". The *Bildunsgroman*, the novel of formation, is without a doubt the model from which Freud establishes the procedures of psychoanalytic therapy. "Talking Cure" deals precisely with breaking the ties between the links in order to reorder the experiences into a narration in which the subject himself is both actor and narrator. It is the narrative structure that returns the lost identity to the patient and this is also the way in which we can imagine the idea of an expression of subjectivity.

It is to this same potential of the novel or of the narration that Appiah (2005) turns in his analysis of the concept of identity. Like Martin Jay, Appiah tries to escape from an insoluble antinomy. In his case we are dealing with the problem of freewill and of the opposition between liberalism and communitarianism, that is to say between the ideal of the autonomy of the subject and the multiculturalist thesis according to which our personal identity, far from being the result of a process of rational deliberation and of freewill, responds rather to the identification with cultural norms. In seeking the way to dissolve this opposition, Appiah has played down the presumption of autonomy, pointing out that the construction of an autonomous personal project is always achieved through the identification with certain specific norms but underlining the idea that, in a global and multicultural society, the subject is free to choose which norms to identify with and can find his "elective affinities". In order to recount this plurality of identifications, from which personal identity is constructed, Appiah turns to MacIntyre and Tylor to recover the idea of novel or narration: One basic condition for us to find sense in ourselves is that we understand our lives in the framework of a narration. It is because we understand our own lives in terms of narrations experienced from beginning to end that the narrative form is appropriate for understanding the actions of others. The identity of the subject in general and of the artist in particular would thus be constructed through what Appiah denominates (using the expression of John Bargh) "automatism of being", that is to say, through unconscious mechanisms of identification with patterns that have remained fixed in diverse tales and that are available for our unconscious assimilation.

If, as Appiah asserts, one of the things that narrations do for us is to provide us with models with which to tell our lives, we will have to suppose that the artist novel has played an important role in the construction of the identity of many particular artists, by offering legends of the artist or models available for, more or less, critical appropriation. The book by Dore Ashton *A Fable of Modern Art* affords a good example of this by studying the way in which the creative personality of Cèzanne, Picasso, Schönberg or Rilke was formed by settling scores with Frenhofer, the painter featuring in the novel by Balzac *The Unknown Masterpiece* (Ashton, 1980). Trying to escape the tragic fate of Frenhofer, who commits suicide when forced to admit the failure of his masterpiece, these artists would have recognised the existence of a limit to expression, of an essential impossibility to express the inexpressible or to bring the ghosts of the imagination to life on the canvas, the page or the music score. The readings that various different creators have made of *The Unknown Masterpiece* establish, therefore, a limit or abyss that should not be crossed, given that doing so implies the certain risk of losing oneself and the danger of artistic experimentation entering the terrain of delirium and sickness[2].

Thus the artist novel offers models that are taken on board unconsciously, but before which it is also possible to establish a critical distance. The irony that the narrator maintains on many occasions as regards the delusions or lyrical excesses of the character establishes a critical complicity with the reader that allows him to come closer to and distance himself from the character in order to construct his own identity through identification and also through differentiation with respect to the model. The artist novel, through vivid descriptions of the works (in the tradition of ekphrasis), makes the experience accessible or communicable and revives it in the reader. It allows one to see and to feel in one's mind's eye, to create a vivid depiction in the imagination, not just of the work in its physical appearance or of the contemplative aesthetic experience but of the creative act in action. Through the narrative temporality, discursive sense is added to the static and fixed character of the perception of the work[3].

Some musicians from novels

We noted the idea that the artist novel, inasmuch as it revives the pleasures and pains of the creative act in the reader, offers indirect access to the procedural and performative aspects of the arts. In this way the artist novel recounts what Agamben (1970), inspired by Nietzsche, denominated "art for artists" in contrast to "art for spectators" . Indeed, the novel does not just recreate the static moment of the aesthetic perception but also the active and procedural behaviour. In the face of the innocence and calm enjoyment of the spectator before the beautiful object, Agamben opposes the riskiness of the experience of the artist, for whom the promesse de bonheur of art turns into the poison that contaminates and destroys his existence. To highlight the particular problems of the expression of subjectivity in the performing arts we will analyse some cases featuring musicians, given that music is the most essentially performative of the arts.

The first constant to be highlighted is that the expression of subjectivity paradoxically appears to be a process of disindividualisation. In the tradition initiated by the Platonic theory of poetic inspiration and taken up again by Romanticism, the artist is presented as a vehicle of expression with a voice which is not his own, possessed by a divine or demoniacal force. But if we understand the term subjectivity in the sense in which it is opposed to objectivity, as something not necessary and evident, but relative and debatable, we find ourselves with the paradox that the artist appears in literature as the creator of original and subjective forms that, nonetheless, seem to obey a necessity. In novels, this idea corresponds with the genius theory initiated in Illustration, in which artistic genius is recognised in the fact that the creator manages to impose his subjective findings with such necessity that they come to be recognised as an indisputable rule; as the best solution to a given problem; as the most successful expression of a specific motif. In this way what starts off by seeming to be extravagant succeeds in becoming something classic.

The musician, as spokesperson for another subject, is the instrument of an impersonal force that tradition identifies as much with the divine as with the demoniacal; such that the artist, the creator subject, experiences an inner division between his own self and that something that imposes itself from within, but also from without. The most recurrent metaphors to depict this split are perhaps that of the double and that of reincarnation, metaphors which, on occasions, are difficult to separate. This is what happens in "Ritter Gluck" the tale by Hoffmann (1809).

The anonymous narrator, who presents himself as a real person thus anticipating indirect free style, relates, as is affirmed in the subtitle, a reminiscence from the year 1809. This piece of information is important, as we will see, because it places the action twenty years after the death of the composer Christoph Williband Gluck. The narrator then recalls his fortuitous meeting with an intriguing character who catches his attention and who turns out to be a composer who admires Mozart and Gluck. The gentleman, whose name is not revealed until the last sentence, tells him of his journey to the "Kingdom of Dreams" and describes some of his oneiric visions in which he also hears some marvellous sounds. The dénouement of the tale takes place in the room where the strange gentleman lives and composes. There he shows Gluck's works to his companion, opens one of them and performs a passage from the opera *Armida* although, to the narrator's surprise, there is nothing written on the musical score. The performance turns out to be surprising because the gentleman introduces "new and brilliant movements... surprising modulations and... melodic melismas". The gentleman claims to have written this music on returning from the world of dreams and finally when asked who he is he replies that he is Ritter Gluck.

The narration always moves within the ambiguity that, for Freud, characterised the literary treatment of the uncanny (*das Unheimlich*): the confusion between fantasy and reality is such that the reader does not know if it is about a madman who believes himself to be Gluck or about a veritable reincarnation of Gluck himself. In the same way as happens to "Pierre Menard, Author of the *Quixote*", by Borges, the reader does not know if he finds himself facing the case of two different people creating the same work without any plagiarism at all. Are we dealing with the ghost of Gluck raised from his grave or with someone who has become so involved in the music of Gluck that he can play from memory and introduce variations in the original score that, nonetheless, seem authentic?

The extraordinary story of "Ritter Gluck" reproduces the paradoxes of performance and of the performing arts, the strange psychic mechanisms that come into play when the performer identifies with the character or when, as is often said, "he gets inside the work". "Ritter Gluck" questions the limits between a performance and a version, and between this and an original composition. Well, was it not the composer who was the transcriber or performer of an inner music that is inspired from outwith? The reference in the tale to the "Kingdom of Dreams" picks up on this topic: the gentleman has heard this music that he plays from the score in this kingdom and the music is, therefore, the manifestation of the truth that remains hidden from ordinary mortals and only manifests itself to the chosen few who have crossed the entrance gate into it. In short, the case of "Ritter Gluck" leads one to think that the musician does not express his subjectivity but that it is precisely his subjectivity what he loses after going into the Kingdom of Dreams. That what really has its own personality is the music itself and not its author.

Thus all composers have their doubles and experience a new reincarnation each time someone performs their works: music does not, therefore, express subjectivity but is rather the subject that personifies a role already written in that marvellous and sinister world of dreams which sounds inhabit. This idea of the autonomy of the work with respect to its author, this need and objectivity of the work in the face of the subjectivity of the creator, constitutes a recurrent motif in many artist novels. It was, for example, in the tale by Stefan Zweig (1927) *Georg Friedrich Händel's Resurrection* in which the composer, during a feverish dream, listens to the music and later transcribes it onto paper. As affirmed by the narrator in indirect free style, "he himself was surprised thanks to what had been presented to him in the dream"; as pointed out by the character, "God was within me" (Zweig 35). At the première of the work, Händel listened to it in surprise because he did not recognise it as his own and he felt a disturbing strangeness: He wanted to supervise and conduct his work, but it shook off its maestro. He lost himself in it, as if he had never heard it before, nor created it, and once more he was dragged along by it (38).

Not just the composer or the performer but the listener also experiences an equivalent loss of himself when he listens and can do no more than be carried away by that torrent of music. This is what we find in the novella by Tolstoy (1889) *The Kreutzer Sonata*. In this short novel the character, transcribing in my opinion some of Kierkegaard's reflections on music using *Don Giovanni* by Mozart as a starting point, asks himself what music is and discovers that music essentially consists of an "irritation" or "excitation" similar to a "hypnotic state". Hence we are referring to the ability to induce sentiments that are not the listener's own, sentiments that would not have emerged from him and that are, therefore, not authentic. The music, as the character affirms, "forces me to come out of myself…to be capable of what I am not actually capable of". The two cited examples tackle, from complementary perspectives, the impersonal character of the work and the loss of the self that the composer experiences: Zweig's Händel does not recognise himself in his work, which he listens to as if it were not his own, and Hoffmann's strange gentleman performs *Armida* as if it were his own and as if he were the reincarnation of Gluck.

The subject of reincarnation in relation to the impersonal character of the music and the loss of one's own identity or subjectivity reappears in a story by Pascal Quignard (1987) entitled "Tch'eng Lien's Last Music Lesson" . On this occasion it is a luthier who is reincarnated, an old Chinese violin maker who states that he knows, thanks to the astrologer, that he will be reincarnated in the 17th century of the Latin era in Cremona, with the name of Tonio Stradivarius in order to inherit the tradition of the Amati. The old man, Feng Yeng, invented by Quignard, in a certain fashion recreates the character that gave the name to the tale by Hoffmann "Councillor Krespel" ., reclaimed by Offenbach in his opera *The Tales of Hoffmann*, (Paris, 1881). The excentric character, also a luthier, wishes to unravel the secret of violin making and to this end he takes an Amati to pieces; but he finds nothing more than the void of his own desire and the old violins remain in pieces in a large drawer. Albeit apropos of the luthier, the composer or the performer, reincarnation is the metaphor with which the idea of creativity having to do with some extraordinary gift that cannot be understood by analysing its parts, as Krespel tries in vain to do, is expressed. Here the creative genius is not something which can be taught and learnt, not even a natural quality handed down from fathers to sons, but something absolutely extraordinary that is transmitted in a magical way through reincarnation. The genius of the instrument maker—in other novels the composer or performer—is presented as a (impersonal) gift which is deposited upon some bearer, whose personal characteristics do not intervene at all. In Quignard's tale the elderly luthier wishes to die and to free himself from this task of being the bearer; he reclaims his right to individuality when wishing his own death. Here the individual is nothing more than the reincarnation of a spirit, the flesh that provides the body for genius but for whom the right to individuality is not recognised.

Reincarnation is not the only metaphor with which literature has approached the paradox of the identity of the musician being formed in a process of disidentification or loss of the self. Musical or theatrical performance has afforded various different opportunities for dealing with the identification between the actor and the character or between the performer and the composer. I shall pause for an instant in the short story "Mr Botibol" by Roald Dahl (1986). Mr Botibol, a comic and even ridiculous figure, is the protagonist of a tale in which the figure of the musician is treated from an ironical distance, in a carefree tone that is very different from the tragic or sinister air that the Romantic novel takes on occasions. It could well be that the humour and irony reveal the way in which the performing arts allow for an experience of subjectivity that escapes from the antinomies that we have seen: no longer a "subjectivity without subject" but rather the formation of subjectivity from the ironical and unprejudiced appropriation of the identity of another.

Let me explain: Mr Botibol, who has just closed a deal selling his business, meets up with the buyer for dinner who gets him drunk with the excuse of celebrating their agreement but really with the intention of making fun of the naïve protagonist. Under the effects of the alcohol, Botibol considers the meaning of his existence. "What have I actually achieved with my whole life?"—he asks himself—and he reviews his failures in love: he has never been in love and he has never got on well with women. Dizzy from drunkenness he goes into his house, turns on the radio and listens to a symphony by Beethoven. The voice of the narrator reproduces the experience of the character: Listening to that marvellous music a clear and conscious idea began to take possession of his confused mind. It was: I am the composer of this music. I am a great composer. It is the first performance of my last symphony.

Then Botibol imagines himself conducting the orchestra and he takes action by waving his arms as if he really did have a baton. He is so struck by this experience that he transforms one of the rooms in his house into a concert hall, with seating, a stage and a podium for the conductor. He buys records of great symphonies and concerts and others with recordings of applause and cheers and, as many record listeners have done at some time or another in the privacy of the home, Botibol fantasises about being Beethoven or Brahms conducting the orchestra at a première. In the music shop he buys a magnificent grand piano but commissions it to be modified so that it emits no sound when touching the keys: the perfect instrument for what we nowadays call play back, a variation of our kararoke. In the music shop he meets a woman and he invites her back to his house to listen to music. Little by little he overcomes his shyness and confesses his hidden passion, showing her the concert hall. There is only one way to listen to music—Botibol says to Lucille Darlington—that in which one achieves two things at once: to imagine that one had composed it oneself and to imagine that the public is hearing it for the first time. Certainly no one can feel the authentic emotion of the music better than the composer himself on the day of its première, Botibol wants to turn into the composer, to steal his music, to take it from him and to make it his own. Convinced of the truth of this, Miss Darlington accepts the invitation to perform her favourite concerts on the silent piano being conducted by none other than the composer in person. Thus together they perform the *Emperor Concerto* by Beethoven conducted by Toscanini with Horowitz as the soloist and after the clamorous applause comes the final surprise: Miss Darlington confesses to being a piano teacher who had always wanted to be Horowitz but who wouldn't mind being Schnabel the following day.

The ending turns what at the beginning seems to be pure sarcasm about an extravagant and ridiculous character into a profound reflection on the psychological mechanisms that awaken musical performance and the performing arts in general. Perhaps the comparison between Dahl's story and that of Zweig will be enlightening. While Zweig's Händel does not recognise himself in the music that he has written, Botibol makes any music that moves him his own and believes himself to express his subjectivity in the music written by another. The difference lays in the position that one or the other adopts. In one case the composer places himself as a passive listener, in the other, the listener almost becomes a performer and conductor. I think that when copying the gestures of the pianist or of the orchestra conductor, Miss Darlington and Botibol do not just seek the emotion of the applause but that their performance takes to an extreme the idea that when we feel music it is because we place ourselves in the position of the creator and that what we call expression of subjectivity implies the appropriation of someone else's feeling. Both the actor who plays the character and the spectator are in some way the character, and only through the loss of the self can the subject recognise his own sentimental identity. Only by ceasing to be Botibol to become Beethoven can our character find the meaning to his existence, appropriating the role as if it were written for him or had been written by him.

The drunkenness of Botibol is equivalent, in the story by Dahl, to Ritter Gluck's dream or to that of Zweig's Händel, such that, in his concert hall, Botibol undertakes his own particular journey to the Kingdom of Dreams. A journey that any listener makes when listening to music that immediately makes his or her own. Botibol's radio and records play an important role in this story because they shift the listening from the concert hall to the living room of the house and allow the listener a new prominence. The radio and any record—not to mention should Botibol have known the digital video editions of the operas!—allow listeners and viewers to feel as if they were in the orchestra or amongst the characters of the scene. It even seems to me as if I have come across Botibol on the bus listening to his last symphony through his iPod earphones. The experience of this strange pair of musicians also anticipates the way in which the spectator relates to pop music today. In pop music the musical performance is not understood without an accompanying body movement. But, unlike what happens in concert halls, the expressive gesture is no longer just the orchestra conductor's or that of the soloist but of each and every one of the spectators who sing and dance with the group thus somehow also becoming a performer.

Although the gestures of the performers or of the spectators are highly stereotyped, they produce the sensation of expressive spontaneity such that by repeating a perfectly coded movement we have the sensation of expressing our own subjectivity through them. We are dealing with a paradox similar to that which Rosalind Krauss (1981) found when analysing the concept of originality in avant-garde painting. In an oil painting by Monet the stroke, the colour, the textures or the rhythms awaken the sensation of spontaneity and originality in spite of being perfectly coded and of being the fruit of premeditated and laborious procedures. Likewise the strokes and colours can also be expressive and personal although they form part of a standardised repertory. As we have maintained so far, the recognition of one's own subjectivity in the arts is partly produced through the appropriation of performative structures or patterns: gestures, movements, interpretations; diverse procedures for the identification of the performer with the character and the musician with the music. The staging or performance revives the original creative act and erases the difference between the original and the copy as well as between the composer and the performer. The performance of an opera two hundred years after its première is never either copy or original, just as the feeling that it provokes is neither the authentic expression of subjectivity nor a ridiculous imitation, in Botibol's way, of the gestures of the composer conducting the orchestra on the day of its première. The apparently ridiculous experience of Botibol, who plays at being the composer and conductor of an orchestra, allows him to find the love of his life and to overcome the inhibition that he felt. Playing the role of the performer is also the best way he finds to feel the music. It is probable that many of us can only aspire towards this secondary form of genius and that only by actively appropriating what has been created by others can we achieve creation. Perhaps in this way all listeners can somehow be performers and all performers, creators. I, just like Lucille Darlington, would not mind being Horowitz or Schnabel tomorrow or perhaps, like Botibol, I would prefer to be Beethoven.

Notes

[1] Frederic Jameson (1984) has suggested that postmodern art breaks down the identity of the subject when conceiving the work as a chain of *isolated signifiers* that have lost the link with the meanings and contexts. The parts of a work function as fragments in a *pastiche*, isolated events that have lost the relation with the whole, like links that are juxtaposed in a chain without beginning, without end and without modulations, that does not manage to integrate itself into a narrative thread. With this, the creative procedure of postmodern art approaches the thought of the schizophrenic, whose experiences are much more intense the more isolated they are.

[2] In my opinion this idea basically coincides with the interpretation that Jacques Rancière 2001 makes of the reading that Freud makes of the artist's novels of Jensen, Hoffmann or Ibsen, a reading centering on the need to re-establish the control of the id or the reality principle over the delirium of the artist. Rancière's proposal emerges from the discussion on the aesthetic interpretation of the unconscious characteristic of Lyotard.

[3] For the etymology of the terms *hypotiposis* and *ekphrasis* as well as for the pragmatic sense of these rhethoric figures of speech see Román de la Calle (2005). Amongst the meanings of the term *ekphrasis* that he analyses one can highlight that it implies the action of "making understood," "making known" and also of "announcing" or "preventing," as well as of "taking out of," "making explicit" and in short of "expressing" what had been hidden.

Works cited

Agamben, Giorgio. 1970. *L'uomo senza contenuto*. Milano: Rizzoli.
Appiah, Kwame Anthony. 2005. *The Ethics of Identity*, Princeton University Press.
Ashton, Dore. 1980. *A Fable of Modern Art*. Berkeley: University of California Press.
Calle, Román de la. 2005. *The Ekphrastic Mirror. The near side of Pictures. The near side of Words. Art Criticism as Paideia*. Lanzarote:

Fundación César Manrique.

Clair, Jean. 1997. *La responsabilité de l'artiste*. Paris: Gallimard.

Dahl, Roald. 1986. "Mr Botibol." In *Completely Unexpected Tales*. London: Penguin Books.

Didi-Hubermann, Georges. 1992. *Ce que nous voyons, ce qui nous regarde*. Paris: Les Éditions de Minuit.

Hoffmann, E. T. A. 1809. "Ritter Gluck. Erinnerung aus dem Jahre 1809." In *Musikalische Novellen und Aufsätze von E.T.A. Hoffmann*. Leipzig: Insel-Bücherei.

—. 1818. "Rat Krespel." In *Musikalische Novellen und Aufsätze von E.T.A. Hoffmann*. Leipzig: Insel-Bücherei.

Jameson, Frederic. 1984. *Postmodernism or the Cultural Logic of Late Capitalism*. Oxford: New Left Review Press.

Jay, Martin. 2005. *Songs of Experience. Modern American and European Variations on a Universal Theme*. Berkeley and Los Angeles: University of California Press.

Krauss, Rosalind. 1981. "The Originality of the Avant-Garde." In *The Originality of the Avant-Garde and Other Modern Modernist Myths*. Cambridge, MA.: MIT Press.

Lyotard, Jean François. 1979. "Le postmoderne expliqué aux énfants." In *Correspondance 1982-1985*. Paris : Galilée.

Rancière, Jacques. 2001. *L'inconsciente esthétique*. Paris: Galilée.

Quignard, Pascal. 1987. "La dernière leçon de musique de Tch'eng Lien." In *La leçon de musique*. Paris: Hachette.

Tolstoi, Leo. 2007 [1889]. *The Kreutzer Sonata and other Stories*. London: Penguin.

Zweig, Stefan. 1927. "Georg Friedrich Händels Auferstehung." In *Sternstunden der Menschheit*. Frankfurt am Main: Fischer Taschenbuch Verlag.

PART III:

DANCE

CHAPTER EIGHT

DANCE, DANCERS AND SUBJECTIVITY:
SOME QUESTIONS ABOUT SUBJECTIVITY
AND THE PERFORMING ARTS

GRAHAM MCFEE

Preamble

Given some themes in my writing, it might seem odd that I have chosen to write on subjectivity in the performing arts. For have I not persistently rejected subjectivist accounts of what goes on in, especially, dance? Thus my book *Understanding Dance* makes clear:

> my commitment throughout…to the idea of judgements, appraisals, evaluations and the like being made within the domain of art as being objective judgements. (McFee 1992a, 21)

And I explained that commitment by pointing out that, for some writers, the subjective was understood as "anything goes." Similarly, my book *The Concept of Dance Education* (McFee 1994/2004, 2-5) began with a section entitled "Against subjectivism"; and now includes an attack on those who explain the values of the arts in education by contrasting its "babble and rhapsody" and "profound acts of liberation" with what the sciences offer in education (McFee 1994/2004, 209). For this "other side of the coin argument" moves from the objectivity of the sciences, with its connection to knowledge, to a corresponding denial of knowledge as a goal in arts education. And such a move is not warranted. Finally, earlier in the year, in Nancy, I railed against "the dismissive subjectivism that bedevils so much discussion in respect of artworks" (McFee, unpublished).

So, to repeat, some might—with some justice—wonder that I am contributing to a discussion of the expression of subjectivity in the performing arts. The answer, of course, lies in getting clear how the topic I shall be addressing here, concerning the importance of the performers, does not, after all, conflict with my rejecting subjectivist (and relativist) thinking: that, to put it bluntly, the topic here recognises (or grants) that subjectivity does not amount to "anything goes," and (hence) does not imply a self-refuting relativism. For the comments from my other writings just mentioned attack that view of subjectivity or such relativism, seen as a consequence of subjectivism. Towards the end of the chapter, I shall return to some related misconceptions. But let us start on a positive note.

Art and experience

We should begin by recognising the sense in which artworks as a whole embody (roughly) the intelligence of their creators[1]—they are made to be meaning-bearing, as I would put it. So there is a sense in which the features or characteristics of any artwork derive from its author or authors—sometimes seen easily and directly, sometimes in a much more indirect fashion. Yet recognising artworks as made for meaning locates a set of personal properties here: that is why the sculpture could be expressive, witty, and so on, while such concepts could not apply to the meteorite (see Ground 1989, 25-26)—even when they could be mistaken for one another, as a pair of Dantoesque "confusable counter-parts" (Danto 1981, 138). But I shall pass over this aspect fairly quickly, merely noting that (for me at least: see McFee 2005) this means something important: namely, that, strictly, artistic properties are not shared with mere aesthetic objects.

In explaining such an artistic/aesthetic contrast, I would point out early on that our appreciation of artworks—our recognising them as art—deploys what the literature calls categories of art (Walton 1978): for one misperceives, say, a Cubist painting if one mistakes it for a work in another style. Further, locating an artwork in its category in this way builds in a certain 'narrative' (as it is sometimes called, since there can be competing ones: see Carroll 2001, 63-74, 75-90) in respect of both artworks and art forms[2]. For how to write the history is, in effect, also how to teach the history and how to judge other works by drawing on that history, employing the categories of art such a history or tradition or narrative suggests or deploys.

So that the distinctiveness of the arts is recognised through noting the possibility of misperceiving an object as either (a) an artwork, when it is not (or vice versa); or (b) as in artistic category X (say, Cubist painting) what was more properly a work in a different category.

Then, first, we must recognise comments in art appreciation as, effectively, comments about the works themselves. As Bob Sharpe (2000 p. 40) put it: "the music itself is sad, not the composer performer, or listener" (2000, 40). This follows, of course, from the transfiguration inherent in objects becoming artworks: when this snow shovel, or this pile of fire bricks, counts as a work of art, things are true of it that were not true before—and are not true of other snow shovels, or fire bricks. And, second, taking an artistic interest in an object is already seeing it (defeasibly)[3] as having some value, of a kind characteristic of artworks. In this context, recognising the force of the artistic is recognising artistic value.[4]

Then, third, our engagement with the artistic is essentially perceptual: that is, perceptual and not, for example, inferential. Indeed, as Richard Wollheim puts it, "perception of the arts is…the process of understanding the work of art" (1993, 142). Those who conflate actors with the characters they portray are right to the degree that we do see the character (which is why, say, one goes to the theatre, rather than just reading a play).[5]

Dancers instantiate the dance

Earlier, I said I would pass over the art-specific aspect quickly. Perhaps "quickly" turned out to be an exaggeration. But the point was sound. For my concern here is specifically directed at the performing arts; and my major interest (among them) is in dance. Then dance, as we shall see, has a distinctive—perhaps a unique[6]—place among the performing arts. Not merely are typical danceworks performables, in the sense that the very same dance can be re-performed on another occasion (despite the differences between such performances), but danceworks depend on the specific physicality of the dancers. Thus musicians fit exactly Urmson's account of performing arts: they bring about "those things…of which the witnessable work consists" (Urmson 1976, 243)—that is, they make or cause the sounds that instantiate the musical work. But dancers do not cause the dance; rather, they are the dance—their movements instantiate it.

Consider here Merce Cunningham saying:

> [y]ou can't describe a dance without talking about the dancer. You can't describe a dance that hasn't been seen, and the way of seeing it has everything to do with the dancer. (1984, 27: quoted Mackrell 1997, 8)

In effect, Cunningham just begins by recognising that one only really encounters the dance itself in performance. Of course, we might quibble here: like the musician, the dancer can confront something by engaging with the score—if he or she can read (say) Labanotation. But, equally, the person seeing only the musical score has not really encountered the work—and the same might well be said for dance! So Cunningham is right that, in a sense, "you can't describe a dance that hasn't been seen." This is why a famous dance critic, asked in my hearing for his favourite danceworks, listed performances rather than (just) works, for the features or details of performances are complete, having made concrete all the places where the work itself under-determines its performances.

Then, when we do see dances, we see the dancers (as Cunningham recognised). So every performance reflects, in some way or other, features of the dancer(s) involved[7]—not only of the dancers, of course; but centrally of them. For many factors impact what movements, and such like, get performed to instantiate, say, Christopher Bruce's *Ghost Dances* (1981)—different casts, different performance spaces, different companies (with differing technical prowess); and even just a different night: differences on Sunday might reflect performers tired from Saturday night's performance. These will be among explanations of differences between performances of the very same dancework. Moreover—just to be clear—the idea of difference among performances is central to the conception of a performing art as composed of performables; works that can be re-performed on another occasion. So, clearly, such differences are permissible within same-dancework continuity—although we can (of course) argue about the degree of difference permissible, given that we end-up with a performance of the very same dancework.

Yet, now, which features of the performance we see—danced by this company on that occasion—are crucial[8] features of the dance, such that we might criticise a performance which failed to include them, and which are the contingencies of this performance? In illustration, consider some cases where compliance with a notated score will generate the dancework. Then imagine a performance uncontentiously of that work, but failing to comply with our score—clearly the score includes some constraints not crucial for the work. So, here, dance-performances based on this score will reflect some features crucial to the dance (perhaps) but also some other constraints. Nor is this case merely a philosopher's fantasy: the Stepanov score for *Swan Lake* presents precisely this situation! In my language[9], this score is not adequate for *Swan Lake* just because it does not identify solely the constraints from the dancework itself, but only for some performances of that work.

To summarise this section so far, we have recognised the key role of the dancer in bringing the dance into a form with which the rest of us can interact: as Cunningham reminded us, "you can't describe a dance that hasn't been seen". But we also recognised that features of the performance may reflect facts about the dancers not themselves essential features of the dance.

Yet much dance today, in being made on the bodies of particular dancers, reflects closely the powers and capacities of those dancers. Then what might—for other works—be mere contingencies of performance seem here to be essentials of these works. Yet we must go carefully, for we do not want to say that, as a matter of logic, only dancer X can perform this work—even if that were the contingent truth at a certain time. Thus, it is widely claimed (compare Mackrell 1997, 7) that Petipa put the thirty-two fouettes in Act III of *Swan Lake* (1895) because at the time he had a dancer, Pierina Legnani, who could perform this, at a time when few could. So here it might even have been true (let us suppose) that at that time only Legnani could perform this segment of the dance: still, the requirement is only for a dancer able to do so. If there were only one, that would just be a practical matter. And that is how we should regard any other requirements here. Thus, Christopher Bruce choreographed a role in *Black Angels* for Lucy Burge taking her as "a dancer of the earth", to utilise her "richer, more sensual way of movement" (in contrast to the "dancer of the air," Catherine Becque: see Austin 1976, 115 [1992a, 207]). So, for that role we would need—or certainly hope for—another "dancer of the earth". And that may be a hard criterion to put on the job advertisement! In fact, almost exactly this problem faced Martha Graham's company, in wishing to retain dances Graham herself could no longer manage—it was not enough to find a dancer who knew the steps, say. Instead, a quality of dance was required that was (fairly) easy to recognise in performers—and especially in those lacking it—but much harder to describe.

In illustration, consider, say, how a merely technical performance of Schönberg's pianowork opus 19 differs from an expressive one. In recognising one performance as 'technical', we grant…well, what exactly? As a first thought, we are granting that the performer sounded the right notes in the right order. But then the difference between this performance and the expressive one seems not to reside in what tones are sounded. Instead, the difference seems to rest simply in what each performer feels.

This just returns us to subjectivist thinking of the kind rejected initially. For what the performer feels is beside the point unless it makes him or her do something different—it must, say, be reflected in the pressure on the piano keys. But when it is reflected in differences in what the performer did (say, in differential pressure on the piano keys), we respond to that difference in contrasting these two performances. So, contrary to our first thought, the performances were not of the same notes played in the same manner; rather, there were differences in the performances. And we acknowledge these differences in taking this performance to be expressive, that one to be merely technical—even when we cannot describe the differences here in any more detail than by contrasting technical with expressive.

Sometimes this is described as being an imperceptible difference: that description is revealing only because it is completely wrong—we perceived the difference well enough; our problem lay in trying to describe it more exactly. And no general account of what more is needed is possible, as what is needed in this case can differ from what is needed in that. In essence, the problem is well captured[10] by an anecdote from Tolstoi's *What is Art?:*

> Once when correcting a pupil's study [the painter] Bryulov just touched it in a few places and the poor dead study immediately became animated. 'Why you only touched it a *wee* bit and it is quite another thing', said one of the pupils. 'Art begins where the *wee* bit begins', replied Bryulov. (quoted in Beardsmore 1971, 12)

The moral here—perhaps unsurprisingly—is that we may not always be able to say how we do these things; but that need not preclude our doing them successfully. Becoming skilled observers will allow us to give due weight to the contributions of individual performers. Thus my problem concerns giving due weight to the importance of the dancer as instantiating the dancework; for, when one sees that work, one always sees it by seeing this or that dancer. So the features of the dancework, as we confront them, are always composed out of this or that troupe of dancers. Then recording the contribution of the dancers is (for me) giving a place to their subjectivity. But, of course, the dancer is as easily over-rated as under-rated. Either move can generate subjectivism of the kinds rejected earlier. And recognising the dancer's physicality concedes that the physicality here is of a dancer—stressing only the anatomy and physiology, or even the neuro-physiology, must be confusing oneself, since those alone do not identify a dancer.

Stressing that these must be dancers involves the recognition, first, that (at the peripheries at least) what is and what is not dance is a matter for debate within a culture—better, within that proper part I call "The Republic of Dance"; and, second, that what is involved in being a dancer for these purposes (and especially the kind of dancer suitable to perform fine art-type dances) is a contextual matter.

This leads us into a later section, where the issue involves precisely clarifying what kinds of resources may be appropriately deployed in understanding dance. There, we should begin by contrasting the conceptual with the empirical; or, if this is different, recognising Frege's point—that: "Error and superstition have causes just as much as correct cognition" (Frege [1918] 1977, 1). That is, granting that (since there is always some causal story) describing the causal basis—or physical substrate—of one's judgement can never be explanatory of the normativity of that judgement. And it is normativity, within dance appreciation, that concerns us here.

As we will see, I am more of a cognitivist on such matters than many writers here: I recognise a cognitive dimension partly by seeing the outcome as rationally explicable, and as thereby incorporating how the event or phenomenon is to be understood (the 'description under which' the action was performed[11]).

'Live performance'

The fact that a dance is instantiated only in a performance has two further features, worthy of mention here. First, performances are needed to concretise that works' under-determined features—yet how do these differ from recordings? If, as a "default position" (Dodd 2007, 5; Caplan 2007, 445), a musical work is identified simply by how it sounds, as a sound-sequence (so-called "timbral sonicism"), this becomes a big issue for music. But dance has no real equivalent of "timbral sonicism," so this possibility is nothing like so important for dance. Still, we may need to discuss the sense in which seeing the video is, and the sense in which it is not, seeing the dance—clearly the dance has lots of features not captured by the video[12].

Second, performances are needed because mere knowledge of danceworks, and their history, is not enough—spectators must experience the work, in order that their judgements be answerable to the work's features; and dancers must put their knowledge into their actions. In this context, this point returns us to our earlier remarks distinguishing the expressive performance from the merely technical one: that difference may be explicable as, say, the particular dancer's conceptual mastery[13], but its reality will be visible in what she does. And we do not require, of course, that these concepts pass through her mind before or, worse, during the performance. For our action, although rationally motivated, was typically explained 'after the fact', in response to a question. So that we should not (and certainly need not) look for a chain of reasoning engaged in prior to the resulting rational judgements, or rational appraisals, of danceworks. And neither should the activities of our dancers be seen as rational only when the product of prior planning and ratiocination. We are first-and-foremost agents: so there is typically nothing more to explain—as Wittgenstein was fond of quoting: "In the beginning was the deed" (OC §403; CV 31). And explanations can be offered when, say, things go awry. But this also illustrates why, from one perspective, what dancers feel is beside the point. If one asks, "Is the feeling of individual corps members at all relevant?", surely the right answer is, "No"—we don't care what they feel: if they think they are behaving in ways appropriate to ensemble, we only care if they are doing so. For the movement's feeling a certain way is not a step to, or a test of, its being right—not least because it can only genuinely feel right when or if it is right. If I want to teach you what it feels like to have your arm in such-and-such a position, I can do so only by getting your arm into that position. And then what you did is important, not what you felt. The same goes for our dancers—except that, having done this many times, they are less likely to be wrong.

Further, we rightly distinguish dancers (as people) from roles or parts: just as one would not let a 'doctor' from a TV soap opera extract one's appendix, one would not avoid—for fear of being transformed into a swan—the dancer who performs von Rothbart, the enchanter in *Swan Lake* (1895). This reminds us that what the character thinks and feels should be distinguished from what the dancer thinks and feels. We need to see the character's animosity; seeing the dancer's animosity would be at best an irrelevance, at worst an artistic flaw.

Issue of virtuoso performers

I have granted the importance of performers in the performing arts—and seen them as persons, rather than merely robot performers. Still, most performers will be relatively invisible except as the work demands it: the work will be appropriately instantiated, and no more needs to be said.

But there are other cases, such as virtuoso performers and the sorts of occasions—I think mainly of dance-galas—where dance offers, as it were, virtuoso roles. The second case is more easily put aside: performing, say, Act III of *Raymonda* (1898)[14] in our gala detaches this movement sequence from whatever (logical) place it had in the dance as a whole—we are not even offering it as part of a dance. Instead, the interest of this sequence is reduced to its portrayal of the technical mastery, and perhaps prowess, of the dancers: that is, we have reduced it to "an acrobatic performance [...just displaying] what tremendous skill it needs" (Rhees 1969, 139). But, really, this is unrelated to the artform of dance, except parenthetically, and, of course, a standard dance performance can be treated as though it were such a gala, if all we attend to in it is, say, how close the dancer's leg is to her ear.

Similarly revealing cases arise—at the other end of the performance spectrum—with choreographic competitions: the judges hope to be able to see the choreography through the performances: and on no other occasion could the dancework itself be confronted. But if the dancers' performances are weak, it will be impossible for the judge to determine, with any confidence, what is a flaw in the work and what, more simply, a flaw in its delivery by this band of dancers. So, just as the virtuoso can lead the spectator's eye away from the dance, so too can poor performance—although here it might be more accurate to talk of poor performance as simply muddying the spectator's vision.

By contrast, sometimes virtuoso performers are important in giving us a view of a certain role (or whole dance, for a solo) which is definitive: so that how we understand the role takes, say, Baryshnikov's *Firebird* (1910) as quintessential (at least for a time). Then the powerful performance *defines* the role (see McFee 1992a, 94).[15] Yet this turns on the nature of danceworks as, somehow, normative: we are looking to what should happen in a good performance, not what does happen in a so-so one. Similarly, some virtuoso performance—in allowing us to see the work clearly—can revise our judgement of it. Indeed, if we take Petipa's choreography in *Raymonda* as "dazzling", our claims derive ultimately from the work "as we know it from Rudolf Nureyev's versions for the Royal Ballet and Australian Ballet" (Brinson and Crisp 1980, 63).

Danceworks as works; dancers as building blocks

To round-off the positive part of my discussion, I will highlight two features not supported by my emphasis here on the importance of the dancer. First, this does nothing to dispute the idea of a dancework; second, it does not identify a role for the dancer as artist in the sense of author of that work.

Again, the first point can be dealt with fairly quickly: even if—on a parallel with Hamilton's comments on theatre (Hamilton 2007, 23-40)—danceworks are "shared cooperative activities" (Hamilton 2001, 566), still, in typical cases, one can return to such-and-such a dance, see it again, and the argument for a dancework is really nothing more than this recognition. Of course, this may not be the most important thing to say about the performing arts—perhaps I stress the essential repeatability of danceworks only because I grew up at a time when 'happenings' (that is, one-off performance events) were an issue. But one inevitably returns to repeatability as among the features of performing arts. That, in turn, localises an aspect of the dancer's role: however unlikely (for reasons mentioned already), different dancers could always perform typical danceworks.

My other claim—that dancers are not artists—needs a lot of clarification, lest it be misunderstood. Since the term "art" in this context means (fine) art, artists are makers of it. Of course, the term "artist" is used in other ways—and dancers might be artists in those craft-mastering ways ("This surgeon is an artist!"); but I am not considering them here. Nor is this claim merely about words: with Wittgenstein, I urge, "say what you choose" (1953, §79), but worry about what contrasts you are drawing.

Since the very same work can, in principle, be performed on other occasions; at other times and in other places, with other casts,[16] works in performing arts are multiples. Then one can make the abstract object either by making a recipe (such as a score) or by creating a ('first') performance. Perhaps only a few dances are composed by writing a score, while most are composed by working in the studio with dancers, i.e. making the abstract object that is the artwork by making a token. In either case, the final decisions will be those of the artist. Thus the artist, as author, has a clear role, even for performing arts like dance.

Then we must put aside some cases where dancers seem like artists in the sense of "authors": First, in respect of some composition, cases where (a) dancers offer movement ideas, but the choreographer decides; or (b) dancers have at best a role in the process other than as dancers: say, I choreography my solo. Then, second, improvisation can be put aside: the order to improvise operative here is a choreographer's order. Third, recognise the number of roles in play: a choreographer may make solos for himself or herself. But even the solo a choreographer makes for himself is a performable (part of a performing art); hence it can in principle be re-performed on another occasion, including (typically) by someone else!

Dancers—like musicians—are of course achieving something praiseworthy (at least in typical cases); so, in denying that dancers are artists, I am not denying that their contributions (and especially their achievements) are laudable. But we must understand both what dancers (and other performers) do achieve, hence what is laudable (when it is), and what they do not—indeed, strictly speaking, cannot—achieve.

As noted already, what dancers achieve is: (a) instantiating the danceworks—without them, there would be no work to be confronted. Then, sometimes, (b) doing that by offering a version or interpretation of the work—what I have called "performer's interpretation" (1992a, 103), as

we speak of Pollini's interpretation of Schönberg's opus 19, contrasting
that with Glen Gould's version. Sometimes we wonder how such-and-such
a dancer would carry so-and-so role: for my generation, the male dancers
for whom this question was raised were Nureyev and, later, Baryshnikov.
Not all performances need be taken as seriously—and hence as
distinctively—as this: We need not insist on a performer's interpretation in
all cases. (Or, sometimes, another dancer might be performing Nureyev's
interpretation.) Both areas of attainment by dancers are laudable,
especially the second. Without the first, there would be no dances to view;
while the second often explains part of our interest in particular dance
performances. Thus we might attend a particular performance in order to
see so-and-so's interpretation of such-and-such a role—as we might also
for a play or an opera.

Since both Pollini and Gould offer 'versions', interpretations, of the
same artwork, a trip to the concert-hall to hear either interpretation counts
as an encounter with Schönberg's opus 19—the artwork itself. Just the
same might be true of our dances. Thus, although the performer's
contribution is praiseworthy, it stands against another contribution;
namely, that of the author of the artwork, the artist. This is the sense that
dancers—like pianists and opera-singers—are not artists. For they do not
initiate the artwork: They are not ultimately responsible for that work,
despite bearing a heavy weight in terms of the work's performance. So the
artist's role as author is crucial, not least because the two roles just
ascribed to the performers only make sense against this background[17].

Suppose we see a particular dance, or play, or listen to a piece of
music, or an opera on Tuesday evening: each counts as one (and only one)
artwork. We acknowledge that fact in granting that, in the same venue on
Wednesday, we can encounter that same artwork again. And this is
typically independent of differences between the performances: both can
be, say, *Swan Lake* despite a wide variety of differences—including being
different performer's interpretations. For being the very same work is not a
matter of similarity here—as numerical identity judgements generally are
not. Thus, the short, hairy boy who bullied me at school is the very same
person as the tall, bald man getting the Nobel Peace Prize—as we grant in
letting him inherit the estate of his (or the boy's) grandfather. So here we
have numerical identity despite radical dissimilarity.

The debate about 'same-work' continuity here, (not our specific topic:
see McFee 1994/2004, 229-231), in effect recognises three kinds of cases:

1. the standard token (say, for Swan Lake, the Ivanov and Petipa
   choreography);

2. the extreme token—properties very different from standard tokens, but still a token of that same type (say, Matthew Bourne's Swan Lake);
3. the new, but similar artwork—a token of a different type (say, the Mats Ek Swan Lake).

Of course, the examples are not crucial; but the thought here is to illustrate sorting candidate Swan Lakes into categories, where the first two preserve work-identity.

Moreover, rehearsing on Monday was (in principle) a rehearsal for all the performances of the work the performers or company would make that week, rather than for only one of them (McFee 1992a, 93). This speaks clearly for our sense of only one artwork here: many works would seem to require many distinct rehearsals.

In practice, a pretty wide range of diversity is granted within 'same-work' continuity for, say, *Swan Lake*[18]: Diversity of company, staging, costume, and even movement. But all of this counts as the very same (numerically identical) artwork. Moreover, one artwork implies one authorship (not necessarily one person, of course; but that point need not concern us here.) So, in our typical dance performances, we recognise only one artwork: hence, at most one authorship. Furthermore, this is the context in which the dancer (or dancers) cannot be artists in the relevant sense, since authorship of the work already exhausts that role. And, to repeat, that authorship is already 'used up'.

In this context, the term 'performing artist' is pretty confusing (and ultimately unhelpful) here: It could pick-out those who instantiate works in the performing arts, such as dance, to recognise their artistry (their craft-mastery); or it could refer to those involved in works of one-off performance art, happenings. But these are very different; we will probably mislead ourselves if we confuse one with the other. Moreover, only the second group might plausibly be thought artists (in some cases, not all)[19] in the sense, previously identified, that picks-out the authors of artworks. By contrast, that is not the right way to see the activities of (typical) dancers.

So my thesis here can now be stated strictly although, as often in philosophy, what I am urging is neither as grand nor as contentious as its first articulation makes it seem. In line with Austin's dictum,[20] the place where I say it (seeming to claim far more) is followed by the place where I take it back. It is that dancers are not artists because dance is a performing art—dancers being artists would, at best, turn dances into 'happenings'.

This conclusion points to a difference only: In particular, I am not rating the activities of artists more highly (nor less highly) than those of dancers; I am valuing each, but differently. Thus, this is not an attempt to downplay the importance of dancers—say, to dis-value the dancer. Rather my plan is to rightly value the dancer. In fact, that is the main thrust of this whole chapter! That means seeing differences between dancer's value and artist's value, without ranking either more highly.[21]

A further case may be helpful here. Thus my stress on authorship as explaining what is central to being an artist allows me to put aside a plausible-sounding counter-example in which an inferior dance becomes recognised as an artwork because of the contribution of an outstanding performer in 'delivering' it. In effect, I would consider this as one of two or three possible cases, reflecting the prior status of the 'inferior' dance. Thus, is that dance an artwork? If it is, then (as a first case) suppose we are happy that the dance we are seeing—although revitalised—is the very same dancework as previous performances: then we will still be ascribing it to its previous choreographer (or whomever): it is still his/her dance, and any plaudits for the dance (or any brickbats) belong to that original author. Here, the revitalised version has allowed us to see the dance for what it was, or to see what is in it. But, in so far as we continue to ascribe the responsibility for the dance to its original author, there is no temptation to think here of the performer as author.

But suppose we imagine that—either wholly or partly—the 'new' dance is a transfiguration of its previous incarnation. The simplest case here might be the transfiguration of a folk dance, so let that be the second case. Here, the 'original' dance was not an artwork; and it is the performer's contribution that makes it one. So it is a bit like finding inspiration in a tree—the tree is not an artwork, but one's painting is. Or perhaps more like a kind of readymade: one writes a name ("R. Mutt, 1917") on a urinal, and then it becomes one's own artwork. But now the 'performer' counts as the author of the artwork. Then, as our third case, imagine a minor artwork brought to life in performance. Since this is not merely a repeat of our first case, the performer must have contributed more than in that example. As this might be expressed, it is not merely his dancing—his performance—that is being admired. But then what is? The temptation must be to say that it is his dance; but now the performer counts as, at least, a co-author—it is his or her dance that is being praised. Of course, in this case, I grant that the dancer could be an artist in the sense under discussion—that is, to the degree that is indeed her dance. (Thus, for analytic purposes, I am separating the performance-role of the dancer from the authorial role.) So, to the degree that we recognise the work as the dancer's, to that degree we see the dancer as author—and hence as artist. But, to that degree, we are no longer regarding that person (or persons) simply as the dancer.

Why is any of this important? In part, the answer lies in trying to accurately assess the areas of possible attainment of dancers—not to offer a comparison (with the achievements of artists) which claims too much for their legitimate activities. Rather, we should celebrate these; and not bewail a failure to attain what was actually unattainable in principle. So we imply neither too much nor to little about them. Perhaps fewer self-proclaimed artists in the world of performing art may mean a happier regime, because fewer prima donnas (at least, that might be a hope.) But due weighing is also crucial to an appropriate valuing of the craft-related attainments of dancers. So that someone might say, with justice and with pride, "No, I'm not an artist—that is because I've spent my time, energy, and creativity on being one hell of a dancer!"

Thus far, I have elaborated places where—for me—the importance of the performers in performing arts might with justice be read as an affirmation of subjectivity. I turn now to three or four unprofitable avenues, where counter-productive claims are made for special roles for dancers, or for a subjective element. And, in general, this reinforces arguments sketched elsewhere.

No place for kineasthesis in artistic appreciation

In *Understandign Dance* (1992a, 264-273) I made clear my reservations about the idea of a kinaesthetic sense (and any similar ideas) under two headings. First, that we did not, in general, have such a sense. My analysis followed Elizabeth Anscombe in noting that the key fact here, of knowing where, for example, one's leg was positioned in space, is simply not something one knows in this (or any other) way: that is, perceptually—once looking in a mirror is excluded. Then, second, that even were there a kinaesthetic sense, it could contribute nothing to the artistic appreciation of danceworks since (at least in typical cases) such appreciation must draw on projective sensory modalities (sight, hearing) rather than on the contiguous ones (taste, touch); this followed from the need for an audience for artworks—the audience should not consist exclusively of those whose limited perspective on the work was that of, say, one of the performers. Finally, I followed David Best (1974, 142) in recognising the absurdity of urging that having danced was a prerequisite for appreciating dances—as though having played in an orchestra were a prerequisite of understanding orchestral music. As Best (1974, 142) pointed out, the correct parallel here would require not only playing all the instruments, but playing them more or less simultaneously. At the centre of the argument here is the requirement for an audience for art:

> [i]t is tautological that art has, is made to have, an audience, however small and special. The ways in which it sometimes hides from its audience, or baffles it, only confirms this. (Cavell 1969, xxvii: quoted in McFee 1992a, 267)

Cavell recognises that a key issue for understanding art and artistic value is: In whose eyes (ears) does this artwork have its impact? Since an answer here seems required if the work is indeed to be art, the transfiguration of (in this case) the movement pattern into dance must be available for recognition. But he also implicitly recognises, first, the variety of different (kinds of) cases here; and, second, that no exceptionless account of the audience for artworks.

Elaborating the idea of an audience, I would mention four issues, highlighting different kinds of cases:

1. What counts as an audience, for these purposes? There is no easy answer. But in the Jack Rosenthal play *Bar Mitzvah Boy*[22], a young man makes the relevant statement, not in the designated place, but in a playground. His sister subsequently argues that, since God is everywhere, God counts as in the audience here. Clearly, that is not a suitable kind of answer here: artworks are human products, requiring the possibility of an appropriate human audience.

2. The point is not whether the work is, as a matter of fact, seen or not: We can imagine running through a dance solo with performance energy to produce a Dantoesque "confusable counterpart" for the performance of that solo. Here, audience or not, this is not performing the work, but rather rehearsing it. And seeing it would not count as being an audience for dance.

3. The requirement here is a logical one: The performance where no-one shows up is, for these purposes, a performance. For we are concerned with the logical possibility of an audience rather than a practical one.

4. The requirement for an audience is, in effect, a requirement that the artwork be understandable (say, in the current climate in the artworld).

Of course, this does not show categorically that artworks require an audience. But it does suggest that many of the concepts we associate with artistic value—its meaning, its intentionality, its publicity—point in the same direction.

Recently, two related views have challenged my position there: one urges that proprioception does, after all, offer a privileged way of *understanding and appreciating* dances. The other postulates a mechanism something like a kineaesthetic sense, ultimately explicable via the neuro-biological hypothesis of mirror neurons. I will comment on each tendency.

Could proprioception be a basis for artistic judgement?

If the claim here is towards proprioception as some kind of motor perception, my view remains unchanged: insofar as there is any perception here, the perceptual modality is visual[23]—thus, in an experiment sketched later, the subjects look at a video of movement sequences. So, it must be wrong to say, "the relevant experience is not a visual one, but a motor one" (Montero 2007, 2). Instead, one needs only a more generous view about what is open to visual perception—that, say, we see the peasants in the Breugel picture dancing. That is, although the visual image is compatible with its being an 'imitate-the-statue' competition, we see the dance, and hence the movement—although, of course, this ascription may be defeated (as there are cases where I say I saw a tomato, but it turns out to be only half a tomato, with the cut side turned away.)

Thus I am very unhappy about such an idea of motor perception, largely because the perceptual mode here is visual: if one blind-folds the audience, they will get none of the effects being talked about. Similarly, at best, dancers might have something like this in their own cases, but (if blind-folded) not for other dancers. Sight and hearing are the only candidate perceptual modes here.[24]

Does anything even suggest that 'proprioception' (granting it some as yet unexplained character and status) offers access to the artistic properties of dances? Montero takes part of her discussion to argue that "proprioception can allow one to perceive aesthetic qualities of one's own movement and positions", commenting "this is an aesthetics...from the point of view of...the dancer" (Montero, 2006a p. 236a). I have reservations about the usefulness of such an idea, even granting its truth, for "the focus on the performer is not appropriate to an artform like dance" (McFee 1992a, 273). As previously, this is explained in terms of the requirement for publicity, for an audience for art. As I said, if one had to choose between the perspective of the performer and that of the audience (a choice that stressing proprioceptive 'understanding' might force on us), it would be right to go with the audience—but my view was that, in general, one did not have to choose because either the two perspectives would coincide or, if they did not, even dancers would grant that the 'final say' rested with the observer. So the dancer must grant that, where ever she thought her leg-position was, she was wrong. Indeed, it would be futile to fill dance studios with mirrors if this were not true. And, of course, some of Montero's own examples support this perspective. Thus when Montero reports overhearing the director of the Royal Dutch Ballet say, "I can tell that that just doesn't feel right" (2007, 2), the right conclusion is that he knew it looked wrong—and that was all he really cared about (he would have re-set the passage on that basis, whatever the dancers said.)

Further, I would emphasise again (McFee 1992a) the emergent character of the understanding of dances: one understands them (to the degree one does) by seeing them as wholes, with a variety of features. That will not be possible if one draws only or primarily on the single dancer's perspective. All-in-all, I see no real case for a proprioceptive sensory modality. Moreover, this is not just about what to call the phenomenon, but about the nature of the phenomenon.

Are the arguments here directed at mere straw figures? It might seem so: surely no-one would think that there was a genuine sensory modality here. In reply, I would offer a three-part commentary: first, the authors do say these things (for example, talk of "motor perception"); and the words I quote (and others like them) appear in major philosophical texts, places where authors might reasonably be expected to say what they mean. And, to repeat, this is what they say (compare also Montero 2006b). Second, if the emphasis were elsewhere, to do its claimed job in this context, this possibility must be (fairly) specific to our dancers, not something the rest of us share (so: not like 'jumping' when being startled). But, seen that way—say, based on a capacity for empathy[25], and for that empathy to express itself through muscular sensation akin to movement—it still needs demonstration; dancers report something here; but what? Further, if the description offered here, of motor perception, is supposed to capture that content, I doubt it. Third, my primary concern is with understanding and perception. So if I were to lose my argument against the existence (or the possibility) of something like a sensory modality here, I would still insist (at least) on my second set of claims: that this is not explanatory of our interest in dance. And that seems to me sufficient reason to put it aside.

The place of the mirror reflex?

Is a discussion of the so-called mirror reflex a useful intermediate step? Certainly if offers another feature apparently explanatory in respect of out appreciation of dance works—and more so if mirror neurons are used to 'explain' the mirror reflex?[26] As Carroll writes, "[w]e have an involuntary tendency to mirror automatically the behaviour, especially the expressive behaviour, of our conspecifics" (2008, 185). And so this capacity thereby: "freely avails itself of our biological heritage" (Carroll 2008, 189). Carroll grants that these are "not fully-fledged emotional states" (2008, 185); but claims that "gestures and postures are also mimicked...in order to gain information about what is percolating inside our conspecifics" (2008, 186). Certainly it might help us to see the force of reference to causal explanatory structures of this sort.

If this account of the miror reflex were true (and, hence, at best), this is just something people do, or have a tendency to do. Applied to dance, perhaps the possibility of our making sense of dance (that is, making sense of an activity of other moving bodies) is partly dependent on such a human capacity. Here, I would offer two thoughts.

First, and in line with previous ideas, I doubt that this is true. After all, the classical problem of 'other minds' (how can one know the thoughts and feelings of another, given knowlededge of her behaviour?) has what force it retains simply because the fact that the person moves in this way is no guarantee of what she is thinking or feeling: hence, our coming to move in that way too must be similarly uninformative.

Second, this propensity to mimic movement cannot function normatively here, such that to manifest it is to be—to that degree—a good dance, and vice versa. For, if there were such a human capacity or disposition, it cannot distinguish our interaction with a good dance from our interaction with inferior ones. As Frege (quoted above) noted, both good and poor have causal stories. So, like sweating, or digesting my food, or breathing, these are not things I can do well (so as to make my behaviour praiseworthy) as opposed to simply doing them effectively—as pneumonia might cause me to have trouble with my breathing. And, more importantly, to relation to this putative capacity cannot separate danceworks that are art from others.

In fact, the absence of the possibility of a normative dimension is fundamental here: a dancework will not be good (or bad) in proportion to its activating or utilising this human capacity. Nor can we infer that what utilises (or draws on) this capacity more often or more regularly is therefore a better (or worse) dance: it is simply a dance which utilises that human 'mirror reflex' capacity. But to understand is normative: what can be understood one can also fail to understand; or, perhaps, misunderstand. So the possibility of 'getting it right' imports also the possibility of 'getting it wrong'. But this contrast cannot be treated solely causally.

This thought has implications when we turn to responses, for instance, to music or movements: one cannot use the need to explain immediacy or an apparently non-conceptual 'content' for one's responses as a justification for requiring a causal account only. The central recognition here must be that such responses to music or movement are widespread. So there is a phenomenon to be explained. But what are our explanatory resources?

It is tempting to see the phenomenon—because immediate and seemingly non-conceptual—as only causally explicable, and perhaps as suitable for causal explanation[27]. To reject this suggestion, we should first recall that what is rationally explicable—and hence cognitive—may yet be immediate; as there need by no 'gap' between my seeing an artwork and my appreciating it (since the appreciation is perceptual). But, second, we must stress ways in which what is conceptual (because cultural) pervades the human world. Thus, for instance, we might accept a biological imperative on humans (as on non-human animals) to eat and to reproduce, amoung other such imperatives. Yet the forms in which these practices manifest themselves are not causal in any straightforward way: we do not simply take a bite from the first available food-source that passes, within grabbing range, across our field of vision. So, if there is a causal basis here, it is well below the surface of typical human actions. Similarly, we do not simply swivel the first object of sexual attraction with grabbing range (even putting aside cultural dimensions of attraction.) Rather, what counts as food here, and how one prepares and eats it, are heavily cultural. In like fashion, the elaborate 'rituals' involved in courtship among humans are not well reduced even to the sorts of causal imperatives operative within the world of other primates. So I would endorse an account of the human resources here as involving how the object of desire (for food as for sex, or love) is necessarily the object as characterised or understood: in this sense, it is conceptual—even if we could not deploy the concepts discursively. That is, I would stress the cognitive dimension in the human versions of the biological imperatives.

This is revealing because it highlights once again what is wrong with appealing to the causal origin of some judgement: as we saw Frege recognise, there will be a causal story for erroneous judgements—hence the causal story alone cannot offer us the requisite normativity: that is, it can never distinguish what ought to go on or what is praiseworthy when it goes on.

What about mirror neurons?

Suppose, then, we postulate, as an explanation of an additional human capacity[28] for awareness of movement in others, mirror neurons, explained as:

> a class of neurons...which are activated when one sees certain types of movement, much as they would be activated if one were to perform the movement oneself. (Montero 2006a, 236b-237a)

That is, as offering the physiological sub-strate for the human powers and capacities—even granting their existence. Notice that the title "mirror reflex", mentioned above, is justfied by the behaviour of humans (and animals) in mirroring the behaviour of others. But no such justification exists for the mirror neurons: their name derives from the behaviours they are supposed to explain.[29]

Then, one question here must be why reference to that sub-strate is revealing when we are concerned with artistic matters. Artistic communication—or artistic interaction more generally—is essentially intentional: we see the artist's intelligence behind it. This, of course, rules out the possibility of its being 'naturally occurring', except where the artist selects such a device. As I have said repeatedly, the cracks in the wall—in so far as they are genuinely cracks—not only do not spell-out my loved one's name, they could not do so: they lack precisely this intentional structure. And the moral from such a case applies here directly: given only the biological (or neuro-biological) sub-strate, one cannot offer anything of genuine interest to any study of artistic communication.

Further, a revealing explanatory note in one paper begins, "The conjecture concerning mirror neurons is based on research with macaque monkeys" (Carroll & Moore 2008: note 23, 425).[30] So why should we take this seriously here, especially since it is conjectural? Of course, the conjecture must have some basis—no doubt at least partly recognising a basis in our neuro-physiology, allowing humans to behave in these ways, to the extent that they do. Perhaps the similarities between our neuro-physiologies and that of monkeys justifies investigating the biological sub-strate of the human powers and capacities by considering first the case of these monkeys. But the capacity for dance (in our sense) is, of course, not one those macaque monkeys share with humans: dance the artform is meaning-bearing in the kinds of social ways precisely unavailable to monkeys—even those ethologists with most enthusiasm for the parallel of monkey-behaviour with humans only concentrate on attenuated human behaviour (say, meetings between strangers sharing a path in the park, compare Morris 1977) rather than, for instance, the elaborate verbal interaction between friends. So too many steps must be taken to connect one to the other to warrant confidence in this as an explanatory structure for a complex human capacity, realisable only within a context—such as the capacity to learn dances (since what counts as dance here is a cultural matter).

There is a pattern here: in each case, the emphasis is on the causal—in some version—at the expense of the rational or normative. As a consequence, insufficient attention is paid both to the specific context of the particular dance 'utterance' and to the broad context within which artistic appreciation and understanding takes place.

Moreover, that paper discusses a TV advertisement, in which "watching music videos on...cell-phones...inspires...[people] to match the movement" (Carroll & Moore 2008, 426). If the point is that much 20th century dance "has been, in one way or another, about the feelings engendered by the music that accompanies it" (Carroll & Moore 2008, 426),...well, the connection is obscure. Of course, music inspires choreographers; of course, many works grow from this—but they do not grow just by Jo and Jane Public responding to music, but only by choreographers (and sometimes, as a compositional technique, dancers) responding to that music. And that is, frankly, a sow with another snout! That one counts as a choreographer or dancer here (or that one's actions count as dance) is, of course, a broadly cultural matter. Not any movement pattern will count as dance;[31] and not just any dance-planning will count as choreography in the sense under discussion. No doubt some biological sub-strate is at work here: but the years of training, the insightfulness of choreographers, the (implicit) reflection on the state of the danceworld, the potential of various dancers...all seem far more fundamental, and much nearer the artistic surface.

At this stage, Montero invokes a particular experiment, reporting Calvo-Merino *et al.* (2005) as follows:

> a team of researchers...asked dancers from the Royal Ballet, experts in capoeira (a Brazilian martial art), and an inexpert control group to watch videos of ballet and capoeira movements while their [the subjects] brain activity was recorded with fMRI. (Montero 2007, 3)

So the context has monitoring of the neural activity of three groups:

> The researchers found greater activity in various motor areas involved in preparation and execution of action when experts viewed movements that they had been trained to complete compared to movements they had not,

while the control group showed the same pattern of neural activity whether they were watching the ballet or the capoeira video.

Faced with this empirical data, the right slogan is: 'Is there no other way to read the results?'[32] So, there is differential brain activity in the Brazilian martial artists, the ballet dancers, and the control groups when faced with images of their own activity (or lack of it). So far, this is what you might expect—that I respond differently to what is most familiar, and so on. What seems to make it stronger is that there was "greater activity in various motor areas involved in preparation and execution of action" (Montero 2007, 3). Well, that is what people say all right. But we do not know enough about the brain to be confident about these claims: for this would only be evidence of anything were these indeed brain areas uniquely associated with 'motor preparation'—and even then we are required to associate 'motor preparation' of this kind with some ability to better perceive the movements of others.

Yet, first, we simply do not know enough about the brain to make such an identification of a unique function to this or that brain area. For instance, there are people with conditions which permit only a small amount of functioning brain, but who manage their lives like the rest of us. So there is nothing absolutely exceptionless here.[33] Hence we do not know enough to say with such confidence what particular patterns of neural firing show. At best, we might comment on what they usually or typically show—if we had sufficient data to determine an uncontentious trend.[34] Further, the claim as reported is only for greater activity—thinking about that seriously highlights how weak a claim it is.[35]

Even those more disposed than I am to give credence to the 'findings' of contemporary neuro-physiology must grant that their account requires an exceptionless application, such that every time such-and-such occurs in the brain, so-and-so is happening. And how could this be demonstrated? In so far as there is evidence about locating human powers in the brain, it offers nothing like this degree of clarity. If someone were to assure me, with his/her hand on whatever is the scientst's equivalent of the Bible (I like it to be Darwin's *Origin of Species*), that this exceptionlessly true of human beings I would withdraw this criticism. But I would want to question how he/she could be so confident, given the nature of available evidence; and I would point out the logic of the situation—that if there is just one human being, past, present or future, for who this was not true, then these scientists are wrong. So this requires more than, say, the 'conjecture' (which I grant) that so-and-so cannot see because he lacks eyes—for that is merely causally necessary, while this is causally sufficient And I do not see how our scientists could have this degree of confidence. Certainly, very many claims made in science are merely stochastic (statistical), showing trends or tendencies.

So its advocates must show not only that a single set of functions are ascribable to particular regions of the brain such that no counter-case could ever be found—and, to repeat, how would this be shown?—but also that there is a dependable relationship between the degree of finding, such that one can infer that, say, is such-and-such electrochemical activity indicates preparation for action (whatever that is), more electrochemical activity indicates more preparation. And this clearly seems a huge stretch.

Then, second, I would stress that, even granting this claim, its relevance to the dance-appreciation case must be demonstrated: what exactly could it show us about the appreciation of the artform dance, when one segment of its data concerns an artform, while another does not. What should we conclude if—like me—we concede the artistic/aesthetic contrast, at least for the normative judgements of art appreciation? But there might well be no general story here widely applicable. Instead, the topic might be one which must be confronted case-by-case, dance-by-dance; and hence, perhaps, the sort of thing best realised in a comprehensive critical biography of this or that dancer or company.

Further, and third, we need to consider the impact of theoretical change in science: Would a claim currently thought exceptionless ever become treated as a useful generalisation but not true exceptionlessly? Or even false in its full generality? (As Newton's Laws were regarded by those who, nevertheless, calculated using those laws in planning the NASA moon landings.) It seems clear that the future of science remains open. And this claim will carry over into that future. For more specific claims about brain structures—mirror neurons being one example—just deploy the theoretical tools of one bunch of these people, likely to be overthrown by later work. And however well these cases describe the neural sub-strate of human activity, they fall far short of describing humans thinking and feeling.[36] Notice Montero quoting a comment about "the brain's response to seeing an action" (2007, 4): that is so dangerous; it means, of course, the brain's response to the person's seeing the action.... and even that is not right, since the brain is a part of the person, and hence it is the brain changes when the person sees (rather than the brain responding either to perception directly or to the person's perception.)[37]

A complication: 'muscle memory'?

One revealing complication here is the idea of 'muscle-memory': this one expression really collapses into two related ideas. The first is properly thought of as a kind of memory[38]: that dancers can learn sequences pretty quickly, and pretty accurately compared to the rest of us—they probably would not become dancers were this not true. So a kind of biological inheritance might be regularly reinforced and 'flexed' in dance training. And this capacity allows our dancer to retain the work of this rehearsal into the next rehearsal, and then into the performances. Moreover, our dancer, asked about the dance years later, draws on this capacity: dancers remember what to do—although they could not, perhaps, have described it to us. But a dancer in a wheel-chair might still mobilise this capacity in recognising a performance by another as deviating from that she had been taught. This capacity seems trained into dancers, but doubtless some predisposition singled them out as suitable for the training. 'Muscle-memory' in this sense is an uncontentious phenomenon—although it might still need to be (further?) explained!

The second idea seems to explain the first: Dancers do this by their muscles somehow remembering. Then this provides the explanation of dancers' capacity both to move from the corrections of the rehearsal room to the final performance and to recall the movement patterns of the dance at some later time. Yet such an 'explanation' seems mysterious—does it really add anything to the first account?

Now, another capacity of persons at least resembles this one: there are lots of behaviours which become 'grooved' for humans, so that they can be performed without thinking. For instance, having been trained to drive a stick-shift, I can change gear at the sound of the car's engine beginning to labour, but be unaware of either noting this fact or acting on it. However, such a capacity does not require further explanation: when I say that I have become so practiced that I can perform this activity without thinking, nothing more need be said. Of course, if you wanted to claim that my muscles remembered how to do it, that would be unexceptionable thus far. But, notice, this is not even as informative as the previous version: in that version, the behaviour was 'brought about' (or 'triggered') by my hearing something—but my muscles cannot hear. So there seems yet more to be explained if we talk of muscle-memory here. But, of course, nothing remains to be explained, beyond noting this capacity in humans—most, if not all, have it to some degree (or they would never learn to drive), but differentially: it comes more easily to some than to others. The point, though, is that, although the mechanisms remain unclear, the human power or capacity is not.

Conclusion

So I have defended the centrality of the dancer as person—and hence the dancer's subjectivity, in that sense—without seeking to over-rate the dancer's role. Thus concern with subjectivity in dance is aligned with the distinctive contribution of the dancers, since artistic appreciation of danceworks—as with any artworks—involves attention to the features or properties of the work itself. That is, understanding dances involves perceptual engagement with the artworks themselves, because the properties at issue should not be located in the artist, audience, or performer. But, unlike typical musical works (where the performers cause the sounds that comprise the artwork), in typical dances the dancers instantiate the dancework. That reinforces the dancer's centrality. To put it bluntly, the dancer is essential—as Merce Cunningham reminded us, we only see the dance by seeing the dancers. That means that the dance reflects features of those dancers. But that does not assign all roles to the dancer. In particular, there is a key sense of the term "artist" (as author of art) which cannot apply to the dancer in a typical dance.

Defending in this way the dancer's role is recognising the dancer as a person, as an agent. And that runs counter to locating special access to the dance for the dancer: say, in kinaesthetic awareness, or its fancy modern counterparts. So my reason for introducing the idea of muscle memory (towards the end of this paper)—as I hope is clear—is that it does not require explanation by the laying out of a complex causal history. Instead, it is a human power or capacity; and, at best, we need to consider the interplay between two factors: does a developed version of this capacity make it more likely that one will succeed as a dancer? Or does dance training develop the capacity? The short answer must be, "both". And a long answer, displaying the phenomenology of particular dancers—and hence their subjectivity—must await another occasion.[39]

Notes

[1] Thus Wollheim writes: "If we wanted to say something about art that we could be quite certain was true, we might settle for the assertion that art is intentional. And by this we would mean that art is something we do, that works of art are something we make" (1973, 112).

[2] Imagine, for instance, that a discussion of whether Milton Avery was "a minor precursor of Rothko or a great master...[reflects] a major debate about how to write the history of modernism" (Carrier 1987, 39) here, amounting to "whether Avery's work belongs in every major museum" (Carrier 1987, 39)—on the

assumption that Rothko's does!

³ For defeasible relation (like *contract* in law), if certain conditions are fulfilled, that relation holds *unless*…So, first, it represents a nearly universal generalisation that, the conditions being fulfilled, the relation holds; second, the burden of proof is on any *objector* who, third, must appeal to the satisfaction of *recognised heads of exception* (McFee 1992a, 61-63).

⁴ So, in summary, such judgement has, at least, a perceptual *base*: my critical remarks about a painting would be rightly dismissed if I had never seen the painting (at best, this would just be someone else's judgement that I am repeating). And, the judgement must take the work to be a work of art: in terms of the previously drawn distinction, it must be artistic judgement *rather than* (mere) aesthetic judgement—this will involve, at the least, both the object's having been intended as art and its meaning-bearing character (see McFee, 2005). Moreover, and relatedly, artistic judgement involves seeing works in the appropriate *category of art*; categories both supplying the concepts through which the perception is mediated, and importing the distinction between standard, non-standard and irrelevant properties for artworks of that kind. Again, reference to *categories of art* implies that, in artistic judgement, the artwork in question is located in its appropriate history or tradition. Further, as we have just noticed, what judgements I can make centrally depend on what I can *see* in the work—as we might say, what I have learned to see. Finally, there is an essentially affective element in artistic judgement. As Peter Kivy once put the point:

> To describe something in artistic terms *is* to *describe it*; but it is to savour it at the same time: to run it over your tongue and lick your lips; to 'investigate' its pleasurable possibilities. [quotation (rectified for the artistic/aesthetic contrast) 1975, 210. See also McFee, 1997]

So we need not deny the essential sensuousness of artistic appreciation. I would add an additional characteristic to this already partial list: that the appropriateness of artistic judgements may vary through time—what I have called *the historical character of art* (McFee 1992b).

⁵ Fourth, as Thomas Reid urged, "[t]his excellence [of an air in music] is not in me; it is in the music. But the pleasure it gives is not in the music; it is in me" ([1785] 2002, 574). For granting that the discussion thus far concerns the properties of the artworks, not simply our responses to them, recognises those properties as themselves response-reliant.

⁶ Opera is certainly different, having a different relation to the music, as well as the power of words; what about theatre? What would Hamilton say? For him, theatrical works seem exactly like dances.

⁷ Even attempts to evade this point ultimately reinforce it. Thus, Alwin Nikolais writes:

> I used masks and props—the masks, to have the dancer become something else; and the props, to extend his physical size in space. But these then *become* the features of the dancer *as we experience them!* (1998, 116).

⁸ Elsewhere, I have sometimes called them "essential features" of dances: both expressions are misleading—the point is simply that their absence would be reason

to *criticise* a performance.

[9] Compare "Dance, Identity and Performance" (McFee, unpublished) read at a conference at University of Nancy, France, May, 2008.

[10] Of course, it is much less clear that a *direct* "artist's hand" would apply for, say, dance. So, looking for a related model, we might look to the artist's *plan*, to his *intention* (or something similar). NB hypothetical intentionalism on which:

> the expressiveness inherent in a painting might be conceived to be that which we would most *justifiably ascribe to the artist as intended emotional communication*, on the basis of the perceptible features of the painting, a complete grasp of its context of production, and a full knowledge of the artist's intentions as to how the work was to be taken, approached, or viewed. (Levinson 1996, 218)

Of course—on my version—this is (a) all we need, once we produce a more robust version (re-reading the "full", "complete"); and (b) as the ordinary kind of understanding of intentional behaviour.

[11] Such "descriptions under which" can play no role in causal explanations, since how we characterise an event does not determine whether or not it will *cause* another, strictly speaking—I do not change the causal powers of a moving billiard ball by calling it "the white" or "the cue ball", nor of (what is in fact) a bullet by describing it differently: say, by giving its chemical composition. And once we see this point, we shall regard fewer and fewer events in the human world as explicable causally, especially those where humans are agents.

[12] Thus, in a parallel way, Wollheim (1987) comments tartly that:

> Since the days of the great Heinrich Wölfflin, art-historians have tended to identify the objects of their enquiry with those properties of a painting which a good slide preserves.

(Of course, Wollheim is never guilty of this)

[13] The point might have been put in terms of "the concepts the spectator has and mobilises" (Wollheim 1986, 48): merely having learned, say, a critical vocabulary for dance or for poetry is not enough—one must be about to *mobilise* that understanding when one looks at dances or reads poems.

[14] Petipa choreography, first danced by Legnani. See Brinson and Crisp 1980 p, 62-63.

[15] Second, what can we say when that performance is no longer *directly* available to us?

[16] With a type/token analysis given of them (see McFee 1992a, 90-99 and 1994, 224-234).

[17] Further, the author typically has a role when the audience considers in which category of art the work is appropriately understood.

[18] As a practical aside: I will retain the example of *Swan Lake*: I know there are objections to it but, if the points are clear (as I hope they are), those worried on *this* point only can supply their own examples. Is *Swan Lake* a good example here? [See also Mackrell: "when works were passed on to new dancers individual steps, and even whole dances, were altered....the choreography is now danced differently" (1997, 7)] In particular, does *Swan Lake* have an author, in the

required sense? First, at worst, this is just an objection to the *example* only; and the example itself has a currency (even if undeserved). Second, the texts I am citing and quoting use this example. Third, the case is much less clear than one might hope. Certainly, by the time Batteaux's categorisation applies. the arts—or, anyway, *most* of the arts, including architecture—had *artists* as authors or creators. Thus, as Mackrell (1997, 36-37) grants, it is only quite *late* in the development of ballet in the modern period that the *achievements* of the choreographers came to be regarded as *appropriately* sacrosanct. But they were certainly given some esteem (and were sought after) by the time Petipa was making dances. Thus, Sally Banes writes, of *La Sylphide*, "[i]t is Bournonville's version that I will analyze here, because I believe that, although it has been altered in obvious ways over the years, it is still the closest we can come to the original Taglioni version" (1998, 15)—the implication being that there is such an original to return to, at least in principle, in the 1830s; and that this 'original' could be ascribed to its choreographer. So I prefer to leave the example.

[19] NB Kivy 2007, 101: performer as "an artistic collaborator": and compare Collingwood (1938, 320-321): "the author...demands of his performers a spirit of constructive and intelligent co-operation...where performers...are not only permitted but required to fill in the details." This seems exactly right: the performers make concrete what is under-determined in *the work itself*. More puzzling is Collingwood's conclusion: "Every performer is co-author of the work he performs" (Collingwood 1938, 321). At best, this is hyperbole for effect!

[20] We can imagine that some of the 'practitioners' involved in a happening are just performers—as typical dancers are: my point is only that there might be some who *are* the artists in such a case.

[21] See Austin who says that:

strange though the doctrine looks, we are sometimes told to take it easy— really it's just what we've all believed all along. (There's the bit where you say it and the bit where you take it back.) (1962, 2).

[22] In a similar vein, when I remarked (McFee 1992a, 104) that the term "creative" amounted to something *different* for dancers than it did for artists, some people thought I meant this to the detriment of the dancers. But this, too, was simply an attempt to recognise important differences.

[23] An award winning play, first shown in the UK on BBC 1 television, on September 14, 1976.

[24] Not just visual: clearly there is also the aural, as for instance in hearing the music—moreover, a fuller account would comment on exceptional cases, such a deaf dancers, for whom sound operates as a kind of projective tactile modality.

[25] And I said much the same thing in *Understanding Dance* (266) in stressing that, at least in typical cases, only "projective" perceptual modalities could be involved in artistic appreciation.

[26] Compare McFee, forthcoming.

[27] Compare Carroll & Moore: "the mirror reflexes that manifest themselves in outward behaviour probably have a physiological substrate in what cognitive scientists have labelled *mirror neurons*" (2008, 424-425).

[28] Much here turns on what is or is not *causal*. If we begin by thinking in terms of what follows from the workings out of the causal ('natural') laws of science, it is clear that causality will be independent of the 'description under which'.

[29] I am aware, too, of debates among neuro-scientsts as to the ascription of mirror neurons to humans: in humans, *the mirror system* might be a more traditional description—let my comments be shorthand for that.

[30] My thanks for sending me this paper in typescript; and for discussioins of aspects of it. Here, as Wittgenstein noted, our mistake lies in thinking that "[s]ometime we *shall* know more about [the "processes and states", even thought , at present, we]...leave their nature undecided" (1953, §308: my reordering and emphasis). In this process, we assume "a definite concept of *what it means* to know a process better" (1953, 308: my emphasis). So that, if we know that our answer lies in a causal sub-strate, we will be in the right region, even if the detail is wrong. But how could we know that? Instead, what we should do is "deny the yet uncomprehended process in the yet unexplored medium" (1953, §308).

[31] It continues with the references: M. A. Umilta, E. Kohler, V. Gallese, L. Fogassi, L. Fadiga, C. Keysers, and G. Rizolatti, "I Know What You are Doing: A Neorophysiological Study", *Neuron* 31: 155-165; V. Gallese, L. Fadiga, L. Fogassi, and G. Rizalatti "Action Recognition in the Premotor Cortex", *Brain*119: 593-609; G. Rizolatti, L. Fadiga, V. Gallese, and L. Rogassi, "Premotor Cortex and Recognition of Motor Actions," *Cognitive Brain Research* 3: 131-141. [In a sense, this is just one reference, round in a circle; the doctrine is something each paper 'tells' the next! So they *appear* to support one another; and do so *psychologically*].

[32] See for example Danto (1987) *passim*; as that paper illustrates, and as Danto appropriate quotes from Wölfflin, "Not everything possible at every time" (1987, 61).

[33] When elaborating some related considerations for the aesthetics of film, Carroll (2008, 171) feels the need to give exposition of two views from the contemporary philosophy of mind: *the simulation theory*—on which "...we understand and explain others...by simulating them. That is, we input their beliefs and desires into our own off-line cognitive-conative system" (Carroll 2008, 172) and *the theory-theory*—which is "...the *theory* that we understand what others are about by applying something like a scientific *theory* to their behaviour" (Carroll 2008, 171). And his critique is partly criticism of these theories. If such a detour through the philosophy of mind is crucial here, it will be essential to select the best alternatives in the philosophy of mind (can that *really* be these?), but also not something to be resolved in a text like this one.

[34] Reflect on the difference between exceptionless causation and stocastic (statistical) causation—as when smoking causes lung cancer; yes, but not in every case. It can *seem* as though the stochastic case is simply of the other, exceptionless kind, but where we lack the requisite information. Now, there will be a single explanation in any particular case; but that could not generate causal laws or generalisations unless cases resemble one another *relevantly*—and that is what I deny occurs generally. Two cases: (1) of course, since I am a physical structure, there is some state of that structure that is, say, my thinking longingly about Nicole

Kidman. But nothing follows about my future states. Of course, if I were in *exactly* that same state again, I would again be thinking of Nicole. But that is actually impossible! Any changes in me—including the physiological ones—mean that I will never be exactly the same again; indeed, this "I" here will always have a different composition in the future. And from my being in *roughly* the same state, nothing follows. (2) If the relationship were described by non-linear equations, we have explained that point (as it occurs previously). For then a slight difference in the initial conditions is granted to permit a *large* difference in the outcome (McFee 2000, 155-157).

[35] Recall how difficult it was to establish a biological basis *even* for the claim that smoking causes cancer!

[36] One of my own favourite examples, although slightly off the point, is a cod map of a section of the human genome which claims to identify a gene for the belief that all bags are carry-on bags—that is crazy; but why? I'd say because it confuses the biological sub-strate with the human explanation.

[37] Greater in wehat respect? Greater by orders of magnitude, or just slightly greater (perhaps not statistically significantly)? In every single case in the study, or just generally? And uniformly? Greater than is typical for that person? All of the above?

[38] As a helpful slogan here, we might begin from 1953, § 281: "only of a human being and what resembles (behaves like) a human being can one say: it has sensations; it sees; is blind; hears; is deaf; is conscious or unconscious." And our reflection should begin by noting that Wittgenstein is here just giving *examples* of the relevant powers and capacities—that others could be added to the list; and that a particular individual might not warrant *all* of these.

[39] For instance, Ryle explained memory as "having learned and not forgotten": the idea here is simply about *how* one learns—about the impact of "learning through doing" (1949, 259).

Works cited

Austin, J. L. 1962. *Sense and Sensibilia*. Oxford: Clarendon Press.

Austin, Richard. 1976. *Birth of a Ballet*. London: Vision Press.

Banes, Sally. 1998. *Dancing Woman*, London: Routledge.

Beardsmore, R. W. 1971. *Art and Morality*. London: Macmillan.

Best, David. 1974. *Expression in Movement and the Arts*. London: Henry Kimpton.

—. 1978. *Philosophy and Human Movement*. London: Allen and Unwin.

Brinson, Peter, and Clement Crisp. 1980. *Ballet and Dance: A Guide to the Repertory*. London: David & Charles.

Calvo-Merino, Beatriz, D. E. Glaser, J. Grèzes, R. E. Passingham, and P. Haggard. 2005. Action Observation and Acquired Motor Skills: an fMRI Study with Expert Dancers. *Cerebral Cortex* 15 (8): 1243-1249.

—. 2006. Seeing or Doing? Influence of Visual and Motor Familiarity in Action Observation. *Current Biology* 16 (22): 1905-1910.

Calvo-Merino, Beatriz, C. Jola, and P. Haggard. 2008. Towards a Sensorimotor Aesthetics of Performing Art. *Consciousness & Cognition* 17 (3): 911-922.

Caplan, Ben. 2007. Review of *Works of Music* by Julian Dodd. *British Journal of Aesthetics* 47 (4): 445-446.

Carrier, David. 1987. *Artwriting*. Amhurst, MA: University of Massachusetts Press.

Carroll, Noël. 2001. *Beyond Aesthetics*. Cambridge: Cambridge University Press.

—. 2008. *The Philosophy of Motion Pictures*. Oxford: Blackwell.

Carroll, Noël, and Margaret Moore. 2008. Feeling Movement: Music and Dance. *Revue Internationale de Philosophie* 62 (246): 413-435.

Cavell, Stanley. 1969. *Must We Mean What We Say?* New York: Scribners.

Collingwood, R. G. 1938. *The Principles of Art*. London: Oxford University Press.

Cunningham, Merce. 1984. *The Dancer and the Dance: Merce Cunningham in Conversation with Jacqueline Lesschaeve*. New York: Scribners.

Danto, Arthur. 1981. *The Transfiguration of the Commonplace*. Cambridge, MA.: Harvard University Press.

—. 1987. "De Kooning's Three-Seater." In *The State of the Art*, 58-61. New York: Prentice Hall.

Dodd, Julian. 2007. *Works of Music: An Essay in Ontology*. Oxford: Clarendon Press.

Frege, Gottlob. 1977 [1918]. *Logical Investigations*. Oxford: Blackwell.

Ground, Ian. 1989. *Art or Bunk?* Bristol: Bristol Classical Press.

Hamilton, James. 2001. "Theatre." In *Routledge Companion to Aesthetics*, eds. Berys Gaut and Dom Lopes, 557-568. London: Routledge.

—. 2007. *The Art of Theatre*. Oxford: Blackwell.

Kivy, Peter. 1975. What makes aesthetic terms aesthetic? *Philosophy and Phenomenological Research* 36: 197-211.

—. 2007. *Music, Language and Cognition*. Oxford: Clarendon Press.

Levinson, Jerrold. 1996. *The Pleasures of Aesthetics: Philosophical Essays*. Ithaca, NY: Cornell University Press.

McFee, Graham. 1992a. *Understanding Dance*. London: Routledge.

—. 1992b. The Historical Character of Art—A Re-Appraisal. *British Journal of Aesthetics* 32(4): 307-319.

—. 1994/2004. *The Concept of Dance Education* (Expanded Edition).
    Eastbourne: Pageantry Press.
—. 1997. Meaning and the Art-Status of Music Alone. *British Journal of
    Aesthetics* 37(1): 31-46.
—. 2000. *Free Will*. Teddington: Acumen.
—. 2005. The Artistic and the Aesthetic. *British Journal of Aesthetics* 45
    (4): 368-387.
—. forthcoming. "Empathy: Inter-personal vs. Artistic." In *Empathy:
    Philosophical and Psychological Perspectives*, eds. Amy Coplan and
    Peter Goldie. Oxford: Oxford University Press.
—. 2008. Dance, Identity and Performance. Paper presented at University
    of Nancy, France, May (unpublished).
Mackrell, Judith. 1997. *Reading Dance*. London: Michael Joseph.
Montero, Barbara. 2006a. Proprioception as an Aesthetic Sense, *Journal of
    Aesthetics and Art Criticism* 62 (2): 231-242.
—. 2006b. Proprioceiving someone else's movement, *Philosophical
    Explorations* 9 (2): 149-161.
—. 2007. "Practice makes perfect: The effect of dance training on the
    aesthetic judge." Paper presented at the American Society of
    Aesthetics, Pacific Division.
Morris, Desmond. 1977. *Manwatching: A Field Guide to Human
    Behaviour*. London: Jonathan Cape.
Nikolais, Alwin. 1998. "Excerpts from 'Nik: A Documentary'." In *The
    Vision of Modern Dance*, eds. Jean Morrison Brown, Naomi Mindlin
    and Charles Woodford, 113-121. London: Dance Books.
Reid, Thomas. 1969 [1815]. *Essays on the Intellectual Powers of Man*.
    Cambridge, MA.: MIT Press.
Rhees, Rush. 1969. *Without Answers*, London: Routledge,
Ryle, Gilbert. 1949. *The Concept of Mind*. London: Hutchinson.
Sharpe, R. A. 2000. *Art and Humanism*. Oxford: Clarendon Press.
Urmson, J. O. 1976. "The Performing Arts." In *Contemporary British
    Philosophy*, ed. H D. Lewis, (Fourth Series), 239-252. London: George
    Allen & Unwin.
Walton, Kendall. 1978. "Categories of Art." Reprinted in *Philosophy
    Looks at the Arts*, ed. J. Margolis, (Second Edition), 88-114.
    Philadelphia, PA: Temple University Press.
Wittgenstein, Ludwig. 1953. *Philosophical Investigations*. Translated by
    G. E. M. Anscombe. Oxford: Basil Blackwell.
—. 1969. *On Certainty*. Translated by D. Paul & G. E. M. Anscombe.
    Oxford: Blackwell.

—. 1980. *Culture and Value*. Translated by Peter Winch, 2nd ed. 1998. Oxford: Basil Blackwell.

Wollheim, Richard. 1973. *On Art and the Mind*. London: Allen Lane.

—. 1986. Imagination and Pictorial Understanding. *Proceedings of the Aristotelian Society Supplementary Volume* 40: 45-60.

—. 1987. *Painting as an Art*. London: Thames & Hudson.

—. 1993. *The Mind and Its Depths*. Cambridge, MA.: Harvard University Press.

CHAPTER NINE

IS A WORD DEAD WHEN IT IS SAID?: RELATIONSHIP BETWEEN TEXT AND PERFORMANCE IN MARTHA GRAHAM'S *LETTER TO THE WORLD*

ROSELLA SIMONARI

Introduction

A dancer enters the stage wearing a period costume with a long wide skirt. There is a door on the right and a white bench on the left. She moves across the stage, she performs some turnings, she bends her torso, jumps, moves in different directions, sits down on the bench and then starts moving again. After this phrase, another dancer comes in, they meet centre-stage and this second dancer utters the following lines:

I'm nobody
who are you?
are you nobody too?
Then there is a pair of us. (288)[1]

The first dancer is Pearl Lang and the second is Jane Erdman. They are dancing in the 1973 video recording *Letter to the World* by the American choreographer Martha Graham. The former dances the role of the One Who Dances (OWD), the protagonist of the piece, while the latter represents the One Who Speaks (OWS), her alter-ego. The above mentioned movements are danced in the opening solo of the OWD.

Letter to the World is a dance piece which Martha Graham created and performed in 1940. It is inspired by the poetry and life of the English writer Emily Dickinson, a figure Graham particularly loved. However, it is not a biographical piece, it is rather the exploration of what Graham used to refer to as Dickinson's "inner landscape" (Graham 1991, 163). The protagonist is split in two, the OWD, originally performed by Graham herself, and the OWS, who utters lines from Dickinson's poetry and letters. There are other characters who embody different aspects of the poet's personality such as the Ancestress (her puritan background), the Lover (her love for life), and March (her childish wit). The OWD struggles against the Ancestress to overcome her own tension as a woman poet. The OWS is a comforting attendant for the OWD and a kind of narrator of the journey she undertakes. Dickinson's fight is in a way Graham's own fight to express her creativity in a world where her dance was not always accepted by critics and audience alike.[2]

In this essay I intend to analyse the relationship between text and performance in *Letter to the World*. The protagonist can be seen as the embodiment of a creative process, she wanders through the avenues of her mind and meets a series of characters who help her to release her positive energies. The spoken lines are used as a *fil rouge* that takes the audience through the dance. For my analysis I refer to the 1941 version of the piece, the version the Martha Graham Dance Company has used for its subsequent reconstructions. I will begin with an analysis of the dance in relation to the spoken lines by focusing on the OWD and the Lover; then I will study the function of the OWS and I will conclude with a reflection on the importance of Emily Dickinson in Graham's choreosophy. In this respect, I will also briefly specify what I mean by the term choreosophy in relation to Graham's work.

The dance and the spoken lines

Letter to the World is nearly one hour long and consists of five sections, which present the poet's inward journey. I refer to the following table for the section titles and the outline of actions:

Sections	Actions
1. "Because I See New Englandly"	Introduction of the characters: the OWD, the OWS and the Lover. The Company dances a Party scene.
2. "The Postponeless Creature"	The arrival of the Ancestress who runs after the OWD and holds her in her arms. The Lover and the Company dance a procession march carrying the OWD who has been 'defeated' by the Ancestress.
3. "The Little Tippler"	Comic solo of the OWD. Playful duet with March. The performances of the Fairy Queen and of the Young Girl who also dances with March.

| 4. "Leaf at love Turned Back" | The OWD dances a solo with a blue veil. She dances a duet with the Lover and then is separated from him by the Ancestress. |
| 5. Letter | The OWD performs a 'white solo' of rebirth. She fights against the Ancestress and wins her (artistic) independence. |

Figure 9-1 Sections in Martha Graham's *Letter to the World*.

The music is by Hunter Johnson with a re-arrangement by Louis Horst, the period costumes are by Edythe Gilfond and the evocative set by Arch Laureter. Each section is highlighted in the programme with a title, which corresponds to a line from Dickinson's poetry. The first section, for example, is entitled "Because I see New Englandly" (285) and introduces the audience to the atmosphere in which the poet wanders. The last section is simply entitled Letter, and is probably taken from poem no. 441, "This is my Letter to the World". It emphasises the final recognition of the poet's creative journey. Graham selected lines from twenty-eight poems, three of them are spoken as a whole, the others are fragments, one single line, a few lines, an entire quatrain and so on. There are also lines from two letters used in the first section in relation to the Lover. The dance develops around each character and around the relationship each of them has with the others. For reasons of space I will only deal with two characters, the OWD and the Lover with brief references to the Ancestress.[3]

As already mentioned, *Letter to the World* is about Emily Dickinson's psyche and the characters represent different aspects of her personality. In this sense, there is an interesting difference between the OWD, the OWS and the other characters. On the one hand, the two main figures embody two clear-cut subjectivities, while the others seem to represent some of its portions. The spoken lines emphasise this aspect by mainly focusing on the mood changes in the protagonist and to present the other characters. Marina Warner has highlighted how splitting has to do with "the severance of the spirit from its bodily envelope" (2004, 120). In *Letter* the idea of a split character emerges in the names of the two protagonists and, at the same time, is connected with what each of them represents. In a way the OWS can be seen as the poet's bodily aspect, in that it is through her voice that she mainly manifests herself. The OWD, on the other hand, can be associated with Dickinson's spiritual presence as her continuous moving testifies. The idea of splitting is then directly connected with that of doubling, which

> is a complex, even riddling concept: it can mean a second self, or a second
> existence, usually coexisting in time… It can mean a look-a-like who is a
> false twin, or, more commonly, someone who does not resemble oneself
> outwardly but embodies some inner truth. (Warner 2004, 163)

In this sense, the OWS represents the outward Dickinson, the dutiful daughter her family and friends knew, while the OWD is her inner part, the poet who wrote most of her work in secrecy. However, their identities are not so different and separate.

In the above mentioned opening scene, the OWS and the OWD bow at each other, they are dressed alike but not in the same manner and the spoken lines contribute to creating an ironical mood. The persona of the poem seems to be making a joke about her identity, "she is nobody" and she meets another nobody with whom to share her irony. These lines are paradigmatic of the non-oppositional relationship between the two figures. Even though their identity is clearly marked by their different function, they are never in conflict; rather the OWS tends to comfort the OWD during her most difficult moments. In the opening scene the spoken lines are uttered after the dance, but in other instances they are spoken before a dance phrase. For example, in the third section, the OWS recites the whole poem "I taste a liquor never brewed" (214) following which the OWD acts like a little girl and performs another intense solo. This time her movements are less fluid and elaborate, she looks as if she is mimicking a comedy act from a variety show rather than dancing. She is funny and joyous and in this she follows what the poem initially suggested.

In the final section, when the protagonist falls into a profound crisis and then reacts to affirm her creativity, the poems are used in a more complex manner, in the sense that they follow each little stage of the poet's rebirth. In this case the spoken lines are uttered during the dance. Initially they denote irreverence towards religion: "Of course I prayed, / and did God care?" (376), then, little by little the lines express a crescendo: "After great pain, / A formal feeling comes" (321) and "Hope is that thing / With feathers / that perches on the soul" (254), until we arrive at "Glory is that bright / Tragic thing, / that for an instant / Means dominion" (1660). The dances change too, initially they are characterised by a "heavy weighted solo" (Capucilli 1999, 7) where the OWD performs movement on the floor beside the bench, then they become more high paced with kicks and jumps which have been synthesised by one of Barbara Morgan's photographs (Morgan 1980, 125). Then the Ancestress comes in and they perform a fight where the OWD finally wins. The closing lines are paradigmatic of the journey she has undertaken: "This is my Letter to the World" (441). After the OWS has said them, the OWD walks across the stage and slowly sits down on the bench.

With regards to the other characters, the focus widens and the notion of the double opens up to its multiple others. According to Marcia Siegel, the Lover

> plays several roles in her [Graham] fantasy, as do most of her characters. In [his] first solo, he evokes her straight-laced father as well as potential husband. (Siegel 1979, 179)

However, this aspect does not emerge clearly from the dancing and Graham does not mention it in the programme note. Siegel also highlights the multiplicity of the Ancestress: "she is death, tradition, parents, iron discipline and blind morality all at once" (1979, 180). On this question, Graham specifies in the programme that the Ancestress embodies Dickinson's "background, puritan, awesome, but beautiful, and is the symbol of the death-fear constantly in her mind" (Graham 1941), so it is possible that she was thinking of creating multiple selves within the same character. Jane Dudley, who was the first to interpret the Ancestress, confirms this view:

> the Ancestress in Letter had several roles. One had to add onto what Martha gave you to dance... In some places, I was like a governess. (Dudley 1996, 58)

Quoting Deleuze and Guattari, we could consider this proliferation of multiplicity as a de-territorialisation of Dickinson's personality where the single identity loses its univocal molar importance to get transformed into molecular multiple selves. According to the two philosophers, the molar "aggregate" (Deleuze and Guattari 2003, 288) is large and organic, it embodies the body with organs, the "statistical and global individual" (Deleuze and Guattari 1987, 49), while the molecular one is the "micropsychic and micrological" (Deleuze and Guattari 1987, 283) body without organs, where the perspective changes and the entity of each organ is dissolved into minor particles, thus achieving de-territorialization. In particular, the way the Lover is presented in relation to the spoken lines, is quite significant.

Before he enters the stage, the OWS says: "I would eat evanescence slowly" (letter 318) which is taken from a letter Dickinson wrote to a family friend, Mrs. J. G. Holland, and which exemplifies her poetic approach to writing letters. This is followed by another extract, "Life is a spell so exquisite / That everything conspires to break it" (letter 389). The Lover, then, enters and the music becomes more dramatic. He performs

some jumps and turnings which accentuate the vertical line of his figure.[4]
There is a contrast between the words spoken before his entrance and his
appearance and moves, in that the former are poetical and surreal, while
the latter are quite intense and tragic. This creates an interesting tension
which may represent the poet's ambivalent feelings towards social life.
She wanted to communicate with the world, but she also decided to live
isolated from it during the last part of her existence. And what perhaps
matters most, she only published a few of her poems during her lifetime.[5]
In this sense, the second set of lines connected with the Lover is quite
ambivalent. Life is exalted as such a magical thing that it almost needs to
be weakened. The Lover then enters and performs his solo. Graham seems
to imply that the Lover does not have a very good influence on the OWD.
And this aspect is further emphasised in the fourth section when he
embraces her from behind as if to control her and the OWS says:

> I'm wife...
> I've finished that,
> that other state...
> How odd the girl's life looks
> Behind this soft eclipse...
> But why compare?
> I'm wife. Stop there! (199).

Significantly, in the end, after the protagonist has won against the
Ancestress, she does not return to the Lover, and her self-fulfilment is
accomplished in the secrecy of her art.

According to Pearl Lang, "the role is in the words, the words feed the
movement" (Lang 2007), an affirmation which suggests a hierarchical
approach to the text/performance relationship, where the words have the
ultimate role and the dance comes afterwards, as a secondary element.
However, Graham selected the spoken lines and she assembled a scenario
for her dance. In 1940 her own embodied language (choreosophy) was
already well developed, Lang presupposes all this when she makes this
affirmation. I would rephrase the question in a different manner, focusing
on how dance relates to the words, how they interact with each other and
what one does to the other. Edward Nye specifies that "dance is poetry in
motion" (Nye 2005, 135), as the two fields have a kind of dynamic quality
in common. Graham was probably taken by the rhythmic sound of
Dickinson's poetry and she used it as another dynamic element in her
dance. The question, then, is not how much her dance 'depends' on
Dickinson's words, but rather what she does to them through her dance.

The One Who Speaks

Through her role, the OWS partakes of the structure of the work. She keeps it together, she is the teller of a story, however surreal. For this reason she is both inside and outside the story. Inside as the sister friend and alter ego of the OWD, outside as narrator, "an observer" (Siegel 1979, 177). At the end of the second section, the OWS faces the Ancestress and, as if she were casting a spell on her, she utters:

In the name of the bee
And of the butterfly
And of the breeze
Amen! (18).

They stand one in front of the other and, while speaking, the OWS moves diagonally from backstage right to downstage left and the Ancestress, taken by her words, steps backwards bending her torso in curving contractions. The OWS is immune from the Ancestress' threatening power and she is even able to dominate her. Through her voice Emily Dickinson's silent poetry acquires a new substance.

In 1930 and 1935 two plays were written on Dickinson, *Alison's House* by Susan Glaspell and *Brittle Heaven* by Vincent York and Frederick Pohl. In those plays there were spoken lines from Dickinson's poems or even allusions to them, but they were inserted in the other spoken parts of the plays. In *Letter* only Dickinson's lines were spoken and their interaction with movement intensified their powerful sense. According to Cristanne Miller, "sound emphatically grounds" (2004, 206) Dickinson's poetry. In the nineteenth-century there was more attention to the sound of poetry rather than to its visual aspect. The former shift mainly took place with modernist poets such as Hilda Doolittle and William Carlos Williams. Dickinson found her inspiration more in the aural characteristics of religious hymns and of Henry Wadsworth Longfellow's poetry, which she often quotes (Miller 2004, 207-213). Even though her poetry has been seen in the light of modernist visual aesthetics and, more recently, scholarship on her has focused on the materiality of her fascicles,[6] in *Letter* it is the sound of her words which emerges with greater strength. The OWS enters in relation with the OWD through voice and movement, but she mainly employs her voice to interrelate with the other characters. It is through her voice that she manages to face the imposing figure of the Ancestress. Dickinson herself had written

A word is dead
When it is said,
Some say.
I say it just
Begins to live
That day. (1212).[7]

From a narratological perspective we can say that *Letter* is a story told
in first person narrative, as most of the spoken lines clearly show, and that
the characters complement the narrative of the OWD in the different
sections. In this sense the role of the OWS is crucial as it creates the
rhythm and mood of each section. As Kaja Silverman underlines with
reference to cinema, "when the voice is identified…with presence, it is
given the imaginary power to place not only sounds but meaning in the
here and now" (Silveman 1988, 43).

The OWS in a way amplifies the presence of the OWD. The use of
words probably helped the audience to better follow the unfolding of the
piece and, in Michel Chion's words, to better remember it.[8] Chion in fact
highlights, mainly with reference to cinema, that "sound enriches a given
image so as to create the definite impression" (Chion 1994, 5) and also
that words are more easily remembered because

> sound is the vehicle of language, and a spoken sentence makes the ear
> work very quickly; by comparison, reading with the eyes is notably
> slower… The eye perceives more slowly because it has more to do all at
> once; it must explore in space as well as following along in time. (Chion
> 1994, 10-11)

When the OWS utters her lines, the music usually stops, so as to create
a suspension in order for the poet's voice to be heard. On some occasions
she is alone on stage as when opening the "Little Tippler" section or when
speaking the final line of the piece. This allows the audience to really
focus on the words and to blend them with movement. For example,
before the arrival of the Ancestress, the OWS speaks the following lines:
"It's coming, the Postponeless Creature…" (390). The OWS utters them
with an anxious tone and running across stage. This creates the
fundamental sense of fear that characterises the Ancestress and is essential
in creating the sense of suspense which anticipates her arrival.

As already stated, the OWS integrates the personality of the OWD and
is in no way her opposite. Rather than presenting the dutiful
daughter/hidden poet dichotomy, Graham stages what we could consider
Dickinson's poetic voice, the OWS, and her creative process, the OWD.
The spoken lines are, in fact, as elliptic as the dance; they mingle with it to

compose the atmosphere of the piece. The division of the two protagonists relies mostly on the specificity of the discipline they embody, that is literature and dancing.[9] Graham wanted to have the lines spoken on stage probably because her intention was to create an imaginary dialogue between her dance and Dickinson's work, a dialogue which continued to feed her creative universe. She repeatedly quotes Dickinson's poetry in her autobiography and one expression recurs more than once, it is "acts of light" (Graham 1991, 7, 170), taken from a letter Dickinson wrote to Catherine Peck in 1884 in order to thank her for her friendship, which she called "acts of light" (Dickinson 1998, 312-313). Graham also mentions it without making any reference to Dickinson, a sign that she had made it hers and, in 1981, she created a piece entitled *Acts of Light* which has not been taken into consideration in relation to *Letter*. It does not include any spoken line, but, in a way, it presents the same 'movement' of "love-death-rebirth"[10] that recurs in her pieces and that is central in *Letter*.

Dickinson in Graham's choreosophy

According to Graham, the past is invariably connected with the present:

> you only find the past from yourself, from what you're experiencing now, what enters your life at the present moment. We don't know about the past, except as we discover it. And we discover it from the now. (Graham 1991, 11)

The present is the time for a dancer to be, to move, to express his/her creativity. It also reveals Graham's belief in life as a continuous flow, "how does·it all begin? I suppose it never begins. It just continues" (Graham 1991, 17). Seen in this light, *Letter to the World* emerges as a work which is dedicated not only to a literary figure, but also to the choreographer's creative process. It is a cyclical journey she herself undertakes to face the problems of creating a dance.[11] There is a phase of initial bliss, a moment of positive energy, that I called 'love'; then there is a crisis, the moment of 'death' which is followed by a re-birth, where the choreographer/poet manages to find the strength to overcome her blocks. The genesis of *Letter* was quite troubled and it required important changes before it reached its 'definite' form.[12] In spite of its initial poor critical review, rather than giving up, Graham insisted on reworking it because the piece was particularly important to her. She probably saw Emily Dickinson as an ancestral figure, another woman who, like her, had challenged the artistic conventions of her time in order to give voice to her creativity, an aspect which was to be analysed by 1970s feminism.[13] The OWD is torn between two different forces, embodied by the Ancestress and the Lover respectively and, in the end, she does not choose either of them. She prefers to be on her own and dedicate her life to her art. This is a very powerful statement on Graham's part, a statement Graham felt was equally valid for herself. Dickinson was also American and this was very important for Graham as her intention was to establish an American dance with its own peculiar style:

> The modern American dance is characterised…by a simplicity of idea, an economy of means, a focus directly upon movement, which is the 'stuff' of the dance art, and behind and above and around all, an awareness, a direct relationship to the blood flow of the time and country that nourishes it. (Graham 1932, 7)

That is why *Letter* was created among other works inspired by American culture, like *Frontier* (1935), *American Document* (1938) and *Appalachian Spring* (1944).

Graham found important resonances with Dickinson's themes like the poet's criticism of religion, her irony and the eroticism of some of her poems. This is evident from the poems Graham selected for *Letter*. Poem no. 376, "Of Course I prayed, / and did God care?" spoken at the beginning of the fifth section, expresses the protagonist's loss of hope at the moment of loneliness and defeat. Graham was particularly critical of Puritanism and the fact that Dickinson was quite irreverent towards God, certainly attracted her attention. At the same time, Graham uses the ironic lines from poem no. 288 to introduce the two main characters: "I'm nobody / who are you?" so as to suggest a light-hearted atmosphere for the journey the OWD is about to begin. Dickinson was renowned for her humour, which she combined with her subtle wit. Last but not least, erotic poems like "My river / runs to thee" (162), which is spoken in the fourth section, mingle well with the eroticism in Graham's dances, an eroticism which she was beginning to develop with works such as *Letter* and which would become a trade mark in her production.[14]

John Emerson Todd has highlighted how some critics have tended "to read whole groups of the poems as biographical allegory" (Todd 1973, ix). Todd shows how Dickinson was not speaking of her experience every time she used the 'I'. She rather posed as different personae, such as the 'little girl', the 'wife-queen', the one embodied by 'death' and so on. Martha Graham could be placed among those 'critics' who interpreted "the poet's inner life through her work" (Todd 1973, ix), because of her use of the spoken lines in relation to the characters. In her own way, she provides a complex portrait where the characters and the sections do not just represent aspects of Dickinson's personality, but also some of the personae discussed by Todd. In the 'Little Tippler' section, the OWD and March create the 'little girl' persona, in the Fairy Queen subsection we have the 'queen' persona, while the Ancestress in the second and second last sections embodies the 'death' persona. Graham was able to give us a picture of what she saw as the main aspects of Emily Dickinson, using her own articulated approach to dance, an approach that I have called 'choreosophy'.

The word choreosophia comes from the Greek *choros*, meaning 'circle' and 'sophia', 'wisdom'. It has been used by Rudolf Laban in *Die Welt des Tänzers* (1920) and in the 1939 preface to his posthumous *Choreutics* (1966) with reference to its use in ancient Greece:

> Choreosophy seems to have been a complex discipline in the time of the highest Hellenic culture. Branches of the knowledge of circles came into being and were named 'choreography', 'choreology' and 'choreutics'. (Laban 1966, viii)

From its mathematical original usage rooted in the work of Pythagoras, the term, with Laban, has come to mean 'movement wisdom or knowledge' and it comprises a whole set of other more specific dance-related types of knowledge: choreography that deals with the actual steps of a piece, choreology, "a kind of grammar and syntax of the language of movement" (Laban 1966, viii)[15] and choreutics, "the practical study of the various forms of (more or less) harmonized movement" (Laban 1966, viii). This notion was also reinterpreted by Aurel Milloss in 1942: "I call Choreosophy the discipline that deals with dance from a moral viewpoint" (Milloss 2002, 64). As Stefano Tomassini has noted, in Laban and Milloss the term has "a metaphysical declination" (in an e-mail message to the author on December 11, 2008) and it has to do with their belief that movement was the basic principle of every kind of life and that the sphere was its most representative figuration (Tomassini 2002, 62). The terminological question is still quite open in the field of dance studies and it testifies to the vitality and richness of this discipline. Alessandro Pontremoli, for example, has created the word "choretics" borrowing its sense from the term "poetics" with reference to the "aesthetical system" (Pontremoli 2004, 83) that characterizes the work of contemporary choreographers or any dance movement.

By using the term choreosophy with reference to Graham's creative universe, I am attempting to find a more comprehensive term to highlight the complex system of embodied thinking that she has created. The

Graham technique is probably at the core of this system, but it is not its exclusive aspect. There is her choreographic work, her written production and her approach to set, music and costumes. All these elements contribute to creating a knowledge rooted in the moving body, a choreo-sophia, which in *Letter* emerges with evocative power.

Notes

[1] The numbers I quote refer to the Johnson edition of Dickinson's *Complete Poems* 1961 [1955]. However, the quoted lines are those Graham used in her piece. They are taken from an unpublished scenario written by Terese Capucilli, one of Graham's former principal dancers and former co-director of the Martha Graham Dance Company. The layout of these poems, in most cases, corresponds to the abridged version in use before the publication of the above mentioned edition in 1955. On the publication history of Dickinson's poems see Betsy Erkkila 2002.

[2] It was in the late 1930s that her dance began to gain a wider audience and a more solid critical appraisal. See Don McDonagh (1973).

[3] I am at present working on a study to the Ancestress and the importance of Puritanism in Graham's work.

[4] This verticality is further expressed in the fourth section when he performs some flamenco-like movements. On the relationship between Martha Graham and flamenco see Simonari (2009).

[5] On Emily Dickinson see for example Gudrun *et al.*, eds.(1998).

[6] See for example Juhasz (1998).

[7] Unlike the other quoted poems, this one is not used in *Letter*.

[8] This aspect also reflects Graham's will to make her work more accessible to a wider audience. This shift towards a more theatrical approach to dance, took place at the end of the 1930s with works such as *American Document* (1938), *Every Soul is a Circus* (1939) and *Letter to the World*. See Don McDonagh (1973).

[9] In this sense, the recently developed adaptation theories could be useful to further unveil this aspect. However, not much is being done on adaptation theory with regards to dance. This is an aspect I plan to explore. On adaptation theory see, for example, Hutcheon (2006).

[10] I first introduced this notion (Simonari 2006), then I re-elaborated it (Simonari forthcoming).

[11] A later piece, *Errand into the Maze* (1947) can be seen as another interpretation of this aspect.

[12] For an overview of the genesis of *Letter* see Simonari (2008).

[13] See for example the landmark essay by Rich (1995). On Graham's *Letter* from a gender perspective see Simonari (2003). My intention is to go back to this aspect in a future study.

[14] For an overview of the Graham technique, see Horosko (2002).

[15] On this term there has recently been a debate during the conference *La disciplina coreológica en Europa: problemas y perspectivas*, Valladolid, Spain, 27-29

November 2008.

Works Cited

Capucilli, Terese. 1999. *"Letter to the World*: Poetry used, characters, outline of action". Fax sent to the author on February 25th, 8 pages.

Chion, Michel. 1994. *Audio-Vision – Sound on Screen.* Translated by Claudia Gorbman. New York: Columbia University Press.

Deleuze, Gilles, and Felix Guattari. 2003 [1972]. *Anti-Oedipus.* Translated by Robert Hurley, Mark Seem, and Helen R. Lane. Minneapolis: Minnesota University Press.

—. 1987 [1980]. *A Thousand Pleatus.* Translated by Brian Massumi. Minneapolis: Minnesota University Press.

Dickinson, Emily. 1961 [1955]. *The Complete Poems,* ed. Thomas H. Johnson. Boston: Little Brown and Co.

—. 1998 [1894]. *Emily Dickinson – Selected Letters,* ed. Thomas H. Johnson. Cambridge: Belknap Press.

Dudley, Jane. 1996. "Jane Dudley." In *Goddess: Martha Graham's Dancers Remember*, ed. Robert Tracy, 50-62. New York: Limelight Editions.

Erkkila, Betsy. 2002. "The Emily Dickinson wars." In *The Cambridge Companion to Emily Dickinson*, ed. Wendy Martin, 11-29. Cambridge: Cambridge UP.

Graham, Martha. 1932. The Dance in America. *Trend.* March, April, May: 5-7.

—. 1941. Programme for *Letter to the World.* Bennington: Bennington College Theatre, 10th August.

—. 1991. *Blood Memory.* New York: Washington Square Press.

Grabher, Gudrun, Roland Hagenbüchle, and Cristanne Miller, eds. 1998. *The Emily Dickinson Handbook.* Amherst: Massachusetts University Press.

Horosko, Marion. 2002 [1991]. *Martha Graham: The Evolution of her Dance Theory and Training.* Gainesville: Florida University Press.

Hutcheon, Linda, 2006. *A Theory of Adaptation.* New York: Routledge.

Juhasz, Suzanne. 1998. "Materiality and the Poet." In *The Emily Dickinson Handbook*, eds. Gudrun Grabher, Roland Hagenbüchle, and Cristanne Miller, 427-439. Amherst: Massachusetts Universiy Press.

Laban, Rudolf. 1966. *Choreutics,* ed. Lisa Ullmann. London: MacDonald&Evans Ltd.

McDonagh, Don. 1973. *Martha Graham.* New York: Preager.

Miller, Cristanne. 2004. "The Sound of Shifting Paradigms, or Hearing Dickinson in the twenty-First Century." In *A Historical Guide to Emily Dickinson*, ed. Vivian Pollak, 201-234. Oxford: Oxford University Press.

Milloss, Aurel. 2002. *Coreosofia – scritti sulla danza*, ed. Stefano Tomassini. Venezia: Leo S. Olschki.

Morgan, Barbara. 1980 [1941]. *Martha Graham: Sixteen Dances in Photographs*. New York: Morgan&Morgan.

Nye, Edward. 2005. "Grace II: Poetry and the choric analogy in eighteenth-century France." In *Sur quell pied danser? Danse et literature*, ed. Edward Nye, 107-135. Amsterdam: Rodopi.

Pontremoli, Alessandro. 2004. *La danza–storia, teoria, estetica nel Novecento*. Bari: Laterza.

Rich, Adrienne. 1995 [1979]. "Vesuvius at Home: The Power of Emily Dickinson (1975)." In *On Lies, Secrets and Silence*, 157-183. New York: Norton.

Siegel, Marcia. 1979. *The Shape of Change. Images of American Dance*. Boston: Houghton Mifflin Company.

Silverman, Kaja. 1988. *The Acoustic Mirror. the Female Voice in Psychoanalysis and Cinema*. Bloomington: Indiana University Press.

Simonari, Rosella. 2003. Martha Graham and Women's Studies. Paper presented at the 5th European Feminist Conference, *Gender and Power in the New Europe*, 20-24 August, Lund, Sweden.

—. 2006. Martha Graham 'atti di luce' con Emily Dickinson. *Danza&Danza* 195: 18.

—. 2008. "Looking Back at Martha Graham's *Letter to the World*: Its Genesis, Its Reception, Its Legacy." *Looking Back/Moving Forward*. Society of Dance History Scholars Conference Proceedings: 52-57.

—. 2009. "Danzare il *cante jondo*: ipotesi di contaminazione fra Martha Graham e il flamenco", *Corpi danzanti. Culture, tradizioni, identità*, eds. Ornella Di Tondo, Immacolata Giannuzzi, Sergio Torsello, 209-230. Nardò: Besa Editrice.

—. forthcoming "'After Great Pain, A Formal feeling Comes': Emily Dickinson's Poetry and Figure in Martha Graham's *Letter to the World*."

Todd, John Emerson. 1973. *Emily Dickinson's Use of the Persona*. The Hague: Mouton.

Warner, Marina. 2004. *Fantastic Metamorphoses, Other Worlds*. Oxford: Oxford University Press.

Oral Documents

La disciplina coreológica en Europa: problemas y perspectivas,
Conference organized by AIRDanza (Associazione Italiana per la
Ricerca sulla Danza), Valladolid, Spain, 27-29 November 2008.

Lang, Pearl. 2007. Conversation with the author, New York: Martha
Graham School of Contemporary Dance, June 12.

Simonari, Rosella. 2003. Martha Graham and Women's Studies, 5th
European Feminist Conference, *Gender and Power in the New Europe*,
Lund, 20-24 August.

Choreographies

Acts of Light, chor. Martha Graham, music Carl Nielsen, costumes
Halston, feat. the Martha Graham Dance Company. New York: City
Center, November 26th, 1981.

American Document, chor. Martha Graham, texts Declaration of
Independence, Song of Songs, Jonathan Edwards, set Arch Laureter,
music Ray Green, costumes Edyth Gilfond, feat. Martha Graham,
Erick Hawkins and the Group. Bennington: Vermont State Armory,
August 6th, 1938.

Appalachian Spring, chor. Martha Graham, set Isamu Noguchi, music
Aaron Copland, costumes Edythe Gilfond, feat. Martha Graham and
the Company. Washington D. C.: Library of Congress, October 30th,
1944.

Errand into the Maze, chor. Martha Graham, set Isamu Noguchi, music
Gian-Carlo Menotti, costumes Martha Graham, feat. Martha Graham,
Mark Ryder. New York: Ziegfeld Theatre, February 27th, 1947.

Every Soul is a Circus, chor. Martha Graham, set Philip Stapp, music Paul
Nordoff, costumes Edythe Gilfond, feat. Martha Graham and the
Group. New York: St. James Theatre, December 27th, 1939.

Frontier, chor. Martha Graham, set Isamu Noguchi, music Louis Horst,
costume Martha Graham, feat. Martha Graham [initially it was part of
Perspectives]. New York: Guild Theatre, April 28th, 1935.

Letter to the World, chor. Martha Graham, text Emily Dickinson, set Arch
Laureter, music Hunter Johnson, costumes Edythe Gilfond, feat.
Martha Graham, Margaret Meredith, Jane Dudley, Erick Awkins,
Merce Cunningham. Benninton: Bennington College Theatre, August
11th, 1940.

Letter to the World, chor. Martha Graham, texts Emily Dickinson, set

Arch Lauterer, music Hunter Johnson, costumes Edythe Gilfond, feat. Martha Graham, Jean Erdman, Jane Dudley, Erick Awkins, Merce Cunningham. New York: Guild Theatre, April 7th, 1941.

Videography

Letter to the World, black and white, chor. Martha Graham, set Arch Laureter, music Hunter Johnson, costumes after designs by Edythe Gilfond, feat. Pearl Lang, Jean Erdman, Armgard von Bardeleben, William Carter, David Hatch Walker. New York: New York Public Library–Jerome Robbins Film Archive–, Compton-Ardolino Films, inc, with the assistance of a grant from the National Endowment for the Arts, December 5th, 1973.

CHAPTER TEN

CAFÉ REASON'S *ORPHEUS*: AN ETHNOGRAPHIC PERFORMATIVE INVESTIGATION OF BUTOH DANCE IN THE UNITED KINGDOM

PAOLA ESPOSITO

In this paper I offer an ethnographic analysis of *Orpheus*, a butoh rock opera, created by Café Reason, a butoh dance theatre company in collaboration with the postrock band Nonstop Tango. My writing is based on fieldwork carried out between November 2007 and October 2008, in the course of my participation in *Orpheus* as a butoh dancer. My sources are drawn in part from narratives and perceptions of the project that I collected while I was one of the participants. But also—and quite crucially—it is my own experience of dancing in *Orpheus*, informed by ethnographic participant observation. As I attempt to retrace the experience lived behind the collective art project, I offer no pretence of objectivity. Those who took part in *Orpheus* may have lived it as I did, as an emotional puzzle, a journey that had slightly–yet significantly–shifted from the centres of gravity of everyday life. Or they may have experienced their own individual emotions.

This production has given me the opportunity to reflect on contemporary interpretations of butoh dance. I shall pay particular attention to the intersection of butoh with musical improvisation, and to the tradition of myth in popular culture. I then discuss backstage events and social interactions. In describing these I also stress how important subjectivity and performativity are to the ethnographic endeavour.

It is generally accepted that butoh originated in Japan as an underground dance movement in the aftermath of the Second World War. It was a manifestation of that generation's experience of disillusion with an established society as well as part of the generalised international spirit of rebellion and re-invention. It has been suggested that the work of

Hijikata Tatsumi, founder of the butoh movement in Japan, expressed a search into the darkness of the soul, the ghosts of the past and into human irrationality (Hornblow 2006). Whilst in Japan Butoh has always been seen as a movement "from below" and typically marginal, since the 1980s it has gained recognition in Western dance and theatre settings and has spread throughout the world of contemporary performance, dance and theatre practice (Klein 1988, Hornblow 2006, Moore 2003). Since then it has not ceased to evolve, changing its shape and dislocating the contexts in which it has appeared. It has been discussed, questioned, named and unnamed. Nowadays more than 100 groups worldwide practice and perform butoh. Today, the very notion of butoh evades conceptual categories or definitions but powerfully informs live performance, and interconnects life experiences with art practices. The characteristic of butoh that is generally accepted to be unique is its absence of a recognisable form; also the fact that it draws its expressive force from internalised imagery. The critic Mark Holborn has written that butoh is defined by its very evasion of definition. Butoh is both theatre and dance, yet it has no choreographic conventions. It is a "subversive force", through which conventions are overturned (Holborn 1987). One aspect that makes butoh challenging and open ended is its ability to expand onto a global landscape and across cultural and social environments (Fraleigh and Nakamura 2006): while keeping its roots in Japanese culture, butoh is soaked with crosscultural vitality. As a practitioner, I find butoh constantly in a stage of becoming, through the plurality of articulations of old and new imageries. As a researcher, I focus on why and how Japanese butoh has found new roots in contemporary performance art, as well as in the everyday lives of practitioners. Undeniably, my research constitutes an attempt to explore my own fascination with the dance.

When I started to research the whys and hows of contemporary butoh, I was filled with urgency to find, first of all, "butoh people" to dance with. Indeed, I could not even think of developing an anthropological perspective on butoh dance without engaging myself in dancing. It is like speaking a foreign language: you can learn the rules of how the language works from a grammar book, but then you'll need to practise it yourself in order to understand how the language really functions in everyday life. Butoh to me works a bit like a language. I understood something of it from my readings, from watching dancers dancing it, and from making short videos of it; in search of the meaning of butoh, I went to Japan for three months. Finally, I came to realise that to understand butoh I needed to dance it myself. So I searched for "butoh people," and found them. I joined Café Reason's weekly classes and gradually, by getting to know the group, I became familiar with their work.[1] The group describes their dance activity in these terms:

> Café Reason is engaged in an ongoing process of exploration through movement. The explorations centre around three questions: Who am I? What is reality? How is my body? And use bodybased, imagebased and environmental stimuli. (Café Reason)

After a few months of training, the group invited me to take part in a theatre project, a butoh rock version of the Orpheus myth. The idea of being part of a staged performance excited me but, not knowing quite what to expect, I decided to turn this occasion into source material for my ethnographic study. The opportunity was to be able to study butoh dance as an insider, through active participation in a performance.

From November 2007, Café Reason joined with Nonstop Tango to commit to production a butoh rock opera inspired by the well known myth of Orpheus and his journey into the Underworld to rescue his dead wife Eurydice. The piece also presented references to the Japanese creation myth of the gods Izanami and Izanagi, which has strong parallels with the myth of Orpheus. Café Reason and Nonstop Tango revisited the myths and paid particular attention to the themes of love and relationships.

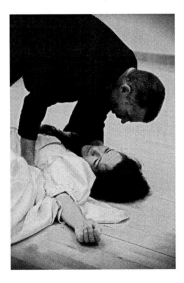

Figure 10-1 Rehearsal of *Orpheus*, 2008. Photo by Dariusz Dziala.

Orpheus also drew inspiration from the film *Orphée* (1949) by Jean Cocteau and *Orfeu Negro* (1959) by Marcel Camus. Café Reason's and Nonstop Tango's *Orpheus* built on this cultural and artistic background by following the same thematic thread of love and death. Their artistic intent was to explore the "archetypal resonance" of these themes across popular culture. The expression "archetypal resonance" is borrowed from an interview with Malcolm Atkins, a musician and composer in the group, and refers to the (Jungian) notion that "the myth captures something that applies to people, that they can relate to in a more 'mundane' environment" (Atkins, November 17th, 2008). The two groups each explored archetypes using their own form of expression: butoh dance (Café Reason) and improvised rock music (Nonstop Tango). The story was delivered through recited text and accompanying singing.

Figure 10-2 Rehearsal of *Orpheus*, 2008. Photo by Dariusz Dziala.

The intersection of expressive levels is inherent to the very definition of *Orpheus* as an opera since it is a mixture of several elements: music, drama, poetry, the visual arts, and at times dance, and where accompanied singing has an essential function (Latham 2002). Malcolm explained to me that the myth of Orpheus is integral to the Western operatic tradition (from Monteverdi to Gluck to Birtwistle) as well as to ballet (Stravinsky). The unique nature of our Orpheus consisted of the juxtaposition of a fairly traditional musical structure on the one hand, and of butoh dance on the other. Malcolm pointed out that there were two different threads running in parallel in the piece. On the one hand, a thread of song and speech, which delivered a fairly straight traditional narrative; and, on the other hand, the choreography of butoh, which broke up the straight narrative, opening the myth to all sort of interpretations. And this "narrative discontinuity" was precisely for Malcolm the strength of the piece, he explained that "there is a clear thread in terms of the songs and the recitation, but the dance actually undermines that." The way butoh reassessed the narrative thread and explored the resonance of poetic acts and movement that transcend the single repetition of story was enhanced by the way the rock band engaged with performance practice from the genres of Western art music, free improvisation, rock and popular music. The Café Reason and Nonstop Tango's *Orpheus* was constructed around the exploration of archetypes expressed through a collage of high and low art techniques in dance and sonic construction (Atkins, November 17th, 2008).

In this section, I attempt to expand my understanding of the social dimension of performance. I particularly refer to the work of Victor Turner (1974) and Richard Schechner (1977) who, in their analysis of ritual, drew connections between Social Anthropology and Performance Studies. Turner and Schechner showed that social and staged dramas are interrelated. Avorgbedor (1999) has pointed out that for both artists "the social substratum is the constant, formative factor that imbues performance with meaning, and that also helps to structure and restructure the performance". In Turner, not only do the major genres of cultural performance originate in social drama (from ritual to theatre and film) and narration (from myth to novel), but they also continue to draw meaning and energy from it. For him, "[a]ll performances, particularly dramatic performances, are the manifestations par excellence of human social processes" (Turner 1974, in Avorgbedor 1999). Avorgbedor argues that one of the major differences between Turner and Schechner is that, while Turner locates drama in conflict and conflict resolution, Schechner locates it in transformation, "in how people use theatre as a way to experiment, act out, and ratify change" (Avorgbedor 1999). For Schechner, "at all levels theatre includes mechanisms for transformation" (Schechner 1977, in Avorgbedor 1999). Schechner devotes much attention to offstage and performance making processes. In the context of analysis, he suggests, we should not pay attention only to the final product, the staged performance, but also to offstage dynamics, such as what happens backstage and during rehearsals. Schechner has drawn attention to the fact that the long processes of preparation that lead to performance have their own socially determined structures (Avorgbedor 1999).

I shall now describe the methodological implications I have drawn from these perspectives. The first is the repositioning of the researcher in relation to the object of study. Referring to performance, Dwight Conquergood (2002) wrote of the need to reduce the gap between analysis and action: "The dominant way of knowing in the academy is that of empirical observation and critical analysis from a distanced perspective" (Conquergood 2002). However, he remarked, that proximity, not objectivity, should become the "epistemological point of departure and return" (Conquergood 2002). The urgency for proximity implies a repositioning of the researcher in relation to the analysed phenomenon. Other scholars have discussed this methodological standpoint: Donna Haraway (1991) contrasts the "vulnerable view from a body" with the "abstract and authoritative view from above", that she finds typical of academic analysis (Haraway 1991). Tamy Spry (2006) offers the notion of the "performative I", to describe the new identity of a researcher seeking to embody the "copresence" of performance and ethnography (Spry 2006).

The second methodological implication consists of "framing the experience". Erving Goffman (1974) used the notion of 'frame' (borrowed from Bateson 1955) and applied it to theatrical aspects of social life. Students of performance, such as Schechner and Turner, used frame to distinguish between theatrical performance and everyday social performances. In my analysis, I use frame to delimit the social dynamics taking place in the context of performance, enacted by performers as social actors. In this respect, the metaphor of frame could be associated with that of stage, that is, the physical space where a performance situation is enacted. I use the expression "performance situation" to embrace the spectrum of interactions that are active in the process of performance: preparation, training and rehearsal, as well as performance as a final product. These interactions can either include the presence of an audience or be limited to the performers. Framing the performative situation can assist the performance ethnographer in her inquiry into these interactions. It also allows her to shift into and outside of the frame of the performance, between active and passive participation, between participant observation and participant enactment, ultimately allowing her to intersect the roles of performer and researcher.

The making of the Prologue gave a first shape to the Café Reason and Nonstop Tango's *Orpheus*. The process took the character of a ritual and an offstage performative encounter. We gathered at the home of the singer of the group, Miles, on an evening in November 2007 in Oxford. As soon as we had all arrived, we were prompted to dress up in evening dress. These were the costumes we would later use in the performance. We took a few pictures, sipped glasses of red wine and started chatting as we would have done at any other meeting or social gathering. I believe that the majority of us were not aware of what was about to happen. Once each of us had put on an appropriate costume, the ritual began. The three organisers of the meeting (Miles, Malcolm and Jeannie) explained the rules to the rest of the group. We were soon going to embark on a "journey into the Underworld". A journey of revelations, in which the participants would find themselves interviewed, one by one, on love and relationships. The interviews took place in the dining room, a space that was largely occupied by a dining table. The interviewers, acting in the role of Underworld creatures, were sitting on a bench at one side of the table. The person to be interviewed would be let in from another room, blindfolded, and guided to sit at the table in front of the interviewers. Then she would be helped to put on yellow rubber washing up gloves, and apply lipstick. Later Jeannie explained to me that the lipstick "was more than what it looked like". It was meant to act as a sort of magical device: "the lipstick meant that you had to tell the truth" (Donald, November 17th 2008). As each came and went, interviewers would turn into interviewees. The interviewee would be asked questions on personal experiences of love and relationships, leading to questions on dream, memory, and loss.

I took part in this ritual like everyone else. Of my interview, I can only remember strongly the odd feeling of being blindfolded in a dark room and guided in front of a group of people I barely knew at that time. I could not remember what questions I was asked, or what I answered until I recently watched the video record of the interviews made by a member of the group. I remember that, after finishing the ritual, I left the house with relief and headed back home. It must have been around 10 p.m. As I was walking, I looked around and had the feeling I was coming from a different dimension: my senses were altered, and the world had suddenly become more real, its textures and sounds were more alive. My own mind had turned into an unusual place, almost as if I were daydreaming. My most inner thoughts had been awoken.

During the following days, I experienced frustration, sadness, bewilderment; these are the words that come to my mind as I read through my notes:

> WHAT IS THIS? I am in a process of shifting… nothing is clear… nothing is safe… nothing to hold on to. How can I make sense of all this? How to objectify, how to put some distance between myself and this whirlwind of emotions?

It later became clear that the ritual had had upsetting effects on all those who took part in it. An exchange of emails conveys the overwhelming emotions experienced by some:

B: "Have to confess felt slightly disturbed, and shaken by the experience...
I hurtled into a really difficult place ... haunted by memories and feelings;
(I had the feeling) of being disempowered, manipulated and... used!"
A: "Rushing back (home)... and arriving in normal setting I felt I'd been
away an age—and in another world. Really a totally different time and
space"
J: "I have been plundering about in the darkness of my own little
Underworld since Saturday—I dropped my torch, lost the end of the bit of
string, tripped over a few trolls, and I was sure I heard drums starting up in
the depths (was it just my heart?)—just, whose idea was it to do that... oh
yes! ... Anyway, I do think we should wait to view the video at least until
the internal dust has settled."

I suggest that putting those subjective experiences into words and
sharing them via email with other participants was an attempt to
rationalise what had happened. Describing those feelings was not just a
display of emotions. It was an attempt to take distance from the event in
order to understand it and, by doing so, regain control over oneself

By giving account of the night of the Prologue, I am attempting to
describe the origins of the making of *Orpheus*. That night we made a first
step within the preconceived structure of the piece, the frame which was to
enclose our moods and thoughts in the following months. In so-called
'role games', each player enacts a role or character for the full length of an
imaginary story. During the game, everyday identity is suspended, and the
player thinks and acts in the terms of the imaginary character he or she is
playing. To be able to discern played identities from real ones is part of
our understanding of the world we live in. In social life we constantly
enact roles, but we instinctively know when to switch from a role to
another—let's say—from the role of parent to that of teacher to that of
brother and so on (Schechner 2002). I suggest that the roles performed in
Orpheus did influence the real life of the participants, and that the tension
required in the piece was often channelled back into the social life of the
group.

There was a point at which almost everyone got almost "fed up" with
everybody else, and more or less restrained discordances came to the
surface. My contention is that those discordances came as consequence of
the structure of interactions in the performance. For instance, the "division
of labour" between dancers and musicians almost took the form of a power
struggle. In an interview on the making of *Orpheus*, I asked both Jeannie
and Malcolm to explain their take on the development of the piece. Their
spontaneous response would reflect the roles they had played in the piece.
Thus, after Malcolm had spoken as a musician, Jeannie could not help
remarking: "The way you [Malcolm] talk about it, it sounds like the music

was the main thing, and the butoh is kind of taking different directions. But for me the dance was the main thing" (Donald, November 17th 2008). I am using this as an example of "negotiation of status" between the two categories—dancers and musicians—within the piece, validated by the different tasks performed. This process would have repercussions on the social life of the troupe as a whole.

Figure 10-3 Rehearsal of *Orpheus*, 2008. Photo by Dariusz Dziala.

Also, I would argue that within each group communication worked differently. For instance, as a dancer I would not attempt to connect with musicians at rehearsals in the same way I would with other dancers. The idea of connection here includes more or less subtle interactions such as greeting someone when entering the rehearsal space. I exclude the possibility that my discriminatory behaviour could have depended on the fact that I knew the dancers better than the musicians. Apart from the fact that I had known most of the people for a relatively short time, I recognised that certain automatisms or unconscious behaviour on my part may have been determined by my need to fit in with the group of dancers. A friend who works in the field of performance once enlightened me, by suggesting that dancers rely mostly on their physicality, and thus greeting each other through physical contact seems more obvious to them than to musicians, who rely instead on the unphysical sphere of sound. Far from attempting to generalise this observation, I cannot deny the lack of consistency I experienced between my interactions with the dancers and my interactions with the musicians. I give this as an example of the way in which the theatrical roles overlapped with the social life of the group during the making of *Orpheus*.

Another example of this came out from a conversation I had with

Malcolm and Jeannie around the experience of *Orpheus*. Malcolm and Jeannie had been, along with Miles, the leaders of the production. In the course of our conversation, they suggested that the making of Orpheus was only partially under their conscious control. For instance, when I asked them why the night of the Prologue they had decided to conduct the interviews, the answer was:

> J: "It seemed just a fantastic opportunity to ask everybody about love really, and what they thought about love ... I did not have any idea how powerful that was going to be, that night."

Apparently harmless acts were described as metamorphosing into something powerful and meaningful:

> J: "I just had this idea of buying the lipstick before we came...I just had to do it as soon as I had the idea I had to do it, but that became such a powerful thing... And in the performance it was really great to use it, such a powerful visual image. But I think it was more than it looked like...I felt the lipstick meant that you had to tell the truth."

And while enacting those acts, they had already lost control over their consequences.

> J: "That night was painful because it was just the start of something we didn't really know where it was going to go, and I think part of the power of it was because I didn't really know what I was exactly planning and I don't think anybody really knew what was going to happen. And I think that's quite an important part of the whole thing,
> that it wasn't like anybody was really in charge of it...I certainly did not know how powerful it was going to be... It felt like that; like that night we were stepping into something that took over then."

In the interview, Malcolm and Jeannie go back to the notion of the archetype. From their perspective, the half—serious game of the ritual had given way to the archetypes. Archetypes are explained as quasi-independent modes of behaviour that one can enact and experience without actually controlling them.

> J: "It sounds very kind of crazy, but it was like these kind of powerful archetypes have got a life, an accepted life, and they kind of wanted to find expression, and they just used us; we were a kind of a vehicle for them to get their stuff out into the world somehow; that's how it feels to me at the moment... I feel like we were just...children playing with fire really."

Malcolm emphasised how archetypes are carried by language, and so they permeate our everyday life and behaviour:

> I see them as templates that you step into (…); I mean, the way I see a lot of these things is that … we have potential for really complex kind of interaction through language. Language is often based on templates of communication. Language isn't just a building box of these expressions; it's actually kind of templates of methods of expression, and I think that the templates of methods of interaction are very *archetypal*, and you slip into these archetypes without realising it. And you get taken over by them, your behaviour gets kind of fashioned by them, without you actually really realising what's happening to you; or you can *rationally* realise what's happening to you, but you can't actually stop going … and that's the base of lots of tragedies, the fact that you slip into a mode of behaviour which actually you can't control."

This is the way these particular performers have theorised the interactions between theatrical roles and wider social life. This adds another level of complexity to my study. In order to develop my theoretical perspective, I will need to interact with the sophisticated theoretical views of these individuals. I am not going to adopt prematurely an overly critical or objective outside perspective because to do so at this stage would be to hinder me from pursuing the experience with this group further.

In this paper I have tried to give account of some aspects of the *Orpheus* production. Following Schechner (1977), I adopted the theoretical standpoint that we can understand much about performance art by looking at the production itself, and at the social dynamics revolving around it. Thus, I paid particular attention to describing *Orpheus'* backstage dynamics. By being actively involved in this production, I attempted to enact the proximity between researcher and researched that has been invoked by Conquergood (2002) and other scholars in the field of Performance Studies. Through this experience, I realised both the limits and the advantages of this approach. By taking part in the ritual of the Prologue, for instance, I could experience the initial stages of *Orpheus* from within. But I had to acknowledge that I was not prepared to distance myself from the repercussions of this involvement. It has taken me quite a time to revisit the event and reconsider it with a fresh mind. From that whole experience, however, I drew the idea that both the experience of fieldwork for an ethnographer and the making of a performance share common aspects: a sense of the unexpected, of the unfamiliar and, at times, of danger. The other side of the coin is that both demand an unconditional sense of curiosity, commitment and trust. Within the

Orpheus team, the dialogue was not always easy, and both differences and discordances came across at certain stages of the production. Yet, eventually, the *Orpheus* show was successfully completed and brought to the Pegasus theatre, in Oxford, on May 30 and 31 2008.

Notes

[1] The butoh dance theatre company Café Reason is based in Oxford and claims to be "the only permanent Butoh company in the UK" (http://www.cafereason.com).

Works cited

Avorgbedor, Daniel. 1999. The TurnerSchechner Model of Performance as Social Drama: A ReExamination in the Light of AnloEwe Halò. *Research in African Literature* 30 (4): 144-155.

Bateson, Gregory. 1955. A Theory of Play and Fantasy. *Psychiatric Research Reports* 2: 39-51.

Café Reason. "Current Work," Café Reason. http://www.cafereason.com.

Conquergood, Dwight. 2002. Performance Studies, Interventions and Radical Research. *The Drama Review* 46: 145-156.

Fraleigh, Sondra, and Tamah Nakamura. 2006. *Hijikata Tatsumi and Ohno Kazuo*. New York: Routledge.

Goffman, Erving. 1974. *Frame Analysis: An Essay on the Organization of Experience*. Boston: NorthEastern University Press.

Haraway, Donna. 1991. *Simians, Cyborgs, and Women: The Reinvention of Nature*. New York: Routledge.

Holborn, Mark, and Ethan Hoffman. 1987. *Butoh: Dance of the Dark Soul*. New York: Aperture.

Hughes-Freeland, Felicia. 1999. Dance on Film: Strategy and Serendipity. In *Dance in the Field: Theory, Methods and Issues in Dance Ethnography*, ed. Theresa J. Buckland, 111-122. Basingstoke: MacMillan.

Latham, Alison. 2002. *The Oxford Companion to Music*. Oxford: Oxford University Press.

Schechner, Richard. 1977. *Essays on Performance Theory 19701976*. New York: Drama Book Specialists.

—. 2002. *Performance Studies: An Introduction*. New York: Routledge.

Spry, Tamy. 2006. A "Performative-I" Copresence: Embodying the Ethnographic Turn in Performance and the Performative Turn in Ethnography. *Text and Performance Quarterly* 26 (4): 339-346.

Turner, Victor. 1974. *Drama, Fields and Metaphors: Symbolic Actions in Human Society*. New York: Cornell University Press.

PART IV:

CINEMA

CHAPTER ELEVEN

SUBJECTIVITY, THE EMOTIONS, AND THE MOVIES

NOËL CARROLL

Introduction

This paper is more of the nature of a contribution to the theory of the motion pictures, rather than to the philosophy of motion pictures. By this distinction, I mean to draw a rough distinction between the formulation of empirical generalizations and/or the specification of causal mechanisms that operate with respect to motion pictures, on the one hand, versus matters of a more conceptual or logical concern, on the other hand. The latter is what I call the philosophy of motion pictures, while the former is motion picture theory. Here I will be talking primarily from the perspective of a motion picture theorist.

The topic of subjectivity in the movies, I believe, was initiated by psychoanalytic-marxist film theorists in the nineteen-seventies. Or, at least, they introduced the discourse of subjectivity to cinema studies. The brand of psychoanalysis that these theorists endorsed was Lacanian, while their marxism was Althusserian. Althusserian-Lacanian film theorists were – and probably still are – convinced that what they called subject-positioning is the philosopher's stone with regard to demystifying the ideological operation of cinema.

One reaction to the grand theorizing of the Althusserian-Lacanians was the turn toward more cognitively oriented, psychological frameworks, including evolutionary psychology and neuroscience. Motion picture theorists—often called cognitivists—of this persuasion have attempted to replace the theories of the Althusserian-Lacanian with ones informed by the cognitive sciences.

In this paper, I would like to chart the transition from the psychoanalytic-marxist discussion of subject positioning to the competing frameworks that are being developed by cognitively oriented motion picture theorists. With reference to subjectivity, I hypothesize that this transition is best understood as the move from speaking of subject positioning to talk of movies and affect, in general, and of movies and the emotions, in particular. Thus, after sketching the Althusserian-Lacanian theory of subject positioning, along with the problems that beset it, I will offer an overview of the cognitivist approach to the affective address of movies, concluding with what I think will become the next important phase in that research, namely, the application of developments in the study of the moral emotions to the movies.

Subject positioning

Subject Positioning was a key concept, if not the key concept, in the Althusserian-Lacanian theory of film that evolved in the nineteen-seventies and nineteen-eighties. The ruling idea was that the devices of cinema—including the perspectival image, narrative, and editing—address spectators as a certain sort of ideological being, and, thereby, position them as a certain sort of ideological subject, or, at least, these devices create the impression that we are the pertinent sort of subject.[1] What sort of subject? A unified, autonomous subject or free agent. What ideological service does the impression of autonomy discharge? It persuades us that we are free, whereas we are actually cogs in the gigantic machine of capitalism.

This effect—the impression of autonomy—is reputedly utterly foundational to the operation of capitalist society. It convinces us that our choices are free rather than determined by the social system. It is a process that induces us to participate in our own subjection by having us suppose, for instance, that our adventures in conspicuous consumption are totally acts of free will rather than the motions of tiny wheels in the social mechanism. Our misrecognition of ourselves as autonomous subjects, in other words, transforms us into subjects in the sense of those who are dominated – that is, subjected to the control of others.

Putatively, virtually every aspect of capitalist culture contributes to the impression that we are unified, autonomous subjects. Movies are important in this regard. They not only reinforce the impression of unified subjecthood by means of characters who appear to exemplify that kind of agency. The very articulatory processes of cinema—such as the perspectival image, narrative closure, and editing (especially point-of-view editing)—also conspire in the illusory construction of the subjectivity of the spectator as a unified, autonomous subject.

Time and space, and, frankly, patience do not permit me to elaborate this conjecture at length. However, let me attempt briefly to suggest some of the ways in which Althusserian-Lacanian film theorists have stated their case.

The cinematic image—the single shot—is pictorial, the sort of thing that Plato claims is produced in a way that is strictly analogous to holding a mirror up to nature. According to Althusserian-Lacanians, the cinematic image re-activates the earlier, psycho-sexual stage of development that Lacan called "the mirror stage." At that stage—around eighteen months or so—the child recognizes himself or herself in a mirror. Whereas previously she experiences herself as a disparate welter of desires and impulses, upon recognizing herself in the mirror, she experiences herself as a unified, complete entity—an individuated body. And unity, of course, is a precondition for our belief in our autonomy, since agency would appear to require unity in order to co-ordinate action. Thus, the mirror-stage-experience provides the foundation for our belief in our free agency.

That is, the young child feels inadequate—feels a lack. The vision of bodily unity spied in the mirror encourages a sense of completeness, the unity felt as a kind of fullness or plenitude where there had been a sensation of insufficiency and disunity.

From the psychoanalytic viewpoint, the human organism is not unified. It is a package of different, often conflicting forces. The unity of the subject has to be constructed. The experience of the mirror-stage of development is the inaugural moment of subject construction which experience itself carries an apparently self-confirming charge of satisfaction.

Our experience of our own bodies as unified in the mirror image is a founding episode in our conviction in our unified, autonomous subjecthood. And the mirror-likeness of the motion picture image, as a replay of the mirror stage encounter, sustains our initial faith in this subjectivity again and again.

Furthermore, the typical cinematic image is perspectival. A perspectival image has a single monocular station point, the point from which the camera recorded the pro-filmic event and which the spectator inhabits imaginarily. This experience of a unitary, centralized viewing position is also thought to bolster our belief in our unified, autonomous subjecthood, insofar as the perspective system that renders the space of the image coherent is also putatively lending a sense of coherence to the viewing subject, himself or herself.

As well, movie editing, especially point-of-view editing, is thought to make a seminal contribution to the spectator's impression of unified subjecthood. In point-of-view editing, we are shown a shot of something— say an apple—and then a shot of the character who is ostensibly seeing said apple. The movie is made-up of discrete pieces of footage. But its fragmentary nature is somehow camouflaged by the editing. Moreover, the fragmentation of the movie might alert the viewer to what the psychoanalyst believes is the actual fragmentation of her psyche. However, by means of the point-of-view structure, this is averted. The spectator is drawn into identifying with the onlooking character who sees the apple, thereby masking the discontinuity in the film strip and reinforcing the spectator's confidence in her unified subjectivity.

That is, the edited film strip is full of gaps or fissures, whose acknowledgment, it is thought, might threaten the spectator's sense of unified subjectivity. The work of editing, especially point-of-view editing, is—to repeat a buzz word from yesteryear—to suture those gaps and fissures by encouraging audience-identification with characters like the one played by Jimmy Stewart in *Rear Window*. Indeed, some avant-garde film makers of the nineteen-seventies and eighties, like the practitioners of Structural-Materialist cinema, maintained that by foregrounding the edited nature of their work, they could loosen the grip of capitalist subjectivity. That is, in the words of Peter Gidal, their mission was to remove the sutures that Hollywood editors deploy to stitch together film strips into coherent wholes which spectators then take to reflect their own subjective sense of unity.

The movie narrative is also rent with gaps and ruptures. According to Stephen Heath, a narrative motion picture begins in a state of equilibrium—perhaps the town in peace, as in the opening of *The Magnificent Seven*. But then that sense of equilibrium is disrupted. Bandits ride into the village demanding extortion money. Some psychoanalytic-marxists describe this turn of events as a violence or a rupture. Gradually, the movie then works its way to a return of the opening state of equilibrium. The bandits are defeated by the Magnificent Seven and the village goes back to precisely the condition of homeostasis with which the film began. The narrative arc sutures the ruptures and disequilibriums introduced by the plot and the ensuing homeostasis imparts an impression of unity in both the film and the spectator by means of the re-activation of the dynamics of the mirror stage of psycho-sexual development. Hence, once again, the unified subjectivity of the viewer is reinvigorated by the recurrent, unifying structures of the mainstream, commercial motion picture.

Although dominant for a time, and still influential, this mode of theorizing has been the target of substantial criticism. One criticism was that it did not appear to have much empirical basis; it was a very armchair affair. Working psychoanalysts at least have their clinical practices which serve as a basis for their speculations. They are able to test their conjectures on their clientele. Yet cinema theorists lacked even this as a platform for their truly ambitious hypotheses.

Another problem was that every phenomenon the psychoanalytic-marxist examined appeared, miraculously enough, to be given the same explanation under the Althusserian-Lacanian dispensation. This or that unity-making feature in the motion picture gives rise to the spectator's misrecognition of himself or herself as a unified subjectivity—a coherently organized, autonomous subject. It's always the same story—the unity of the device induces a sense of unity in the subject, despite the fact that the devices look to be very different structurally. For example, an A/B/A narrative structure—one that goes from so-called equilibrium to disequilibrium and back to equilibrium—would appear to be very unlike a point-of-view editing structure, not to mention a perspectival image. And yet, all three stimuli are worked into the same coherence-in-the-object/impression-of-unity-in-the-subject scenario.[2]

Furthermore, this problem seems connected to another. The language of the Althusserian-Lacanian theory strikes one as vague, often metaphorical and associative. "Unified" is obviously covering a lot of territory—probably too much. It is just too easy to find unity everywhere. "Suture" is metaphorical and thus can be applied to very different phenomena figuratively, while the sense in which the cinematic image is a "mirror," akin to the one in the famous mirror phase, is completely free-associative. That is, because the language of the theory is vague, metaphorical and associative, the theory can be made to appear to explain everything which, of course unfortunately, is tantamount to explaining nothing.

Of course, an even deeper objection to the psychoanalytic approach to motion picture theory was that it ignored a cardinal principle of psychoanalysis, although a cardinal principle often ignored by Freud himself—namely, that a psychoanalytic explanation is a kind of last resort. One only appeals to the operations of the mechanisms of the irrational after all manner of rational, cognitive, and somatic explanations have been exhausted. Just as the Catholic Church in investigating sainthood, does not count something as a miracle that can be explained biologically; so one does not psychoanalyze the silence of a mute, if that is due to his defective vocal chords. Nor would a patient's inability to read be psychoanalyzed, if his intelligence quotient were not up to it. That is, it is analytical to the notion of psychoanalysis that it focuses upon phenomena that cannot be explained either cognitively or somatically.

However, it is exactly this desiderata that Althusserian-Lacanian film theorists ignore. That is, they never ask whether there are cognitive or biological explanations of the phenomena—such as pictorial recognition and narrative comprehension—that concern them. They plowed ahead with their psychoanalytic model without ever considering the possibility that it might be constrained in such a way that they had a sizeable burden of proof to lift along the way.

The cognitivist alternative to Althusserian-Lacanianism emerged as a very natural dialectical response to the dominant paradigm. For, obviously one way to de-rail an Althusserian-Lacanian approach to any phenomenon is to field a plausible cognitive and/or biological explanation of the phenomenon in question, since a plausible conjecture of this sort trumps the need for psychoanalysis.

Initially, cognitivist alternatives to the story of subject positioning were readily advanced with respect to the spectator's negotiation of the cinematic image, and to the spectator's comprehension of cinematic narration and editing, including point-of-view editing. Nevertheless, there did seem to be one aspect where the psychoanalytic approach had a clear-cut advantage over the cognitive approach. That was the domain of affect.

Motion pictures clearly engage the feelings and the emotions. And the realm of feeling at least seems to belong more squarely to psychoanalyst, rather than to the cognitivist.Indeed, the emotions have often been characterized as at odds with cognition. But, if that is the case, then the cognitive movie theorist would appear to have little to offer about a very important element of the address of the motion picture to its audience. Would the affects, most notably emotions, then, be the last bastion of the subject-positioning model? Or, could this remaining aspect of what the psychoanalystic theorists called subjectivity be handled within the conitivist framework?

Affect, emotion, and cognition

Psychoanalytically informed film theorists exploited the psychology of Lacan in order to attempt to explain the way in which movies abetted the construction of the capitalist subject. Whether movies—especially at the level of their formal devices—made much of a contribution to the construction of the capitalist subject is something about which I have always been skeptical. Nevertheless, in the course of pursuing this grand project, these theorists offered accounts of the nature of pictorial recognition, of the comprehension of narrative, and of film editing. As we have seen, these theories leave much to be desired. However, in order to challenge them effectively, it was not enough to demonstrate their errors of fact and logic. Althusserian-Lacanian film theory would remain attractive so long as there were no alternative theories to take their place. Thus, cognitive theorists began to field alternative approaches to these matters.

A leading figure in this regard was David Bordwell whose article "Cognition and Comprehension: Viewing and Forgetting in Mildred Pierce" (2008) and then his book *Narration and the Fiction Film* (1985) provided an alternative, constructivist model of narrative comprehension to the reigning psychoanalytic one. Likewise rival accounts of pictorial understanding and point-of-view editing were developed by cognitivists. But one area where cognitivism seemed ill-equipped to afford much insight was that of feeling and the emotions. Cognitivist theory seemed obviously suited to explain cognitive processes, such as narrative comprehension. But, what about our intense affective reactions to movies?

The lacuna was brought home to me especially during a conversation with Annette Michelson, one of the founding editors of the journal October. Commenting upon the development of cognitive cinema theory in the eighties, she noted that she felt that something was missing. Cognitivists had little to say about how it is that we can be so powerfully moved by movies. In failing to address this issue, she suggested, cognitivists had ignored that which particularly attracted film theorists of the nineteen-seventies and nineteen-eighties to psychoanalysis in the first place. Michelson contended that psychoanalysis at least gave film theorists a leg up on what they rightly regarded as a phenomenon that called-out for sustained consideration by cinema theorists – namely, the way in which movies engaged so intensely the feelings and emotions of viewers.

I am not sure that the Althusserian-Lacanians were actually very helpful in shedding light upon the affective address of cinema, since the only feeling state that seemed to preoccupy them was the feeling of wholeness that came with the re-activation of the Mirror Stage in the viewer. Nevertheless, the main thrust of Michelson's observation was correct. If cognitivists hope to develop a comprehensive theoretical approach to the movies, they would have to have something to say about the affective impact of movies upon the subject; they would need to explain how motion pictures manage to stir up so reliably the subjective feelings of audiences.

It may strike some of you as strange that cognitivists would take the study of affect in cinema to be part of their charge. For, as often noted, from ancient times onwards, the emotions have often been characterized as outside and even opposed to the realm of the cognitive. So even if cognitivists wanted to deal with the emotional address of movies, it might be thought that they would, in principle, be unable to do so.

However, we have traveled a long way since Plato introduced his tripartite soul with its battle between reason and the emotions. Contemporary theories of the emotions do not draw such a stern and antagonist division between the emotions and cognition as the one endorsed by Plato. Despite their many differences, most contemporary theories of the emotions regard the emotions as involving appraisals or evaluations of their objects, where appraisals and evaluations entail cognitive processes, which, at the very least involving pattern recognition. There is a great deal of disagreement about the nature of these appraisals and their relation to cognitive processes, but inasmuch as the emotions can be said to involve assessments or judgments of some sort, they involve forms of cognition and, thus, belong to the domain of cognitive psychology, or, more broadly, cognitive studies.

In the sixties, the influence of behaviorism began to wane, and psychology was said to have taken a "cognitive turn." But within that gyration, there was also housed an "affective turn," moving in tandem with the cognitive turn. Many psychologists and philosophers advanced the idea that the emotions had cognitive constituents, even as they debated the nature and role of these constituents. This research then became available to theorists of the motion picture, who, by the nineteen-nineties began construct alternative theories of the affective and emotional address of the movies. Some of these theorists include Ed Tan, Gregory Currie, Carl Plantinga, Murray Smith, Gregg Smith, Jinhee Choi, Deborah Knight, and others. Cognitive theorists of the moving picture have proposed accounts of the ways in which various genres address the emotions—including the genres of suspense, horror, melodrama, and comedy.[3] Various models for understanding the relationship between the fictional characters in movies and their audiences have been developed—including notions of sympathy, empathy, and simulation.[4] Likewise, various analyses of the formal devices of cinema have been advanced, including theories of point-of-view editing, movie music, and the close-up. Indeed, ironically enough, the study of the emotional impact of movies is one of the most active research programs among ciné-cognitivists.

One approach—namely, my own—to the analysis of the emotional address of movies begins with the presupposition that the emotions size-up situations and the things that give rise to them and elect differential reactions to the aforesaid stimuli on the basis of antecedent computations, whether immediately upon exposure to the pertinent circumstances or after some interval. That is, these computations may occur on contact at the initial level of perception or they may be processed cognitively in the forecourts of the mind, either tacitly or consciously. They may engage the frontal cortex of the brain or they may bypass it entirely and may be relayed directly to our behavioral-response centers. It is the function of these affective systems to evaluate the actions, events, and states of affairs in which we find ourselves with respect to certain recurring existential themes – like loss – and to prepare us to respond to them accordingly. The emotions appraise our environment in terms of our interests and prime us to act tactically so as to protect or advance our welfare.

For example, if the stimulus is appraised to be harmful, our emotions set the organism to flee or to fight or to freeze. This response, of course, is what we call fear. Similarly, if the situation that confronts us is one in which we perceive a wrong done to ourselves, or to those whom we hold near and dear to ourselves, or to our interests, then we are prepared to "get even." This, perhaps needless to say, is anger. Other affective responses in this neighborhood include sorrow, pity, indignation, reverence, awe, hatred, love, shame, embarrassment, guilt, humiliation, comic amusement, loyalty, patriotism, and so forth.

Emotion is the domain of affect in which differential computational appraisals of stimuli relative to certain interests give rise to visceral feelings which typically prime behavioral tendencies to act. Or, to put the matter graphically, the perception of danger (an appraisal of a large hulking thing in our vicinity) leads to a chill down my spine (a visceral feeling) which makes me freeze in place (an evasive behavior). Altogether these components add up to an instance of the emotion of fear.

The emotions are a good thing to have from an evolutionary standpoint. Compared to processes of conscious, rational deliberation, the emotions are very fast, "down and dirty," decision-making routines. They scope out the situation quickly and ready the organism to react, sometimes within the blink of an eye. By the time you reason your way to the best way to deal with a charging bull, you could be trampled. But in virtue of your emotions, you are moving out of harm's way without a second thought, often, quite literally, before you know it. The emotions, in other words, are of no small advantage when you're in a tight spot.

Of course, the emotions may sometimes be mistaken. What I may first size up as a large, potentially dangerous creature lurking in the shade might turn out to be nothing but a curiously shaped bush. However, way back when in the environmental circumstances of the African veldt, where the emotions evolved, it was better to be safe than sorry.

The emotions were evolved by natural selection in the first instance to respond to the percipient's conception of the situation. That is, if the percipient believed that the large shape in the shadows was a dangerous creature, then she was thrown into a state of fear, even if the stimulus was really just a bush. But the emotions do not only respond to what one believes about one's circumstances. One can also react emotionally to counterfactual or contrary-to-fact situations—to situations imagined.

Thus, the tribal elders could frighten their children away from the nearby stream by narrating a tale about one of the young boys being eaten by an alligator when he got too close to the river's edge. In this way, the fact that the emotion system can be activated by imaginings was also adaptive, both for purposes of warning and of planning. Moreover, it is this feature of the emotions that is relevant to the way in which movies engage viewers emotionally, since it is the ability to be moved affectively by that which we imagine that enables us to be frightened by horror movies and thrilled by action-packed races and chases.

That is, many, if not most, of the things that we call movies are fictional. Fictions, in general, and movie fictions, in particular, mandate that we imagine – that we entertain as unasserted—certain propositional contents, such as, with regard to the opening of *Vertigo*, that Scottie Ferguson is dangling from the ledge of a building in San Francisco. The capacity to be moved by what one imagines, which originates as a boon to survival, in other words, can be mobilized for the purposes of art and entertainment. Just as the tribal children could be thrust into a state of fear by imagining being devoured by an alligator, so we can be frightened on behalf of Scottie Ferguson when we imagine that he is on the verge of plunging to his death.

But how exactly are our emotions elicited by movies—how are our imaginings transformed into emotings? In order to answer this question, it is useful to recall certain features of the emotions. Emotions, as indicated, are evaluations of certain situations, made with an eye to protecting our enhancing our interests, typically by disposing us toward acting in a way that promotes our welfare or the welfare of those with whom we are aligned – lovers, family members, friends, fellow citizens, etc. When I assess an action as unjust, I feel indignation. When I appraise a state of affairs as potentially harmful, then I feel fear.

As these examples suggest, emotions are appraisals and, as appraisals, they are governed by evaluative criteria. In order for my psycho-physical state to count as fear, the object of that state should be harmful or, at least, potentially harmful. I cannot be in a state of fear, if I do not apprehend the object of that state as harmful or potentially harmful. If I do not believe, imagine, nor otherwise apprehend wet noodles to be dangerous, then I cannot be afraid of them. For an emotion of a certain sort to obtain, the object of the emotional state must be cognized under the right category. To be angry at x generally requires, in everyday life, that I have been wronged by x or, at least, that I think I have been wronged by x. To be comically amused by y, I must apprehend y as an instance of perceived incongruity.

Emotions can originate near the site of perception and prime bodily action without a further need for computation: the groom slips on the banana peel and we burst into laughter. Or, the emotion may arise after being cognized over time, either tacitly or cognitively. Professional envy regarding your office-mate's executive bathroom privileges probably requires a lot of cogitation, in contrast to the flash of fear elicited by a sudden movement. Motion pictures afford opportunities for the emotions to erupt through a variety of routes—some mediated by conscious cognitions, some by tacit ones, and some more immediately.

The quickly advancing, dark figures may immediately send the icy rush of fear down my spine. On the other hand, in order to admire the bravery of the speaker, we must cognize her performance under the concept of courage—something that may require quite a bit of observation, discrimination, and thought.

Nevertheless what all these emotional states have in common is that they are evaluations or appraisals relative to certain criteria. In the ordinary course of events, we attend to this or that state of affairs and subsume it—either mediately or immediately; consciously or tacitly—under the appropriate criteria, and feel fear, anger, sadness, and so on. In everyday life, it is up to us to organize, albeit often automatically, the stimulus in light of the appropriate criteria.

But motion pictures are different. In movies, situations come already organized or predigested emotively in terms of the relevant criteria of appropriateness. If the movie makers want to elicit anger from the audience, then they design the scene in question in such a way that the wrongness of the villain's actions is made salient. Since wrongness is criterial for anger, structuring the scene in a way that it wears its wrongness on its sleeve, so to speak, is, all things being equal, likely to spark anger in the spectators.

I call the process of making salient the features of scenes and sequences that are criterially apposite for eliciting from audiences the pertinent emotional states criterial prefocusing (Carroll 2000) That is, the movie makers focus upon elements of the scene or sequence in such a fashion that what stands out for viewers are details that mesh with or meet the criteria of the emotional state the movie makers desire to provoke in us.

In life, in contrast to fiction, our emotions have to select the pertinent objects upon which to focus from a plethora of largely unstructured stimuli. But in fictions, including movie fictions, the fictioneers have done much of the selection for us with an eye to foregrounding those features of the situation that suit the criteria for the emotional state the movie makers wish to trigger in the audience. With regard to motion pictures, our emotions are not called upon to organize the situation before us, so to say, de novo. To a much greater extent than in our experience in everyday life, events and states of affairs in fictional motion pictures have already been emotively structured for us by the movie director and his team. We do not typically have to depend from the first instant upon our emotions to organize the fictional events and states of affairs as much as we rely upon our emotions to perform this task on a daily basis. For, in the main, the states of affairs and events in motion pictures have been emotionally predigested for us by the creators of the movie.

That is, the creators of the motion picture have already done a great deal of the work of emotionally sculpting scenes and sequences for us by carefully designing and making salient the features of the fictional situation that satisfy the criteria for drawing forth the emotional state intended by the production team. Details that suit the criteria for the desired emotional response have been selected, filtered, foregrounded, and emphasized in the narrative, dialogue, composition and through the camera positioning, editing, acting, musical commentary and so forth.

In contrast to the way in which the emotions generally have to start from scratch when it comes to ordinary experience, when it comes to the typical run of movies, the events on screen have been emotively prefocused for us by the production team. The director and his associates have selected the elements of the scene or sequence that they think are emotively significant and thrust them, to put it bluntly, in our faces. The means to this end at the movie makers disposal include: camera position and composition, editing—including what I call variable framing[5]—lighting, the use of color, and, of course, musical accompaniment, acting, dialogue, and the very structure of the script or narrative.

But what does it mean for a scene or a sequence, an action or an element thereof, or a character to be emotively prefocussed. Again, here the fact that emotive appraisals are governed by criteria is crucial. To be happy for my cousin, for instance, I must be convinced that he is doing well. If he is doing poorly, and I am apprized of this, then I cannot be happy for my cousin. Moreover, just as the emotions in daily life are governed by certain evaluative criteria of appropriateness, thusly must the emotions in movie fictions be so governed. Hence, a situation or character in a motion picture is emotively prefocused by being criterially prefocused—that is, by being structured in such a way the descriptions and depictions of the relevant objects of our attention in the movie clearly, aggressively, and decisively satisfy the criteria for the emotional state intended by the creators of the motion picture.

For example, the makers of zombie movies hope to put us in the emotional state of horror. Horror is a compound emotion, involving fear and disgust.[6] As already noted, harmfulness is a criterion for fear; impurity, on the other hand, is a criterion of disgust. Therefore, in order to provoke horror in the audience, the makers of a zombie movie will emphasize certain of the properties of the zombies—specifically, those that count as fearsome and disgusting. Consequently, the zombie will be shown arrestingly to be dangerous or harmful in terms of its murderous implacability, its cannabilism, and its contagiousness, while its impurity—for instance, its open, decaying wounds—will be given a close-up look.

Once we perceive the objects of our attention under the criterially pertinent categories—such as harmfulness and impurity with respect to horror movies—the intended emotion, horror, is apt to be raised in us. That is, as a result of entertaining the appropriate appraisals—typically the ones implicated by the criterial prefocusing—we are likely to undergo the bodily responses that the movie makers planned.

Movies and the moral emotions: A program

So far the discussion of the way in which movies engage the emotions and shape the subjectivity of viewers has involved a summary of conclusions that cognitive motion picture theorists, like myself, have been developing over the last two decades. But in this section of my paper, I would like to look ahead to future research and to outline, somewhat programmatically, a way in which cognitivists might continue their investigation of movie emotions into the future. This involves turning to recent work in moral psychology, with special attention to evolving theories of the moral emotions.[7]

Obviously, exercising our emotions is one of the primary functions of motion pictures, especially the ones we call movies—that is, popular, mass-market narratives. Many of the movie genres take their name from the emotion they are intended to engender – such as thrillers, mysteries, tear-jerkers, and horror fictions. But maybe less obviously, perhaps the most pervasive emotions engaged by movies are the moral emotions. For the moral emotions are addressed by every kind of movie, genre notwithstanding. Thus, focusing on the moral emotions is likely to tell us a great deal about how motion pictures work, most notably about how mass-market movies are structured. And this is where contemporary research in moral psychology enters the picture.

The elements of moral psychology that concern me today involve the study of the moral emotions. Certain previous conceptualizations of the moral emotions would seem hard to square with our relation to moving pictures. For example, the notion—that moral judgments follow upon moral reasoning which, then, once conclusions are delivered, ignite moral emotions—would appear to be too slow and deliberative a process to be operating with respect to a rapidly edited, action movie. However, recent research into the moral emotions indicates that this is not the way the moral emotions are always or possibly even usually elicited. Rather, the moral emotions, according to social psychologists, like John Haidt, are fast, automatic, intuitive appraisals.[8] That is, upon recognizing certain patterns, the stimuli are processed immediately, resulting in a flash of feelings of approval or disapproval. Reasoning and reflection, if they enter the process at all, generally come into play after the initial intuitive appraisal is issued, monitoring our immediate assessments and sometimes modifying them. These intuitions are cognitive insofar as they involve pattern recognition, but they need not be front-loaded by reasoning. Indeed, some moral psychologists maintain they never are.

So, in other words, William James's picture of the emotions may have been more accurate in certain respects than that of cognitivist theorists of the emotions, like me, who in the past have criticized James. But, in any event, something like a neo-Jamesian approach to the provocation of moral emotions in response to an often fast moving, temporal art like cinema appears to afford a better model for understanding our affective responses to movies than do theories that propose that the moral emotions always result from reflection. For my own part, I would still maintain that reflection can cause moral emotions to erupt—unlike some neo-Jamesians, like Jenefer Robinson.[9] Nevertheless, I would agree with the view that many or even most emotions only involve fast intuitive appraisals. Part of the evidence for this is that people are so bad at identifying the variables that are causing their moral responses, as in cases in which the way a question is framed can prompt contradictory rationalizations, or, as they are sometimes called, confabulations.

Moreover, from the perspective of cinema and media studies, the idea that the emotions can take the form of rapid intuitive appraisals accords with our experiences of motion pictures far better than the reflection model, since the vast majority of motion pictures allow little time for deliberation.

That the emotions are connected to moral assessment should be no surprise, since the emotions are naturally selected adaptations for making assessments rapidly. That is, the emotions are a form of value judgments. Thus, insofar as moral judgments are evaluative, albeit ethically, it is predictable that they bear some relation to the emotions in general. On my view, the moral emotions—like indignation—are a variety of moral judgment. And, furthermore, even emotions that are not moral, narrowly construed, can be enlisted to moral effect, as when we find the object of a moral prohibition to be loathsome.

The constant making of moral judgments pervades everyday life. We are always judging the character of the people we encounter as well as their actions. This experience is as pervasive, if not more so, with respect to movies. And it is even more condensed in the typical motion picture, since movies possess the resources—particularly what I previously called criterial prefocusing—to shape the characters and actions screened with such surpassing legibility. The moral emotions are part of the motion picture maker's tool kit. And contemporary moral psychology can tell us something about what is in that tool kit.

Specifically, contemporary moral psychology can provide students of cinema and media with a map of moral affect. Moral psychologists, for example, have hypothesized that there are five cross-culturally recurring or nearly universal domains of moral concern.[10] These include a concern with treatment of others in terms of harm, on the one hand, and benevolence or care, on the other. We might call this the welfare scale.

Those who inflict harm—particularly in terms of pain, and especially, where the victims are the young, the defenseless and the vulnerable—provoke fast, intuitive, other-condemning, emotive appraisals, such as anger, indignation, loathing, contempt, and disgust (disgust as in the expression "he is so cruel that it makes me sick."). The character played by Tim Roth in Rob Roy is perfectly designed to raise the audience's collective gorge through his virtually gleeful zest for inflicting harm—in terms of pain and humiliation—upon others. We do momentarily waver in our loathing for him when he tells a woman he is seducing of his unhappy childhood, but our ire is renewed with interest when we learn that he is lying to her.

Moreover, the audience is not only apt to greet the perpetrators of harm with anger. The victims elicit compassion, which John Haidt, calls an other-suffering emotion. So at the same time that the audience's concern with harm provokes anger toward the Cossacks in the Odessa Steps sequence of *Potemkin*, compassion is elicited for those who are massacred. Interestingly, they include two children, a group of elderly petitioners, two mothers and finally the older woman whose face is slashed by the horseman's saber. Here the director, Sergei Eisenstein, is obviously exploiting the outrage that occasions the abuse of the most vulnerable.

The welfare scale not only predicts intuitive negative appraisals in the form of hatred in response to characters and situations that mete out undeserved harm to others. The welfare scale is also sensitive to acts of benevolence, generosity, helpfulness or just concern. These gestures are likely to provoke felt, intuitive appraisals of admiration of various magnitudes. Where the act of benevolence involves some sacrifice on the part of the benefactor, the emotion of admiration can become quite elevated as in the case of those mothers in melodramas, such as *Stella Dallas*, who forgo all for the welfare of their loved ones. Acts of kindness positively dispose us toward characters and these acts can be as subtle as the gunfighter who treats his horse with concern.

At this point, some of you are likely to be mumbling that there does not appear to be any difference between the findings of what is alleged to be moral psychology and folk wisdom. Under the behaviorist regime in psychology, millions of dollars in grants were dispersed in order to confirm that if rats were rewarded, they learnt faster, and, even faster, if they were punished. Did we really need experiments to prove that hypothesis? Couldn't we have asked our grandparents?

Similarly, does this fancy talk about a welfare scale do any better? Do cinema and media theorists really need it? We don't need university-certified psychologists to tell us that the suffering caused by the so-called "gods" in 10,000 B.C. is likely to piss off the audience. And isn't it also just as obvious that that beneficence, all things being equal, elicits admiration and, if it is great enough, even awe?

Let me make two responses. The first response appeals to the explanatory value of isolating widespread, almost universal moral interests. The specification of the welfare domain of moral concern and the enumeration of the emotional responses and the factors that give rise to them are not merely limited to our tribe, that is to say Western culture. The claim is that the welfare domain and others are nearly universal moral touchstones that recur across diverse societies. Furthermore, there seem to be good evolutionary explanations as to why the concern with harm and care, and the other domains of moral focus to be discussed, should occur cross-culturally. Consequently, since cinema and the other mass visual-media are predicated upon soliciting and securing vast audiences, especially through the mobilization of the emotions, we would expect them to be preoccupied with human interests that are extremely widely distributed. For, that will help explain the success of cinema and other forms of mass media which harken to these concerns. Thus, the discovery of the welfare scale as a nearly universal moral touchstone will play a role in an account of the power of movies.

Second, from the descriptive point of view, all that is being claimed here is that the clarification of domains of ethical concern, like the welfare scale, and the moral emotions they enlist provides a broad map of the territory. They alert cinema and media theorists about the kinds of things for which they should be on the lookout inasmuch as we wish to determine what cinema and mass media need in order to command large audiences emotionally.

But subsequently it will remain up to cinema and mass media researchers to produce maps of greater refinement. Protagonists should be designed in such a way that they elicit fast intuitive appraisals in terms of admiration for their beneficence. Cinema and media scholars can determine the range of tropes of benevolence and the regularity of their re-occurrence with respect to various traditions and relative to diverse audiences. Isolating the domains where one should search for these regularities is a valuable first step. No one claims it is the last step. As the last step it would be banal. But as a first step, it is enabling. It directs research.

In addition to the recurring concern with welfare across ethical systems in terms of harm and concern, other cross-cultural domains of moral interest include: a justice scale which is sensitive to issues of fairness and reciprocity; Westerns, like Shane, appeal to this scale by emphasizing the cattle owners flagrant disregard for the rights of the farmers. There is also an authority scale which governs the apportionment of respect, including the amount of respect due one with regards to her position in a hierarchy. It is this scale that is invoked by movies like Prince Kaspian, in the Narnia franchise, in which usurpers are defeated and rightful rulership restored. In addition, there is a loyalty scale which mandates the emotional appraisals of individuals within the group versus those without as in the case of the emotion of patriotism; this scale can be especially important in war movies. And lastly, there is a disgust scale where the objects of disgust may not only be ingestibles, but also moral actions.

Disgust, in the first instance, is an emotion that protects the intimate borders of our bodies—our mouths, our nasal passages, our genitals, etc. Foods, odors, sexual acts and practices are the objects of disgust in its perhaps primary sense. However, the presence of sexual practices on this list indicates that disgust can be elicited by things other than ingestibles. The domain of disgust can be extended beyond the objects it was originally evolved to protect. It can be dragooned for the defense of the boundaries of the other moral domains.

For example, disgust can function as the reverse side of in-group allegiance by stigmatizing members of the out-group as abominable sub-humans. Thus, the provocation of disgust may be a lever of moral rhetoric when it comes to the representation of outsiders such as the Jews, gays or outright enemies, like the Japanese during World War II. The scene of the black-dominated legislature in Griffith's *Birth of a Nation* is an obvious example here.

Indeed, disgust can be enlisted as a toxin protecting the borders of the entire gamut of moral domains insofar as we are often disposed to describe any infliction of wanton harm, injustice, disrespect, or disloyalty as sickening, nauseating, or disgusting. Although western liberals are prone to discount disgust as a moral emotion, not only is this response to violations of things like dietary taboos in traditional societies regarded as on all fours with infractions in the other moral domains, but even the modern liberal will use the vocabulary of disgust in order to characterize or, perhaps better, to dramatize her abhorrence of, say, injustice, as well as perhaps to articulate something of the phenomenology of her feeling.

In each of the recurring moral domains, breaches of the relevant norms typically elicit other-condemning emotions such as anger, contempt, indignation, loathing and disgust. Adherence to the norms in each domain trigger other-praising emotions ranging from feelings of approval to admiration and in instances of extremely supererogatory acts—think Jesus Christ here—even wonder.

Time does not permit the presentation and analysis of more examples of each of the cases that this general framework for the moral emotions isolates. But perhaps that is not really necessary, since I'm sure most of you can readily think of examples from everyday life and/or from cinema. That may lead you to complain again that there is no benefit to be had from familiarizing yourself with this developing branch of moral psychology. However, it isn't my point to announce some astounding discoveries like "Killing some people in either life or movies will make some other people angry."

Rather, the advantage of this psychological theorizing is that it provides a framework for organizing a research program into the rhetoric of the moral emotions as they occur in movies as they are. These categories of moral concern systematically guide us toward where to start to look for the operation moral rhetoric. This then puts cinema and mass media theorists in a position to chart which sorts of moral emotions are engaged most often, which strategies are favored for raising moral emotions, in which genres and in which national cinemas are said strategies dominant, and what significant convergences and variations in moral-emotive address are there across genres, historical periods, regional styles, and so forth.

One reservation regarding the appropriation of this framework might be that it may be said to rest upon the dubious assumption that morality everywhere is the same which assumption is obviously false. Different places and times have clearly constructed different and sometimes conflicting moral systems.

Yet that is not something that this approach to moral psychology denies. Rather what is being claimed is that these moral domains recur as domains of concern cross-culturally. This is consistent with different societies formulating different perspectives on, for example, harm. Sometimes this may be due to the differential weight alternative cultures place on the different domains in the basic package.

Just as biology prepares children to be language users rather than the user of a particular language, so it appears that people are generally born with the generic capacity or innate preparedness absorb the morality of the society in which they are enculturated, insofar as such moralities are built-up upon the sensitivities connected to the five domains that we have been discussing. Hence, the framework I am rather programmatically recommending now abets research in areas where the moral rhetoric of different cultures overlap, while also being able to help pinpoint where the cultural difference between alternative motion-picture-making traditions rests upon different ways of negotiating the five basic moral domains.

A brief summary

Briefly summarizing then: the discourse of subjectivity entered cinema studies as a concept employed by psychoanalytic-marxist film theorists. They used the notion in their accounts of the construction of the capitalist subject, especially in terms of the operation of such cinematic phenomena as the perspectival image, narrative comprehension, and point-of-view editing.

Cognitive theorists of the motion picture were quick not only to criticize the psychoanalytic hypotheses of the Althusserian-Lacanians, but also to field alternative cognitive theories of the recognition of the perspectival image, narrative comprehension, and point-of-view editing. The cognitivists were a bit slower in developing accounts of the ways in which movies address the emotions, a topic of which it might be thought the psychoanalysts have prima facie advantage.

Nevertheless, cognitivists have since shown themselves to be capable of providing theories, such as that of criterial prefocusing, that are of arguably even greater specificity than anything produced under the aegis of marxist-psychoanalytic film theory. Moreover, the cognitivist research program into the topic of movie emotions will, I predict, be supplemented and enriched by the evolving frameworks recently available from contemporary moral psychology which research, by dissecting the moral emotions, may afford even further insight into the subjectivity of movie viewers.

Notes

[1] For an extended introduction to and criticism of Althusserian-Lacanian Film Theory as it evolved especially in the United States, see Noël Carroll (1988).

[2] Indeed, generally it is the only unity of the cinematic devices that the Althusserian-Lacanian is able to describe with any precision; the impression of the unity of the subject seems totally parasitic descriptively upon the descriptions of the relevant devices. The Althusserian-Lacanian does not seem to have independent access to the unity-experience of the viewer. Of course, I do not mean to suggest that the viewer feels disunified before the onset of the pertinent cinematic devices. The spectator undoubtedly feels unified way before she enters the movie theater. But that is hardly due to the operation of cinematic devices that she has not yet encountered.

[3] See, for example, my "Film, Emotion, and Genre" (2006).

[4] See, for example, Plantinga and Smith, eds. 1999.

[5] See Carroll (2008).

[6] See Carroll (1990).

[7] For a helpful overview, see Prinz (2007).

[8] Haidt (2001).

[9] Robinson (2005).

[10] See Haidt and Joseph (2004). See also Rozin *et al.* (1999), Shweder *et al.* (1997), and Prinz (2007).

Works cited

Bordwell, David. 2008 "Cognition and Comprehension: Viewing and Forgetting in Mildred Pierce." In *Poetics of Cinema,* ed. David Bordwell, 135-150. New York: Routledge.

—. 1985. *Narration and the Fiction Film.* Madison, Wisconsin: University of Wisconsin Press.

Carroll, Noël. 1988. *Mystifying Movies: Fads and Fallacies in Contemporary Film Theory.* New York: Columbia University Press.

—. 1990. *Philosophy of Horror.* London: Routledge.

—. 2000. "Art and Emotion." In *Beyond Aesthetics*. Cambridge: Cambridge University Press.

—. 2006. "Film, Emotion, and Genre." In *The Philosophy of Film and Motion Pictures*, ed. Noël Carroll and Jinhee Choi. Oxford: Blackwell.

—. 2008. *The Philosophy of Motion Pictures*. Oxford: Blackwell.

Haidt, John. 2001. The Emotional Dog and its Rational Tail: A Social Intuitionist Approach to Moral Judgment. *Psychological Review* 108: 814-834.

Haidt, John, and C. Joseph. 2004. Intuitive Ethics: How Innately Prepared Intuitions Generate Culturally Variable Virtues. *Daedalus* 133: 55-66.

Plantinga, Carl, and Gregg Smith, eds. 1999. *Passionate Views*. Baltimore: Johns Hopkins Press.

Prinz, Jesse. 2007. The Emotional Construction of Morals. Oxford: Oxford University Press.

Robinson, Jennefer. 2005. *Deeper than Reason*. Oxford: Oxford University Press.

Rozin, Paul, Laura Lowery, Sumio Imada, and Jonathan Haidt. 1999. The CAD Triad Hypothesis: A Mapping between Three Moral Emotions (Comptent, Anger, Disgust) and Three Moral Codes (Community, Autonomy, Divinity). *Journal of Personality and Social Psychology* 76 (4): 574-586

Shweder, Richard A., Nancy C. Much, Manamohan Mahapartra, and Lawrence Park. 1997. "The 'Big Three' of Morality (Autonomy, Community, Divinity) and the 'Big Three' Explanations of Suffering." In *Morality and Health*, eds. Allan Brandt and Paul Rozin, 69-76. London: Routledge.

CHAPTER TWELVE

HOW DO DOCUMENTARIES RAISE EMOTIONS?

SALVADOR RUBIO

The aim of my paper[1] is to provide some keys to answer the question "how does the documentary arouse emotions?" To do this I will combine two approaches: the first starts from some theoretical reflections on philosophical aesthetics (specifically, Noël Carroll's theory of fiction and Richard Wollheim's theory of emotions), and the second analyses a fragment of a very particular documentary film, one of the founding classics of the genre, *Las Hurdes. Tierra sin pan* (1933) by Luis Buñuel.

My contribution is part of a wider research activity into the subjectivity of the documentary which has already provided some results[2] and which does not stop at the classical documentary but seeks to reach beyond and find some of the keys to what has become known as the "new documentary", and in particular the "new Spanish documentary" (Torreiro 2006). The limitations of this paper oblige me to restrict myself to the example I have cited. In the broader research mentioned I have upheld that the new documentary today is characterized by at least two features: hybridization (generic and discursive) and emotional involvement (or subjective involvement, on the part of both the maker and the viewer). This statement is perfectly coherent with a conceptual and even historical consideration of the documentary, according to which (even when starting from an assertive and modal declaration on the documentary) the emotional involvement in the documentary text not only does not put in check its "documentary nature" nor move it towards a mannerism of the documentary, but rather reaffirms it and embraces it more deeply. Adopting such a posture supposes, on the one hand, an avoidance of the obstacles which prevented fixing a characteristic (if not a rigid definition) of the documentary discourse, but, on the other, it eludes the dangers of an exclusively cognitivist or informative conception of the same. Buñuel's film, with its recognized foundational character, yet at the same time complex and indomitable, seems to me to be simultaneously an example and a precedent of the hybridization and the subjectivity of the new documentary.

There are still five, very general, suppositions of my perspective that I would like to clarify as regards this issue before broaching the matter proper.

First, saying that the documentary image causes emotion may (rightly) seem to be an obvious thing to say. We feel emotions when we see the photograph of our past, of a loved one who is no longer with us, or a press photograph reporting current news can arouse feelings in us. Similarly, we respond emotionally to a nature documentary or when we see what our town was like during the years of the Spanish Civil War. Clearly this more or less daily emotional experience has its keys (in the diversity of its functions, aims and modes) and it deserves particular study, but it is not the specific aim of this contribution. My object is rather the documentary film (short or feature length) which is developed and exhibited as a film of creation (to some extent, author) which has burst onto the current cinema scene, albeit in minority circles, and in particular into recent Spanish cinema and its preceding tradition, which includes "authors" (with all the opportune nuances) like Buñuel, Vigo or Flaherty, to name but three among many.

Secondly, I accept Nichols' (1991, 2001) now classical approach[3] to the definition of documentary cinema, opting for a modal characterization which distinguishes between six sub-genres (expositive documentary, observational, poetic, participatory, reflexive and performative). Other theoreticians (Weinrichter 2007) argue for a terminological approach to the problem of distinguishing between the documentary film and the fiction film, and they prefer to talk about, non-fiction films, essay films (distinct from documentary films), or even narrative documentary as a distinct category from the essay film. I believe that the purely terminological approach solves nothing, in that it reproduces the traditional definitionist task of searching for some definitive criterion or taxonomy, but forgoes the positive lesson to be learnt from such a search.

Thirdly, I accept a definition of the documentary as a discourse which is fundamentally characterized by its assertive character, in line with the Documentary as Assertion[4] theory, defended, with some nuances, by authors like Wolterstorff, Carroll and Ponech (i.e. the documentary as a discourse characterized by its asserting something, in whatever modality, about an aspect or a fragment of the world). For Carroll (1997), the documentary is seen as a film of presumptive assertion, or as a film which is received as asserting something about the world.

Fourthly, I find it surprising that, given the fruitful aesthetic reflection on emotions which is an ongoing issue in the debate between cognitivists and non cognitivists within the framework of the so called theory of fiction, there is practically no theoretical reflection on emotions in the documentary discourse, and the more so since there are positions in this debate (like the cognitivism detailed by Carroll) that could be singularly strengthened, I believe, by analysis of the functioning of the emotions in the documentary discourse, and not just in the fiction discourse. The answer, I believe, is related to success (and all that it implies) of the so called "fiction paradox", to which I will be referring later.

In the fifth place, I believe that the research into the emotionality of the documentary acquires a clearly performing character to the extent that it pivots crucially on the articulation of a time that the filming represents (which includes shooting, montage and history) and a time for the film's projection (on which the time of its reception is built).

Now I can go on to the subject proper of my paper.

My main hypothesis is, in synthesis, that the idea upheld by Noël Carroll (1991, 1998) which refers specifically to the so called "fiction paradox", which states that "emotions may rest on thoughts and not merely upon beliefs" (Carroll 1998, 273), has an interesting application for the emotional functioning of the documentary (particularly for the cinematographic documentary). And this, in spite of our assuming, from Carroll (1997) himself, that there is a characterization of the documentary as an assertive discourse.

I will, very synthetically, reconstruct Carroll's proposed response to the fiction paradox. As is well known, the fiction paradox asks how it is possible for us to respond emotionally to the fictional work of art, since we know that the events are fictitious. The fiction paradox especially affects the classical cognitivist conception of emotion, according to which the cognitive state that is most responsible for an emotion must be a belief. If there is no belief in fiction, how can emotion be produced? Carroll's answer lies in a corrected cognitivism insofar as he rejects "the supposition that emotions require beliefs in all cases" (1998, 272); i.e., Carroll accepts that emotions require a cognitive element,

> but, I would argue, the form that that component may take is diverse, including not only beliefs, but thoughts and perhaps even patterns of attention. And, furthermore, the form of the cognitive component that is most relevant to understanding our emotional responses to fictional narratives is thought, not belief. (1998, 272)

While belief implies "a proposition that is kept in mind in an affirmative sense", a thought "consists of maintaining a position while not affirming it", and so the fiction author is saying to us "suppose p" or "imagine p" or "think about p without affirming it".

I believe that there is a perverse effect of the great success that the fiction paradox has had on aesthetic reflection, and it is the following. If what is startling about the fiction paradox is its insufficiency of beliefs to explain the arousal of emotion in a discourse such as the fictional one, in which there is a "suspension of belief", then it seems as if in the discourse which is centrally characterized by belief (i.e. by the assertions about certain areas or aspects of the world and the belief that such assertions are either True or false) there would be no call for any question about the generation of emotions. To put it another way, it as if the emotions were something given naturally (or at least not aporetic, not to be explained) in the documentary discourse. But if, as Carroll rightly believes, radical cognitivism is wrong in "supposing that emotions require beliefs in all cases", then this should hold not only for the fictional discourse but also for the documentary one.

My working hypothesis is that in the case of documentary cinema there is an important (but not unique) mechanism for generating emotions which is also based on the generation of thoughts in the viewer. One crucial distinguishing feature with fiction is that these thoughts do not take the form of imaginations in the sense that Carroll says that fiction proposes that we imagine certain propositional contents ("imagine that Manhattan is made of pizza" or "suppose that Albania has conquered the United States"), but it does induce inferences and associations that arouse simple and complex emotions in the viewer. Such thoughts (and, why not "attention modes", if we use Amelie Rorty's denomination) can be articulated through sequences of ideas, narratives, redundancies, rhythms, contrasts, oppositions, etc. which generate expectations in the viewer in a way that is perfectly compatible with the assertive tonic of the documentary.

I believe that Wollheim's theory of s (despite its differences with Carroll's one) offers a complementary aspect which covers precisely the part that Carroll's approach does not theoretically cover, since Richard Wollheim gives us keys as to how emotion is articulated, in terms of mental disposition, from the most basic mental states (thoughts, desires) which Carroll pertinently underlines for the case of fiction. What is interesting here is how belief, in the documentary case (and in contrast to the fiction case) occupies a central position in thoughts and desires.

Let me sum up this second theoretical support. Wollheim (1999) (coinciding in part with the line of B. Williams) postulates that emotions are mental dispositions (which often presuppose mental states, such as feelings and thoughts).

This is so, because precisely the role of the emotion is to provide the creature —or, as we might now get used to saying, the person— with an *orientation* or an *attitude to the world*. If belief maps the world, and desire targets it, emotion tints or colours it: it enlivens it or darkens it, as the case may be. (1999, 15)

Thus, emotion is formed on belief and on desire, and they are essentially interactive.

A desire forms. We are thereby sensitized to the world. The world satisfies or frustrates our desire: we experience the impact of the world. We respond to this impact by forming an attitude. But this attitude, we must recognize, anticipates a reaction from the world. And to this reaction, we have in turn some idea of how we would expect ourselves to respond. And so on. (1999, 223-224)

Wollheim devotes one chapter to the so called moral emotions (like shame and guilt).

Let us move on now to our example. Luis Buñuel made the first version of his film *Las Hurdes. Tierra sin pan*[5] in 1933. From its birth it was mythical and it remains so today. It has never ceased to arouse controversy and opposing reactions, even amongst specialists of the documentary genre. There is one aspect in which, in some way or another, all students of the film coincide (even if they do not in general grant it the relevance and attention it merits). It is precisely its evident vocation to not leave the viewer indifferent. This way of appealing to non indifference includes important nuances between the actors. Mercè Ibarz (without doubt one of the best experts on the film) alludes, for example to the "anti-emotional character, the base of the sound montage" (1999, 153). It is clear that the cold tone of the off screen voice (well perceivable in the French), and likewise the clinical-intoning descriptivism tone that runs through the text of the commentary seek to provoke a reaction in the viewer that is not exactly one of empathy. Then there is the distancing effect (in the Brechtian sense) of the music of Brahms. Yet the result, rather than anti-emotional, is one of a non empathetic, non direct emotional nature. Only form such a realization can the effect this film continues to produce today be understood.

For Buñuel is not seeking to make a mere ethnographic documentary, but rather an anarcho-surrealist—or even surrealist-communist as Herrera (2006) would say—exercise in an action that goes towards the mind and the guts of the viewer within a very specific sociopolitical context—an acid criticism of the republican social action, of the centre-left in fact. In addition, there is a timeless utopian (in the etymological sense of the term, i.e. with no real place) discourse against poverty and good intentions. It also goes against the regenerationalist imprint which was already present in the Freinetian pedagogical experiments which were carried out in the schools of las Hurdes Bajas (as in Caminomorisco), which had been set up to a large extent as a consequence of the royal visit in 1922. This Freinetian pedagogy had been driven by Ramón Acín (producer of the film) and Herminio Almendros (Néstor Almendros' father). References to education in *Las Hurdes. Tierra sin pan* have, without doubt, to be understood in this context. In a similar vein were the activities of the Misiones Pedagógicas (Pedagogical Missions) and the Museo del Pueblo Español (Museum of the Spanish People) with the famous documentaries shot and mounted by José Val del Omar in those years. Both cultural and educational institutions had been promoted by the Republican government. The anarcho-surrealist approach of Buñuel's film was openly radical, of direct action (if the goat doesn`t fall, shoot it), and not reformist, like the roots of the missionist documentary, or the North American documentaries of the Farm Security Administration during the Great Depression, or those of the English social documentalism of Grierson. Buñuel also takes a stance against Unamuno's praising of the inhabitants of Las Hurdes as heroes of the fight against hostile nature (however much the fragment we will analyse emphasizes this aspect, it has to be taken in the context of the whole film.

The peculiarity of *Las Hurdes. Tierra sin pan* is, as many examiners have pointed out, that it is not so much an assertion about a particular area (Las Hurdes) but a more general and abstract statement on human wretchedness—including, of course, the area in question. The map of the poverty stricken regions of Europe with which the film begins is highly significant.

In the final part of my paper I would like to unfold a small analysis of what I have called the emotional trigger of Las Hurdes. Tierra sin pan, in other words, of the specific building up of the viewer's non indifference. For Buñuel not only seeks the viewer's non indifference *tout court*. Rather he aims to shy away from mere sympathy, in terms of pity or commiseration. (In some way this is a forerunner to Buñuel theme that would explode in all its fury in *Nazarín* (1959), that of the perverseness of "good feelings." So Buñuel designs an emotional mousetrap in which the viewer becomes caught in a mixture of at times conflicting emotions (desolation, indignation, even beauty) which all converge to give a feeling of discomfort. There is an important role here for the "Yes, but…" which Ado Kyrou (1962) had already seen in his interpretation of the film, of the "the better, the worse" which traps the characters, but fundamentally the viewers. "The dramatic architecture of the film is founded on the utterance: 'Yes, but...' In other words, Buñuel starts by presenting a scene which is unsustainable and then throws in a ray of hope, only to dash it" (Ibarz 1999, 223-224). The filmic complexity is "the result of three elements: image, commentary and music, a singularly potent and explosive mixture" (Ibarz 1999, 168). The music and the tone of voice employed by the narrator are distancing elements which contribute decisively to avoiding mere sympathy; however much the narration may adopt different roles which are contrasted by the images—what Bonitzer has called "the radical test of the dominion of the commentary" (Quoted in Ibarz 1999, 175).

The documentary does not exhaust its assertiveness in a mere exposition of beliefs which may or may not be believed by the viewer (as the naïve notion of the documentary seems to assume), but rather builds the desire which leads to emotions on the soil of beliefs. These emotions in turn generate a complex set of interactions with the desires and the beliefs through their relation with the rest of the text and through their inter-textual references, and also through the overall assertive nature of the film.

There is a sequence in *Las Hurdes. Tierra sin pan* which shows how agriculture in *Las Hurdes* functions[6]. After the opening shot of the river there is a shot which starts from the river water and shows us a couple of locals working in an area of shrubs. "We come now to one of the essential parts of this report", says the narrator. Then the voice asks and explains: "What do the men of Las Hurdes do to construct the land which will provide them with food? They begin by choosing a spot near a river and next, with the help of their wives, relations and friends, they clear it of all its usual vegetation of heather and rockrose." (fig. 12-1)

Figure 12-1 Luis Buñuel, *Las Hurdes*, 1932.

We see the men filling sacks, in a short long shot, while the narrator continues: "Once the land has been cleared, they raise walls, one stone on top of another, with no mortar. This wall will protect the field from the winter floods. Once the wall is built, they will be off to the mountain in search of soil for plants." (fig 12-2)

Figure 12-2 Luis Buñuel, *Las Hurdes*, 1932.

In a medium shot, we see a local carrying a full sack on his shoulders, with the comment "They put it in sacks, and then carry it through the thistles to their fields." A long shot shows us a band of crops in diagonal (fig. 12-3). In comes the narrator: "All the fields of Las Hurdes have the form of narrow bands along the river. The hard winter wipes out the work of a whole year in an instant." A final aerial shot shows us the fields enclosed by the meandering of the river.

Figure 12-3 Luis Buñuel, *Las Hurdes*, 1932.

In this micro-sequence Buñuel not only describes a constructive process, at the same time he generates an emotional trigger (which fulfils its relative role in the film's overall emotional trigger). The level of belief (the map of the world which is proposed) is supported by the illustrative evidence of the images (of which the commentary offers a generalization), by the logical coherence of the process, even by the its similarity with other techniques for constructing similar terraces or farmlands to those that are surely familiar to the viewer, since they are common in many areas. It is on this initial level of belief that a desiring mechanism is built in parallel. The viewer witnesses a constructive crescendo, which is pierced by effort and difficulties, which means that he can harbor hopes of success in the hard struggle of the locals to survive. In this crescendo an important role is played by the initial question, the trigger of the process, which is positively formulated: "What do the men of Las Hurdes do to work the land that will provide them with food?" As well there are the allusions to the collaboration required of the "wives, relations and friends", the detailed description of the patient way of building the walls ("walls of stone, one on top of another with no mortar"), the promise of protection that these offer against the winter ("This wall will protect the fields from the winter floods"), the explicit illustration of the effort through the image of the local burdened with his sack, underlined by the narrator's, "which they carry through the thistles", or finally the diagonal shot of the strip of land surrounded by scrub. The crescendo phase is abruptly cut short by a phase of decrescendo that has the effect of neutralizing the hope in the viewer, because of the hard work, in the mid term, which is wiped out by the rising winter waters. Although this neutralization is not systemic (the viewer may suppose that the winter floods do not infallibly occur each year, for the good of the precarious survival of the locals), the emotional effect for the viewers is, however, effectively that of denying the positive approach of the initial question ("What do the men of Las Hurdes do to build the land that will feed them?"). Thus the emotional effect in the viewer of this frustration of the desirous crescendo, it is one of despair, the quashing of hopes, a blind alley which entraps the people of Las Hurdes.

Buñuel's cinematographic genius can be observed especially in the visual counterpoint that he has created for this neutralizing crescendo-decrescendo at the level of the commentary. The whole sequence is constructed, at the level of images, through two procedures are repeated again and again: the lap dissolve[7] and the pan[8]. If the lap dissolves serve to exert an inertia on the visual continuity which internally unites the images making up the constructive process that Buñuel describes, the pans install the pillars of this series, literally, in the river water, from the first shot of the sequence through to the final shot of the fields enclosed by the meandering of the river. The quashing of all hope at the sound level (represented by the allusion to the winter floods) is perfectly supported by the visual level, by the presence of the river water in all the nuclei of the description of the constructive process. Let us recall a detailed list, at a purely visual level, showing the presence and the role of the underlined cinematographic resources (pan and lap dissolve):

- Fade-in from black. Shot of the river and pan upwards to the lands to be cleared.
- Lap dissolve. Closing in shot of the work of clearing.
- Lap dissolve and pan from the cleared land down to the river.
- Lap dissolve. The stone wall from the river. Lateral pan across to the building of the wall.
- Cut. Short long shot of the soil collection.
- Cut. Long shot of the soil being carried from the hill.
- Cut. Medium shot of the soil being unloaded. Small descending pan.
- Cut. Shot of the river water. Ascending pan to the cultivated lands.
- Cut. Pan running along the terraces beside the river.
- Cut. Aerial shot of the meander with a small circular sweep. Fade-out into black.

This strategy is repeated in the next sequence, the search for manures. Again an event of startling emotional efficiency serves to quash the constructive process of hope: the adder bite (reinforced by the physical evidence of the local who has been bitten) interrupts the solution of the collecting of manure from the mountain. Buñuel rubs it in with the fact that, according to what is said, the seriousness of the bite is not intrinsic, but is due to the infections that will follow.

In Wollheim's terms, this emotion taints or colours the world and models in the viewer an attitude or a direction towards the world. (I insist that this micro example does no more than fulfil a role that is relative to the film's overall emotional mechanism). The emotion again interacts with beliefs and desire insofar as it drives the viewer to believe in a more general map of the reality of the world and to harbour desires for an improvement or change in it.

In short, the aim of the film is to assert a certain state of things: the wretchedness of Las Hurdes, and to force the viewer finally to have some belief about it. This belief has to motivate a human and political conscience that moves the viewer and reactively awakens a desire to change the state of things, as corresponds to the declaredly political character of the film. Yet at a micro-structural level, the analyzed sequence works with a subtle interactive balance between beliefs, thoughts, feelings and desires. The image and the sound assert micro-states of things which make up the farming practice of the locals, a process which is imprinted with a progressive inertia which leads to feelings of hope to be harboured by the viewer, hopes which end up being dashed by the blind alley, the fatally closed circle, of the wretchedness of Las Hurdes. The outcome is the assertion of a microstate of things: the blind alley of the local agricultural productive progress. But the filmic work of constructing the sequence (at both the visual and the sound level) aims, at the same time, to taint or colour the world, and to model in the viewer an attitude or a direction towards the world: an emotion. And this emotion is not merely commiseration or pity, but something closer to deep indignation (beyond a fleeting feeling), since one feels upset, even on the verge of anger.

What is most interesting about the above analysis is precisely how the construction of the mechanism of beliefs and emotions, which is in turn connected to the film's overall mechanism, rests on thoughts, feelings, associations and micro-assertions which make up a subtle and complex audiovisual mesh constructed from the weapons of cinematographic morphology, syntaxes and semantics (the metaphorical role of the water, the pans and the lap dissolves, the narration of the process, the buttress and the sonorous counterpoint of the off screen voice and the music...).

Of course, I am not denying either that the NODO[9] or the TV nature documentaries (which usually end with a warning about the danger of extinction of some species or region with which we have just sympathized) remain at the level of mere belief, of the map of what is real. If my hypothesis works, it will have to be researched how this network of beliefs and emotions is woven into other types of the documentary discourse.

I return to *Las Hurdes. Tierra sin pan*. Javier Herrera, quoting Pierre Lefevre (1937), says in a passage of his study on the critical reception of the film in Europe during the Spanish Civil War:

In short, if we adhere to the references cited, we find that Buñuel achieves all that he pursued, which was nothing else than to produce an emotional impact in the viewer and to arouse in him a radical unconscious reaction, be it favourable or contrary to his thesis; as Pierre Lefevre, perhaps the sharpest critic of the film says: «*Tierra sin pan* is perhaps —and I say perhaps because I am not very sure of myself — a disagreeable work, but

Luis Buñuel, its author, knows how to look at the world through a lens, and in such a manner that we cannot escape from the way in which he presents it to us; he recreates everything for us, he obliges us, whether we like it or not, to see according to the law he imposes. We become his slaves...» (Herrera, 198)

The significant thing here is, we can add, that he continues to trap the viewer of the XXI century, which demonstrates the endurance of that interpretative palimpsest soil which is his emotional trigger.

Lefevre's apt remark uncovers, in passing, some of the black points of the film which, effectively, enslaves the viewer who is trapped in its aesthetic-emotional device. So converting the film also into a precursor in this, and only this, aspect of the modern propagandist documentary (whose greatest exponent is, perhaps, the American Michael Moore), although also, let us not forget, that of the social revindication documentary and the poetic documentary. In passing, it likewise enslaves the people of Las Hurdes, who are instrumentalized by the filmic device and who are at no time given voices.

The new documentary (and in parallel with it, the current theory on the documentality of analytic aesthetics) have uncovered the congruence of a deep subjective dimension of the very concept of documentality (a congruence which is not new, but which was already in a variety of ways in Flaherty, Vigo or Vertov). Buñuel had unveiled it as a strange typological simplicity in a barely known text, an academic autobiography which he sent to the MOMA before his brief American venture and which Aranda quotes in his book on Buñuel:

In my view, there are two types of documentary films: one, which may be called descriptive, in which the material is limited to the transcription of a natural or social phenomenon. For example, industrial manufacturing, the construction of a road or the operations of an airline, etc. Another, much less frequent, type is that which while being both descriptive and objective at the same time, seeks to interpret reality. That is why it can attract the artistic emotions of the viewer and express, love, sadness and humour. Such a documentary is much more complete because, as well as illustrating, it moves. Although there are themes which lend themselves more easily than others to such a proposition, none is a priori excluded from this emotional possibility.

It is an approach for the "emotional possibility" which would function as a common denominator of the metamorphoses of *Las Hurdes. Tierra sin pan* that film's scholars, such as Ibarz or Herrera, have described. The reasons why we might have "forgotten" (in inverted commas) something like this (something so simple?) lie in the historical-ideological operation that has traditionally reserved the function of moving us by the fictional discourse, which paved the way to lifting up the documentary as a cold, objective discourse which is susceptible to being evaluated exclusively in terms of True or False. This uncovering is today more necessary than ever, insofar as, in parallel to the complex hybridization process of the documentary genre, the ingenuous objectivity and the presumed emotional neutrality of the current documentary discourse continue to be drawn out on the one hand, but on the other it continues to be necessary to distinguish truth from distortion and subjectivity from manipulation. *Las Hurdes. Tierra sin pan* is an extreme and very particular example. Its particularity does not make it an especially clear example, but quite the opposite, a highly complex one (as I have tried to show in this paper). Its complexity enfolds an enormous richness which is only opened up to us precisely because we are aware of the complexity.

Notes

[1] This work was possible thanks to funding from the Spanish research projects HUM 2005-02533 and FFI 2008-00750/FISO, from the Fundación Séneca 03089/PHCS/05 and 08694/PHCS/08, and through my collaboration with the *Phrónesis* research group.

[2] See, for example, Rubio (2006, 2007ª, 2007b).

[3] Nichols (1991, 2001). I am following the synthesis of Nichols' classification made by Plantinga (2005).

[4] Plantinga (2005) provides a good proposal for the classification of these theories, including the theory of the *Documentary as Assertion* (DA).

[5] I use a standard denomination and dating for the film, steering clear of the complicated variations of both that are not relevant to the purpose of the example here.

[6] What follows is not a strictly detailed list of the sequence but rather a mere description which substitutes (as far as possible) the viewing of the same. The stills are purely illustrative. I have translated myself the French sentences by the narrator into English.

[7] A transitional editing technique between two sequences, shots or scenes, in which the visible image of one shot or scene is gradually replaced, superimposed or blended. (http://www.filmsite.org/filmterms7.html). Also known as "cross fade".

[8] Abbreviation for *panorama shot*; it refers to the horizontal scan, movement, rotation or turning of the camera in one direction (to the right or left) around a fixed axis while filming. (http://www.filmsite.org/filmterms14.html) We will include occasionally in the concept vertical movements around a fixed axis as well.

[9] Obligatory actualities for the Spanish cinemas during Franco's period.

Works cited

Aranda, J. Francisco. 1975. *Luis Buñuel. Biografía crítica.* Barcelona: Lumen.

Carroll, Noël. 1997. "Fiction, Non-Fiction, and the Film of Presumptive Assertion: A Conceptual Analysis." In *Film Theory and Philosophy*, eds. Richard Allen and Murray Smith, 173-202. Oxford: Clarendon Press.

—. 1991. *The Philosophy of Horror.* London / New York: Routledge.

—. 1998. *A Philosophy of Mass Art.* Oxford, USA: Oxford University Press.

Herrera, Javier. 2006. *Estudios sobre Las Hurdes de Buñuel. Evidencia fílmica, estética y recepción.* Sevilla: Renacimiento.

Kyrou, Ado. 1962. *Luis Buñuel.* Paris: Seghers.

Ibarz, Mercè. 1999. *Buñuel documental. Tierra sin pan y su tiempo.* Zaragoza: Prensas Universitarias de Zaragoza.

Lefevre, Pierre. 1937. Signé, Louis Buñuel. *Avant-Garde*, Brussels, June 11. My translation.

Nichols, Bill. 1991. *Representing Reality: Issues and Concepts in Documentary.* Bloomington / Indianapolis: Indiana University Press.

—. 2001. *Introduction to Documentary* Bloomington, Indianapolis: Indiana University Press.

Plantinga, Carl. 2005. What a Documentary Is, After All. *The Journal of Aesthetics and Art Criticism* 63 (2): 105-118.

Rubio, Salvador. 2006. La imagen verídica: algunas reflexiones sobre el nuevo documental desde la estética analítica. *Daimon* 39: 169-179

—. 2007a. Film documentaire et subjectivité: l'émotivité de l'image assertive. *Les cahiers du CRICC* (Centre de Recherche Images Cultures et Cognitions) 1: 48-67. http://imagescognitions.univ-paris1.fr/spip.php?rubrique3.

—. 2007b. ¿Existe una emocionalidad específicamente documental? *Enrahonar* 38: 37-44.

Torreiro, M. 2006. Esa cosa llamada el documental español contemporáneo. *Minerva* 3.

http://www.circulobellasartes.com/ag_ediciones-minerva.php?ele=7

Weinrichter, Antonio. 2007. "Introducción." In *La forma que piensa. Tentativas en torno al cine-ensayo.* Pamplona: Punto de Vista.

Wollheim, Richard. 1999. *On the Emotions.* New Haven and London: Yale University Press.

PART V:

ON PERFORMANCE

CHAPTER THIRTEEN

AESTHETIC DISTANCE IN THE PERFORMING ARTS

ALESSANDRO BERTINETTO

Introduction

The aim of this paper is to discuss the challenge launched by (certain conceptions of) performing arts, and especially some recent forms, against the aesthetic conception of art. Some theorists maintain that performing arts cannot be understood in terms of aesthetic experience, aesthetic differentiation and aesthetic distance, because performing arts – and especially the new forms of performing arts – are not primarily based on "works", but on "events".

I will argue rather that we still need the concepts of aesthetic differentiation or aesthetic distance to understand art experience in general. It is certainly true that performing arts differ in many ways from non-performing arts. This difference is due especially due to the fact that they involve the audience more directly, sometimes to the extent that the performance engenders a feedback loop, which can blur the roles of artists and beholders. Nonetheless, I will maintain, this feature does not make the notion of "aesthetic distance" obsolete, useless, or mistaken. On the contrary, we still need this notion to properly appreciate and understand performing arts as art.

Performing and non performing arts

In the first place it is useful to think about the general difference between performing and non-performing arts. In a very broad and loose sense one could actually say that every encounter with an artwork is a "performance". In fact, watching films, attending art exhibitions, reading novels are all real activities that take place in real time. The reader, the spectator, the beholder must do something, must be in some ways active, in order to have the right experience of the artwork. Hence, in this broad sense, every art experience involves a performing event.

Nonetheless, we do customarily distinguish between performing and non-performing arts. In fact, in a more specific sense, the locution performing arts designates those art forms in which one group of people (the performers) using transitory materials (sounds, actions, bodily movements) "perform live before a second group, i.e., an audience" (Saltz 1997, 119). So the public reading of a book by the author or by an actor in front of an audience falls within the class of performing arts, while the private reading of a book does not.

Dance, theater and live music are typical cases of performing arts. In these cases "not only the audience's encounter with the artwork is an event, but the work encountered is itself an event" (Saltz 1997, p. 119). A person or a group of people do something on the stage and the audience watch and listen to what happens in front of them. Hence, in performing arts, the aesthetic object, i.e. the object of aesthetic attention, is human behavior: the audience pays aesthetic attention to what human beings do on stage during a certain lapse of time. The aesthetic object is the event, i.e. the live performance of actions. The audience listen to the music or watch the play or the dance that are taking place just in front of them, and this experience is in various degrees an experience of aesthetic satisfaction[1].

New forms of performing arts

The point I will discuss is the following. Today some performing art forms challenge the idea that works are played by some performers in front of an audience who is supposed to experience them aesthetically. I will focus my attention especially on E. Fischer-Lichte's book Aesthetik des Performativen, which until now is, as far as I know, one of the main philosophical attempts to grasp the particular aesthetic character of contemporary performing arts. By maintaining, like other theorists do, that new forms of performing arts (performance art, happenings, recent forms of theatre) radically defy the traditional ways to understand art, she argues that we need a different and new conceptual frame to understand them. The aesthetic conception of art grounded on disinterestedness and distance, she argues, is valid only in the case of a "work"-based art; but performing arts are not art forms based on works, they are based on events. Improvisational art forms as well as performance art and happenings involve, accordingly, a different kind of performativity; one that can not be appreciated from an aesthetic distance. These art forms follow, as it were, completely different rules.

According to Fischer-Lichte, the performativity at issue in such art forms is the direct production of actions. It does not consist of the expressive or representational accomplishment of semantic and emotional contents previously established and fixed in steady forms by an author or by a composer. The performed actions' aim is not to present to the audience meanings, contents or emotions represented or expressed by those actions. Performed actions do not mean or are referred to something else: they rather mean and are referred to themselves. They are not signifiers for signified meanings that could also be presented otherwise. They mean what they do.

Hence, Fischer-Lichte argues, in performing arts like happenings and performance, the dualistic distinctions between reality and fiction and/or illusion, between nature and culture, event and work collapse. There is no longer a presentation of a fictional story set in a previously written (or somehow produced) work through a real event, happening in real time (the actions performed on stage); on the contrary, we are facing actions that mean what they really are, without any reference to meanings or contents produced before the performative event. They are self-referential.

Moreover, this kind of performativity implies that also the spatial and physical separation between performing artists and audience as well as their social and conceptual distinction disappears, or at least tends to disappear. The audience actively participates in the actions performed. Artists and audience become both interacting performers. Hence the main feature of this kind of performativity is the interaction between artists and audience and between the members of the audience. It is no longer a situation in which one or more artists do something in front of an attending audience. Artists and audience interact and the artistic event is the result of this interaction.

Hence those performing arts are self-referential and auto-poietic:

Performances are self-referential because there is no work to be performed: the actions performed do not present us with semantic or emotional meanings in some ways existing, before the performance, in a previously composed work. The actions performed are the performance's meanings. This fact rules out the possibility that the actions performed by the performers' bodies express or represent meanings and/or emotions. The physicality and the materiality of the performers' bodies and actions exceed their meanings. So, according to Fischer-Lichte, any expressive and symbolic meaning does not matter for the success of the performance as performance.

Performances are auto-poietic events in which a particular feedback loop occurs. The behaviour and the actions performed by the artists affect the reactions carried out by the spectators. The spectators' responses influence other spectators' reactions and, in turn, affect the subsequent artists' actions. The performing event is referred to itself in the strong sense that it engenders and feeds itself, as it were, from the inside and it is not the actual token of a pre-existing type. Hence it produces itself: in this sense it is auto-poietic.[2]

Performances as auto-poietic systems

In referring to the performativity of happenings, performances and the like as auto-poietic and based on feedback loops, Fischer-Lichte employs the notion of self-organizational complex-system—originally used by Francisco Varela and Humberto Maturana to explain biological systems like the living cells.

A complex system is self-organized and auto-poietic because the system produces the components that, in turn, produce the system, and so on, to the extent that the product of the organization is the living system itself. The system generates its own components as much as its boundary. Hence, "whether a given system is capable of making its own boundary or not is often the most discriminating criterion for recognizing whether a given system is auto-poietic or not (allopoietic)." (Luisi 2003, 51; Schlee 2007, 102).

An auto-poietic complex system is hence well-characterized by two circular relationships:

1. The circularity between "producer" and "product"
2. The circularity between "being" and "doing".

Due to those circularities, an auto-poietic system is autonomous, because it generates its own rules and boundaries.

Now, Fischer-Lichte argues that performances, happenings and the like are auto-poietic in this sense. As a matter of fact, situations in which there is an audience in front of the performers make the interaction between them possible. This factual possibility distinguishes performing from non-performing arts. Feedback loops do not occur in painting or carving in the normal case. In the normal case the beholders' responses, their perceptions and judgments of a certain painting do not influence the way the painting is painted. They certainly can influence subsequent paintings by the same artist (and naturally also by other artists) as regards the interpretation thereof given by other people. Nevertheless, that painting remains the same, after the beholders' emotional and interpretative responses. On the contrary, in performing arts the audience response can influence the performance which is taking place at the same moment at which that response is produced.

Hence, the fact that during classical live music performances, theatrical plays or dance shows this interaction, in a lot of cases, does not seem to occur is due to social, cultural conventions or customs rather than to a factual impossibility. In many cases, I think, the interactive nature of a performance is a matter of aesthetic precepts. Especially, but not exclusively, in performing arts based on previous written works, the precept to execute a work faithfully has as a consequence the normative prohibition and the factual reduction of interactions between performers and audience.

So, what Fischer-Lichte's thesis seems to mean is that the new performance arts (since the avant-garde) exploit the possibilities of performing arts to an extent that was not "allowed", as it were, before. She seems to claim that these changes largely depend upon the fact that before the age of the avant-garde performing arts were still art forms based on "works" already composed or created. The art product was the work produced by a composer, by an author, and he/she was the real artist; the performer should follow, if possible with artistry, the instructions prepared by the author and he/she should represent or express what the author wanted his or her composition or play to represent or express. The feedback loop should be avoided or at least narrowed. This was the precept.

Now, things have changed. We have art forms in which not only performers directly invent what they perform, but that also intentionally explore and exploit, rather than intentionally trying to limit, the resources of the feedback loop between artists and audience, to the extent that often the audience participates in the artistic event, contributing to its realization. Extending a distinction proposed by Peter Kivy for music, before we had "arts for spectators", now we have "arts for participation" (Kivy 2001, 180-182).

In those art forms there is no rigid difference between artists and spectators. On the one side, improvisation is one of the main features of many contemporary performing arts (jazz, living theatre, happenings, etc.); on the other, often the spectators' reactions as well as their influence upon other spectators and upon the "artist(s)"cannot be controlled by the artists. So, even the spectators/artists difference tends to vanish, or at least be less rigid. There are not only several possibilities of reciprocal contact between artist(s) and audience: the spectator is often a performer in his/her own right, who not only enjoys the performance, but contributes to making it.

According to Fischer-Lichte, in new performing arts the performance is auto-poietic in this sense because it makes itself: it is not the exclusive product of the artist's actions and intentions. It does not need to follow external instructions by means of expression or representation to be what it is. Performances do not refer by means of expression or representation to emotions or symbolic meanings. Like in everyday life, meanings and emotions occur, as it were, only as performed actions. So, in happenings, performances and the like one experiences and lives situations that are not fictional or imaginative, but, like scientific experiments, real situations, in which one can experiment with reality, while living it. They are "laboratory situations", which are no longer differentiated from everyday experiences, because they are at the same time parts of life and its models (Fischer-Lichte 2004, 359). They are *ad hoc* provoked and purpose-made real life situations which give the participants the chance to live the events of life with special intensity and directness, but without any detachment. In everyday life, you are continuously involved in feedback loops, because your behavior is a response to other agents' behavior, which, in turn, is affected by your response, and so on. The same thing, seemingly, happens in today's performative practices. So, what happens in a performance is not the interruption of the everyday experience, but its continuation: there is no real separation between art (from the one side) and the social, economic, political, ethic world (from the other side).

Hence, the self-referential and auto-poietical nature of this kind of performativity are the main reasons offered by Fischer-Lichte and others in support of the idea that art forms based on events, and no longer on works, involve the audience in forms of participation which make it impossible to aesthetically experience the event in a "distanced" and "disinterested" way.

These ideas about the performativity of performing arts raise some interconnected questions.

The first one is whether work-based performances are really devoid of feedback loops, that is, whether feedback loops are exclusive features of explicit improvisational and interactive performing practices.

The second question is why the new performing arts are not expressive or representative.

The third question, finally, is whether the participatory and interactive nature of a performance (based on feedback loops) prevents its experience from being an aesthetically disinterested experience to the extent that its artistic character could only depend on its institutional nature.

In the remainder of the paper I will try to answer these questions (§§5,

6, 7). §8 tries to answer to some possible objections against the position I endorse and presents some conclusive remarks.

The performative process

The first question is whether performances based on the interactive feedback loop can not be founded on "works". This is not the case, because, in a certain sense, every performance, although interactive and producing and produced by feedback loops, is not completely improvised. In fact, even performing arts based on improvisation and actively involving the audience are in some sense founded on programs, instructions, projects or leading ideas that are the starting point of the performance. In other words, there is no completely improvised performance or, rather, the improvisation is not a kind of creatio ex nihilo[3]. Hence the interactive and improvised performance is maybe not the instance of a previous written or composed work (opus), but some previous work has to be done as the performing events' baseline or guideline.

Even in extreme cases, when the player goes on stage without any idea of what to play and to improvise, the way he/she improvises depends, in an important sense, on the work he/she did before, learning how to improvise. As in the case of improvised music, "a definition of improvisation in terms of complete spontaneity is far too restrictive" (Young and Matheson 2000, 127).[4]

On the other hand, even if the performance is supposed to be the faithful execution of a previous composed work or play, which establishes all the instructions for the execution, without permitting any allowance for performers' interpretation, certainly the mood of the evening, the audience behavior and other social and environmental factors will influence the performative process, to the extent that there will hardly be two completely identical performances of the same work. (cf. Sparti 2005, 30) Also, in traditional live performances based on previously produced works, performers perceive in some way and to some degree the audience's emotional response to what they are doing. This affects their performances and contributes to the originality of every live performance (of the same work). Although sometimes normatively banned in performances that are accomplishments of previous composed works, interactions based on feedback loops may remain almost unperceivable, but they actually occur in every performance. And vice versa, it can happen that interactions do not occur or, rather, that they occur in a very less noticeable way—even if the performance is the result of an improvisation and even if the audience is supposed to actively participate in the performance.[5] This means that the separation and the absence of interaction between artists and audience is a gradual matter: it is not due to a factual impossibility.

Emotions, meanings and contents

Furthermore the claim about the complete self-referentiality of the significance of a performative event, i.e. the idea that performativity rules out expressivity and representationality, is not convincing. According to this claim, art performances are completely free and improvisational events, which do not bring emotions and meanings to the scene by means of expression or representation. Allegedly, only real actions and reactions executed by real interacting human beings count.

This is a mere wrong presupposition. Even if there is not an already well processed work to base the performance on, the expressed emotions, the referred meanings or the represented contents are not produced and transmitted in the same ways as emotions, meanings and contents you come across in "extra artistic" situations. The fact that in a certain performance real interactions between flesh and blood persons happen in everyday places, as much as the prominence of the materiality and the physicality of the performers' bodies and actions, may contribute to the performance's artistic success and its innovative, disruptive, playful, etc. aspects. This is part of the ways that performance communicates meanings and emotions, i.e. one of the performance's aesthetic features, and it does not rule out at all its expressive or representational powers. These ways to communicate emotions, meanings and contents, by performing actions you may possibly participate in, are exactly what you appreciate in art performances. Hence, also in interactive live performances, you appreciate the ways emotions and other semantic contents are expressed and represented (inclusively the ones expressed and represented by your performative contribution to the performance). Anyway, you are not functionally and instrumentally interested in the real existence of the represented and expressed emotions and contents and you know that you are in a kind of play. Unless you notice some (representational or expressive) difference in the performer's emotional or semantic behavior in comparison with the emotional and semantic behavior of people in everyday life situations, either you are probably not attending to or participating in an art performance, but making some other experience, or it is an art performance of little artistic value.[6]

Aesthetic experience

So, the last question I would like to answer to is maybe the main one, considering the point I am committed to arguing. The problem is precisely whether improvisational and/or interactive performances based on feedback loops can or cannot, in principle, be aesthetically experienced for their own sake in a disinterested way. Many authors answer negatively. They say that in performances, happenings and the like there is no longer aesthetic differentiation. In fact, they maintain that there are no works upon which performances are based and the dichotomy signifier/signified collapses, while only the performed actions matter, and not what they could express or represent. So, the argument goes on, there are no rigid boundaries between 1. art performances, 2. non art, but aesthetic performances (like TV shows, sport events, etc), 3. rituals and, more generally, there is no clear difference between 4. art and life, but rather something like an unstable "threshold" (Fischer-Lichte 2004, 357). And, given this situation, only art institutions can confer the art status to a performance, which, otherwise, could not be regarded as an art performance. In other words, in order to distinguish between art performances and everyday events, you should turn to the "institutional theory of art". Like Duchamp's readymades, commonplace objects that receive the art status from the art world, performances are artistic if they occur within artistic contexts.

I think I have cast some doubt on the validity of the premises of this argument while answering the first two questions. Hence I can anticipate my answer to the third question. The feedback loop can occur in an art performance without causing the end of the aesthetic differentiation between art and life. If the spectator participates in the art event, even to such an extent that he/she decisively, while expressing his/her emotions and/or communicating meanings, contributes to the way the performance succeeds, therefore becoming an essential element of that performance, he/she can still regard his/her participation and the whole interaction as aesthetic. His/her aesthetic experience is certainly not only a contemplation of the event, but an active participatory contribution to its success as art event.

Nonetheless Fischer-Lichte maintains that the attempt to understand a performance after having participated in the performance is no longer an essential part of the artistic appreciation of the process (Fischer-Lichte 2004, 270). The reason she provides to argue for this view is that this attempt to understand is not part of the performance: it takes place after the performance and it cannot add anything to the feedback loops that constitute the performative process.

She defends the view that we have to experience the performance and this experience rules out subsequent understanding, because performances cannot be contemplated, but lived through. She argues that both successive linguistic descriptions of a performance experience as well as your remembering the experience you have had are constitutively insufficient to get the significance of the performance as performance. In fact, they cannot give you back what was happening hic et nunc; they cannot make you live the experience (Fischer-Lichte 2004, 270-280).

Certainly, having an experience is different from describing or remembering one. But, apart from the fact that remembering an experience and linguistically describing it can retrospectively add, through a kind of temporal feedback loop, something to the subjective quality of experience you participated in, I can't see any reason to argue that the direct interactive experience rules out any attempt to understand what is happening and what you are doing while participating in the performance.

The "spectator" can reflect on what he/she is doing or on what he/she has done during the performing event, that he/she in a certain degree contributes to create; in this way, he/she can aesthetically enjoy through the distance produced by reflection what they are doing or what they have done, noticing the aesthetic qualities of the experience they are/were making. They can enjoy as aesthetic object their response to the actions as much as the entire interaction between all the subjects involved in the performance. And they may be also aware that this performing event, the interaction between themselves and other spectators and between themselves and the artists, has/had something particular to it, something that makes it an artistic event. In this way, a spectator's awareness of his/her contribution to the aesthetic success of the performance can be a big part of the aesthetic pleasure he/she takes from this experience.

Therefore, the performance is neither less artistic nor is the experience thereof less aesthetic, if the audience interacts with the "artists". You do not cease to have an aesthetic consciousness of an art event if you directly take part in the way it happens. You can have an aesthetic consciousness of the participatory interaction that constitutes the performance. The aesthetic object is this performative participatory interaction (cf. Saltz 1997, 123).

Hence, if somebody who participates/participated in the event does not aesthetically enjoy the event, by experiencing it as a special kind of event –as an event that, in a certain sense, is different from other events of the life experience–, then he/she is probably not involved in an art event, but rather in something else.

Actually, the recourse to the "institutional theory of art", that, according to Fischer-Lichte and others, is the only way to explain the art nature of some performance, not only makes the claim about the disruptive character of arts based on performativity in the context of artistic practice and in art theory very troublesome, it also raises problems with regard to the auto-poieticity and self-referentiality of the event performed. Since, as we have seen, a performance event is (or at least should be) auto-poietic, it should set itself its own boundaries, since it is autonomous. But, if art institutions are the pre-established social, economic, cultural frames that provide the event with its conceptual quality as an art event, then the auto-poietic character of the event is limited. The performative event takes the rules it follows (or part of them) from its institutional frame, even if during the performance those rules are broken. Hence, in absence of aesthetically appreciable features, it is regarded as artistic only because of its context: the consequence would be that, if it is an artistic event, then its artistic nature comes, as it were, from the outside: it is no part of the auto-poietic event. Under this aspect, the institutional character of the event and its auto-poiecity conflict with each other.

Moreover, the fact that the performers often play with the institutional backgrounds of the performance in order to provoke the audience's behavior, to the extent that sometimes you don't know anymore if you are involved in an art event or in something else, proves that the performance is not a completely self-regulative organism: there is a plan followed by the performer. The art-institutional character of the performance is in this case part of the performance: but whether the performance is or not artistic does not depend upon its art-institutional frame. It depends upon the way its performative reflection on (and maybe denouncement of) its own institutional character occurs and is experienced. Like a lot of very important and valued artworks, its experience can be also shocking because it crumbles the buildings of art institutions. Anyway, this shock can be an important part of its artistic value, providing that it is an aesthetic shock.

Now, an aesthetic shock, like other aesthetic experiences, is an experience that involves our imagination and intellect not in a functional (or dysfunctional) way, but rather in a playful way, implying and producing a distance from the "seriousness" of life. Through this distance we can enjoy our participation in an interactive performance event and regard it as art performance.

So art events are events that are appreciated for their own sake: in some degree they possess features and aspects, which are not a function of something else, but which in an important sense can be appreciated per se.[7] The fact that an improvisational and/or interactive performance is, in a certain sense, like the interactions we are involved in everyday life, because to a certain degree every action and interaction is an improvised (inter)action, which produces and presupposes feedback loops between the interacting people, does not imply that an interactive and/or improvisational performance can not principally, under some aspect, turn out to be detached from the stream of ordinary experiences and appreciated in a distanced way and for its own sake, i.e., aesthetically.

The experiences of artworks

Unfortunately, the concept of a "disinterested", "distanced" aesthetic experience as well as its application to art is itself strongly disputed and many people are not ready to accept it, especially in the lack of further clarifications.[8] However if you understand disinterestedness not as a psychological, but as a logical condition of the aesthetic experience of artworks and art events (see Crowther 1996, 2001, 2003 and Zangwill 1992), it is easy to understand why this concept is useful to grasp the proper character of the experiences of artworks and art events. It means that, although an object or an event may have important practical values, you can also enjoy it "without taking this value into account" (Crowther 2003, 128). This means: you can enjoy it for its own sake. And art phenomena are particularly apt to this kind of experience.

Thus, an aesthetic "for its own sake" experience of a performance you participate in can certainly be a "laboratory-experience": but if you enjoy it as an art experience it is differentiated from the stream of ordinary experience, obviously without ceasing to be a factual, a real experience. The question remains as to how can it be reasonably argued that such a participatory interactive experience is distanced, given that while making the experience of the performed event you participate in its accomplishment to the extent that you are responsible of (part of) the way it happens. As is well known, according to Bullough, the idea of aesthetic "distance" counts only in the case of traditional staged performances, theatrical plays performed on stage and the like, that is, in the case of situations in which a person

> is not actually engaged directly with the object. She is out of direct involvement with the object, experiencing it as if it were 'out of reach' where she cannot affect any changes that would alter the object, and the object cannot affect any changes in her. (Fenner 2003, 51)

It is as if there were a "fourth wall" separating performers and audience.

But what if objects or events, "through the way they were constructed or the way they function, invade the psychical or even physical space of the audience member?" (Fenner 2006, 51-52) What if "the fourth wall" falls down? Would the experience be in this case less distanced? If it were so, according to what I previously argued, it would be difficult to characterize it as aesthetic. But I think that, although you are physically not distanced from the object/event you experience, in an important sense, you can have both: your interactive, transformative and productive participation in the performing event and the distanced, disinterested, differentiated experience. Actually, while the art event is taking place, the audience taking part in it can experience it like a viewer that is located inside the picture he/she is painting (cf. Sparti 2005, 49). He/she contributes to the production and the turning out of the event, and he/she reflectively experiences what he/she is making, his/her interactions with other performers (the artist(s) and the other members of the audience) as much as the entire course of the performance, per se, for its own sake.

In art events and performances based on improvisation and/or interaction the product that is aesthetically valuable is the creative, interactive and improvisational process itself, with its feedback loops, and also with its possible mistakes, incoherencies, etc. Therefore, certainly, those art performances cannot be appreciated in a formalistic way. (cf. Sawyer 2000 and Brown 2000). But this does not mean that they cannot be appreciated in an aesthetically distanced way. Interactive live performances can be aesthetically experienced and judged according to aesthetic criteria like intelligible or surprising development, internal unity, coherence, originality, ingenuity. As in the case of jazz performances, what is aesthetically experienced and judged is the action as it is being performed, i.e. the creation rather than the artifact, including the elements of risk and frailty. Perhaps the more interactive and improvisational the performances are, the higher the risks the performers necessarily take are (cf. Alperson 1984, 22-23, 26). In any case, sometimes, the successful experience of something is more valuable, if that something involved risks. This is maybe a good reason to take part in, experience and enjoy improvisational and interactive live performances.

Performances, even disturbing and shocking ones, are artistic if they can be aesthetically experienced and appreciated. If not, they are not art performances. Those experiences can surely be so powerful and intense to the extent that, due to their perceptual qualities, their forms, their meanings, they transform you, your thinking, your sensibility, exactly in the same way as the experiences you make with other artworks (including works of non performing arts). They can perhaps be tagged as Dionysian rather than Apollonian experiences or as experiences of the sublime (or even of the ugliness, of the unpleasant) rather than as experiences of the beautiful. Nonetheless you take a performance as art performance if you experience it aesthetically, appreciating and valuing it for its own sake, that is, making an experience that, as it were, stands out "as a distinctly singular experience in contrast to the stream of ordinary experience" (Schusterman 2006, 222).

Hence, although the notions of aesthetic experience and aesthetic attitude do not enjoy today very good health on the philosophical stage, I think that –explicitly or implicitly, intentionally or unintentionally– erasing the aesthetic distance practically thwarts the pleasures offered by art as much as giving up the notions of aesthetic difference and aesthetic attitude theoretically hinders the possibility of understanding any artistic phenomenon.[9]

Notes

---

[1] Some theoretical problems arise when the events are not happening live, but they broadcast to the audience through media like radio, TV, the Internet. In these cases you have a live performance, but there is still a real physical distance between performers and audience. Since the theoretical question I am concerned with here is the experience of live performances which are not broadcast through technological media, I will not discuss this point.

[2] Cf. Fischer-Lichte (2004) and Mersch (2002).

[3] For example, even in the case of jazz–a music genre that thrives on improvisation–the improvisation is hardly absolute as "improvisers do not create ex nihilo". Also extreme forms of improvisatory music, like free jazz, exploit, despite their creativeness, "a stock of material" (Brown 2000, 115-116). See also Alperson (1984), Sawyer (2000), Sparti (2005).

[4] I agree with Young and Matheson:

"[...] an improvised performance is one in which the structural properties of a performances are not completely determined by decisions made prior to the time of a performance... The structural properties of a performance include its melody, harmony, and length (in bars, not in temporal duration). A structural property is to be understood in contrast to an expressive or interpretive property. The expressive properties of a performance include tempo, the use of rubato, dynamics, and so on. We believe that the line between expressive and structural properties is a fuzzy one, but it must be drawn if we are to avoid the conclusion that virtually every musical performance involves improvisation." (Young and Matheson 2000, p. 127)

[5] In fact sometimes the required audience participation fails to take place:

"Participatory theater and happenings represented an attempt to invite audiences into the process, but rarely was that actually possible... the gap

---

between the performers-whose relationships and performances had developed over a long time-and the "outsiders" was often too great to overcome" (Saltz 1997, 124).

[6] People arguing against the expressive and representational features of performances sometimes support their point by giving as examples real performances during which performers executed really dangerous actions (for themselves or for the audience) that ended up by inducing the spectators to stop the performance or by stopping the performance, because the performer themselves, whose lives were in danger, could not go ahead. This happened for instance in some M. Abramovic's performances. In my opinion, this possible situation does not prove at all that, in those art performances, only the actions performed and their materiality matter but not the expression and/or representation of meanings or emotions through those actions. It only proves that at a certain moment an event, that maybe before was artistic in nature, cannot be experienced anymore as such. The artistic expression and representation ends and gives way to simply real occurring events, which are what they do. This is not another kind of art. It simply is the factual end of (that) art (event). The "game", as it were, is simply over.

[7] Surely, they can be aesthetically experienced and valued, i.e. appreciated as and like art events, even if they are not, in origin, (performed as) art events: "For example, while the desire for victory may impel a tribe to perform a war dance, it is surely possible for the participants to be caught up in and to enjoy the rhythms and drama of the dance for its own sake, rather than in terms of its anticipated practical consequences. In such a case the logical ground of the dancers' rapture is disinterested, even if their feelings are Dionysian. Indeed [...] it is the very power of such *aesthetic* rapture that can explain why dancing and other forms of artifactual imaging are taken as having effect on practical outcomes" (Crowther 2003, 128). See also Stecker (2006, 8). Not only disruptive and revolutionary art events, but also rituals and other performing practices, which are not principally artistic, can be aesthetically experienced like and as art events, if they have features and aspects you can enjoy and understand in the same way you enjoy and understand artworks. On the contrary, as we have seen before, if the actor or the "main" performer of a supposed art event performs actions that provoke the collapsing of the aesthetic difference, the event ceases to be an *art* event.

[8] See for example Beardsley (1982), Carroll (2000, 2002), Shusterman (2000), Stecker (2006), Bertinetto (2007), Scruton (2007).

[9] I am deeply indebted to Paolo Calvino, Maria José Alcaraz León, James Hamilton and Graham McFee who commented and criticised the paper, giving me important suggestions.

Works Cited

Alperson, Philip. 1984. On Musical Improvisation. *The Journal of Aesthetics and Art Criticism* 43: 17-29.
Beardsley, Monroe. 1982. *The Aesthetic Point of View*. Ithaca, N.Y.:

Cornell University Press.

Bertinetto, Alessandro. 2007. "Art as derealization." In *Imaginacija, čutnost in umetnost / Zbornik referatov III. sredozemskega kongresa za estetiko,* Proceedings of the III. Mediterranean Aesthetik Kongress, 22-27.

Brown, Lee. 2000. "Feeling my way": Jazz Improvisation and its Vicissitudes – A Plea for Imperfection. *The Journal of Aesthetics and Art Criticism* 58 (2): 113-123.

Bullough, Edward. 1912. Psychical 'Distance' as a Factor in Art and as an Aesthetic Principle. *British Journal of Psychology* 5: 87-118.

Carroll, Noël. 2000. Art and the Domain of the Aesthetics. *The British Journal of Aesthetics* 40: 193-208.

—. 2002. Aesthetic Experience revisited. *The British Journal of Aesthetics* 42: 145-168.

Crowther, Paul. 1996. *Critical Aesthetics and Postmodernism.* Oxford: Oxford University Press.

—. 2001. *Art and Embodiment: From Aesthetics to Self-Consciousness.* Oxford: Oxford University Press.

—. 2003. Cultural Exclusion, Normativism and the Definition of Art. *The Journal of Aesthetics and Art Criticism* 61: 113-123.

Fenner, David. 2003. Aesthetic Experience and Aesthetic Analysis. *Journal of Aesthetic Education* 37 (1): 40-53.

Fischer-Lichte, Erika. 2004. *Aesthetik des Performativen,* Frankfurt a.M.: Suhrkamp.

Luisi, Pierre L. 2003. Autopoiesis: a review and a reappraisal. *Naturwissenschaften* 90: 49–59.

Kivy, Peter. 2001. *New Essays on Musical Understanding.* Oxford: Clarendon Press.

Mersch, D. 2002. *Ereignis und Aura. Untersuchungen zu einer Ästhetik des Performativen.* Frankfurt a.M.: Suhrkamp.

Saltz, David Z. 1997. The Art of Interaction: Interactivity, Performativity, and Computers. *The Journal of Aesthetics and Art Criticism* 55 (2): 117-127.

Schlee, C. S. 2007. Poetry as Compass: Chaos, Complexity, and the Creative Voice. *Forum* 1: 101-112.

Scruton, Roger. 2007. In Search of the Aesthetic. *British Journal of Aesthetics* 47: 232-250.

Shusterman, Richard. 2000. *Performing Art.* Ithaca/London: Cornell University Press.

—. 2006. Aesthetic Experience: From Analysis to Eros. *The Journal of*

Aesthetics and Art Criticism 64: 218-219.

Stecker, Robert. 2006. Aesthetic Experience and Aesthetic Value. *Philosophy Compass* 1: 1–10.

Sawyer, R. Keith. 2000. Improvisation and the Creative Process: Dewey, Collingwood, and the Aesthetics of Spontaneity. *The Journal of Aesthetics and Art Criticism* 58: 149-161.

Young, James O., and Carl Matheson. 2000. The Metaphysics of Jazz. *The Journal of Aesthetics and Art Criticism* 58: 125-133.

Zangwill, Nick. 1992. Unkantian Notions of Disinterest. *The British Journal of Aesthetics* 32: 149-152.

CHAPTER FOURTEEN

WITNESSING THE PAIN OF OTHERS: HOW PERFORMANCE ART IS PERCEIVED

DORIS KOLESCH

My contribution focuses on a special feature of the expression and experience of subjectivity in contemporary art since the 1960s: Witnessing and experiencing pain. Pain appears to be an anthropological constant, in the sense that there is no known culture or era totally devoid of experiences or concepts of pain, even though what is conceptualized and experienced as pain appears to be extremely varied in each case. As both a physical and mental phenomenon confronting individuals and societies, pain certainly shows signs of being an anthropological constant; one aspect, however, that is absolutely not constant and in fact extremely variable and dependent on a host of historical, cultural, social, technical and media factors, is how pain is perceived; how it is presented, understood and conceptualized, and finally how individuals or whole societies deal with the existence and experience of pain.

This preface to the topic is important to me, because my subsequent reflections are based on the premise that the depiction and perception of pain are also dependent on media factors; by which I mean how or by which media and techniques pain is addressed as a subject and conveyed within a society. With this focus on the media dimension of both the experience and expression of pain in performance art since the 1960s, I hope to contribute to a better understanding of the specific aesthetic experience that such artistic events have offered and are still offering today.

Why has pain made such a career in performance art? This question is certainly one worth addressing. In 1962, Yoko Ono continually hit her head on the stage floor rhythmically to the music of *Wall Piece for Orchestra*, and a few years later, in 1969, Ben Vautier banged his head hard against a concrete wall until it started to bleed. Valie Export in 1971 crept naked over glass fragments strewn across the floor during her performance of *Eros/ion*; 1973 Chris Burden arranged a similar situation in *Through the Night Softly*, when in the dark of the night he crawled undressed across a street in Los Angeles covered in broken glass. Peter Weibel sewed photographs onto his own body in his 1970 *Photo Haut Gedichte* performance, while Vito Acconci bit himself on the arm in his *Trademark* performed the same year. Several such performance artists, including Gina Pane, Günter Brus and Marina Abramovic, scratch or cut their skin open with knives, razor blades or jagged glass, flog themselves with whips or subject themselves to open fire or flames. Other performance artists starve themselves and fast for several days, often with limited freedom of movement. They have themselves pierced with needles or nails or even, as Chris Burden did in *Trans-Fixed* in 1974, nailed in the manner of a crucifixion to the roof of a VW beetle, with the engine roaring at full throttle into the night as part of the performance. And last but not least, performance artists like Marina Abramovic, Peter Weibel, Denis Oppenheim, Timm Ulrichs and once again Chris Burden, subject themselves in some of their works to the potentially fatal risk of electrocution, a loaded pistol or even a shotgun.

This brief list could be extended almost infinitely; it is neither systematic nor comprehensive. I simply want to demonstrate that crossing boundaries and breaking taboos in the form of physical injuries and self-inflicted wounds, along with castigation, self-mutilation and auto-aggressive acts—particularly from the 1960s to the present day—are by no means isolated incidents, nor do they represent the exceptional acts of individual performance artists, frequently denounced by a wide range of critics and the general public as pathological manifestations of psychological problems, masochistic tendencies or sexual dysfunction. Quite the reverse, in fact, is true: the acts and behaviors cited, which in the early days of the 1960s and 1970s were usually classed as body art, represent to this day a significant and definitive stream of performance art, which is by no means a marginal, fringe element.

Such performances have shocked and fascinated audiences in equal measure, and some of them continue to do so today. In performance art, theatre and fine arts studies dealing with such artistic events it has become common to tone down or neutralize the shock and puzzling incommensurability of such performances, by seeking to apply a particular explanatory or interpretive model to them. For instance, Gina Pane with her obsessive self-injuries, is taken almost without exception to be a feminist artist who—depending on the particular interpretation adopted—is either voicing criticism of patriarchal power structures and gender-specific role fixations, or perpetuating the myth of the link between femininity and masochism—two at least conflicting interpretations, which are also completely at odds with Pane's own explanations and ignore countless aspects of her performances that go beyond any individual interpretations placed on them. Interpretations which claim that Chris Burden turned himself into a shaman or exemplary sufferer in *Trans-Fixed* or *Shoot*, in order to convey extraordinary experiences to the public, seem rather implausible and leave us at a loss to know why any artist in the presence of an audience would willingly allow himself or herself to be shot in the arm—not to mention the discrepancy between the violent act and the banality of its depiction in a photo and on 16 mm film.

In view of these things I would like to take a different focus, although I do not claim to be able to give any kind of definitive or adequate explanation for the above-mentioned phenomena. In view of all the taboos broken, boundaries crossed and painful practices that numerous performance artists have adopted and still do today, I am sceptical of any all-too coherent and definitive explanation. And in my opinion one of the aims of analyzing such artistic events should be conceding their element of defiance and incommensurability in any commentary, description or reflection.

My contribution highlights a factor that is seldom given enough attention. The above list of performances that, in a host of different ways, have depicted, featured, and perhaps even induced or demonstrated pain, is not only incomplete and unsystematic. It leaves out perhaps the most crucial element of all, by completely ignoring the audience and their reactions in each case.

My starting point for the following reflections is that the historic significance of performance art not only lies in the way it has expanded the themes and tools of presentation, nor in its mixing and hybridizing of hitherto separate art domains and disciplines. An essential factor seems to me to be the attempt to establish a completely new relationship between artist and audience, between the theatrical event and the way it is perceived. We now find ourselves in an art, theatre and performance art scene, which—from a theatre studies point of view—at the very least can be described as post-postdramatic. Essential impulses and innovations of performance art of the 1960s to 1980s have since found their way into the theatre and everyday culture. Even in some of the very conservative city theatres, the audience's reaction now tends to be one of bored dismissal when an actor urinates on the stage floor—and not because such a scene is considered disgusting, inappropriate or even unpleasant, but apparently because it has been seen so many times before that the element of provocation and scandal is gone—to say nothing of the immensely popular reality TV shows like *Big Brother* which after all are nothing more than television and consumer exploitation and trivialization of artistic practices developed in the 1960s at the very forefront of the neo-avant-garde movement. In view of these historic developments, it is worthwhile pausing for a moment to remind ourselves what the driving force and motives were that led to the emergence of performance art in the second half of the last century.

Performance art is a hybrid form which arose as a result of individuals crossing the boundaries between established genres, when artists with backgrounds in a number of different disciplines—from music and dance to sculpture, painting and photography—were searching for new ways to present and articulate their ideas and, regardless of all their differences, were focused on the performative execution of these ideas. Certainly it is no coincidence that performance art was primarily initiated and pursued by artists with no particularly close connection to theatre or, for instance, by artists who had undergone no training as actors or directors. Nevertheless it is indisputable that performance art established its own identity as something clearly distinct from traditional bourgeois theatre. Performance art shies away from both the practice and the clichéd image of conventional theatre, with its proscenium-arch stage and the associated physical separation between what happens on the stage and the audience in the auditorium, as well as its process of creating an illusion and its models of presentation and perception. From here on in, I will confine myself to commenting on the presentation and perception models.

With regard to the aesthesis of presentation, it is precisely the "as if" form of theatrical representation that performance art rejects. The actor is not Hamlet or Iago or Antigone, but acts out the character, slips into the role and acts as if he were Hamlet, Iago or Antigone. For this reason, the unspoken pact between actor and audience in theatre is absolutely clear: the injured, murdered or deceased figure undergoes a miraculous resurrection no later than the time of the final curtain call, and reappears in his or her embodiment by the actor completely unharmed on stage, albeit with the significant ambiguity of being both the character played and the real-life actor at the same time. Representation and presentation of the character, along with the actual identity of the actor, exist concurrently for that short moment, while over the course of the preceding theatrical performance, the tendency is for the representation of the character to eclipse the identity of the actor, or attempt to conceal it completely.

A performance artist, on the other hand, is not presenting a fictional character or role but initially is presenting only himself or herself—which should not be taken to mean that the *persona* of the performer is identical with that of the private life of the performer. The time in which he or she performs the act does not represent another fictional period of time, and the physical space does not primarily stand for a different space. Instead, the performance occurs in the here and now in this time and place, which first and foremost refers only to itself.

Linked to this rejection of the dominant mode of "as if" presentation is the rejection of the established perception code of the theatre. After all, the "as if" is aesthetically coupled with an attitude of aesthetic distance on the receptive side. The pleasure, achievement, fascination and also the limitations of theatre lie in the fact that the people watching are in fact observers, and to a lesser extent also listeners. With an attitude of aesthetic distance, the audience can follow what is presented and feel free of the pragmatic limitations and pressures of everyday communication and interaction: in theatre I can shamelessly gawp at a woman's breast—at least while she is on stage; I can stare adoringly at people and hang on their every word—a behavior we frown on in the real world, and one that even young children learn to give up at an early age. In theatre I can lean back in my seat, and, without any obligation to intervene, take a stand or do anything at all, I can sit and watch while one character on stage murders another.

The title of my address, "Witnessing the pain of others," is an explicit reference to the last book published by the great essayist, Susan Sontag, whose *Regarding the Pain of Others* (2004) is an in-depth reflection on war photography. Susan Sontag, with her lucid thoughts on this subject, and also on the way society deals with illness and Aids, is undoubtedly an important source of inspiration for the issue under discussion here. And her two essays on Antonin Artaud are among the best, in my opinion, of all the research on offer about Artaud. Nevertheless, I am about to disagree with Sontag, too, in the sense that it makes a big difference whether I see images of suffering, torment and pain, or whether I see performances that not only depict suffering, torment and pain but also demonstrate and present it. To give some clue at least to the general tenor of my argument, I offer the following: my theory is that performance art changes the relation between what happens and what is witnessed, to the point where the audience becomes a participant and an integral part of the performance and no longer a spectator at a safe distance. Performance art—and not because of its inherent subject matter, but because of its formal structure or power as a medium—is not just about witnessing the pain of others. Rather, a different and more wide-reaching form of perception is provoked that extends to comprehension; to sensing the pain, and even to the point of being physically affected and affronted by it, even though no form of physical contact with the audience takes place.

However, it is important to stress that this reconfiguration of the relation between performance art and the audience does not equate to the simple removal of aesthetic distance. The *noli me tangere* (touch me not), which contemporary art has developed and cemented as a transforming continuation of ritual and religious practices over the centuries, is not something that can be eliminated by a few performance artists. Visitors to museums, exhibition spaces and galleries come across these friendly admonitions all over the world: "Please don't touch"; "*Bitte nicht berühren*"; "*Prier de ne pas toucher*"; "*Si prega di non toccare*"; "*Se ruega no tocar*". The message is that any contact with art should be restricted to eye contact only. Sensory perception and touchy-feely experiences of aesthetic phenomena, or aesthesis in the etymological sense of the word, have largely been banned from the established range of receptive options. Anyone who does dare to reach and touch an exhibit will trigger an alarm system, field a reprimand from surveillance staff, the disapproving and disbelieving glances of other visitors or, in the worst case scenario, find themselves denounced as little better than willfully destructive art vandals or art thieves.

The situation is similar in the theatre. I sit there quietly on my seat in the darkened room, my eyes and ears completely trained on the raised, illuminated stage. The social community of my fellow audience quickly reveals itself to be a social disciplinary body, if I should dare to whisper too loudly, move about too much or engage in other activities that fall outside the strict framework of my role as a member of the audience. The "no touching" rule applies here too. The actors are exposed to my glance and I am allowed to indulge my curiosity, my rubbernecking tendencies and my longing to watch their every move without fear of censure. However, should I storm onto the stage to touch a fascinating figure, feel the fabric of a costume or seek direct contact with a character, I would be breaking a taboo and creating a scandal. I would have to have taken leave of my senses, (yet still be using them and be enthralled by them), to even dare to do such a thing—and incidentally quite physically fit, in order to be able to leap over the actual, architectural threshold of this symbolic border, or invisible fourth wall.

Just how much the "no touch" rule has become culturally entrenched and internalized in aesthetic contexts is evident from the performance art and theatrical acts of the past few decades, which have employed a host of different strategies and techniques to break down the barriers between actors and audience, and encourage the audience to go beyond observing to the point of taking part and taking sides. From the safe distance of someone who is told about such situations, who reads about them in newspaper reports or books, or thinks about them at their desk, it is hard to imagine what a complex mix of conflicting impulses, decisions, habits, expectations, doubts and self-doubts is experienced by anyone finding themselves in such a situation of being caught in the middle. The supposedly aesthetic question, of whether I should intervene, join the performers, detach myself from the group of curious and expectant onlookers—whether I should change sides, so to speak, for a moment—becomes a burning, existential and ethical question, which is not only capable of shattering my understanding of art, but also my attitude to the world, and my own sense of self.

It should not be underestimated how central the references to historic images and presentation models, and to the iconographic traditions that are familiar to us from painting, film and television, are to many works of performance art. One could say that presentations of pain re-enact what has been seen thousands of times before and translate it into physical evidence, making it a graphic, obtrusive reality, which is by no means devoid of medium nor unmediated, but on the contrary—at least in performance art involving pain—puts the spotlight on the body as the medium. And which, from an audience's point of view, is embarrassing and sometimes even painful, for the simple reason that the onlookers have none of the established and comforting perception models to fall back on that they have collectively practiced when viewing paintings, photography, films and television images. Susan Sontag claims in *Regarding the Pain of Others*:

> Images have been reproached for being a way of watching suffering at a distance, as if there were some other way of watching. But watching up close—without the mediation of an image—is still just watching. (2004, 117)

The argument Sontag uses to underpin this claim is that observation always requires a certain distance to be taken; that it implies a space between the observer and the thing observed. While I agree with her in principle, I want to argue in what follows that perception of performance art is not adequately described if it is understood as watching, and nothing but watching. This is why I have deliberately chosen not to publish any of the many available photographs of performance art by Marina Abramovic, Vito Acconci, Chris Burden, Günter Brus, Valie Export, Yoko Ono, Gina Pane, Ben Vautier, Peter Weibel and others, since they would convey very little of the actual medium itself, and in some cases say nothing about the aspects of our perception of performance art that are central to this discussion.

What, actually, does happen in performance art? Such performances, by revoking the notion of a representational aesthetic, undermine the perceptual convention of aesthetic distance that is fundamental to conventional aesthetics. Members of the audience become participants who are responsible for what they have seen, heard and experienced—and I mean this in two ways: firstly, by taking part in what happens and secondly by the associated responsibility for the events that occur, and for what they have heard and seen in each case, since no central perspective, no dominant version, and no authoritative interpretation is offered. The onlookers become witnesses and this act of witnessing gives rise to a responsibility in terms of their response: responsiveness and responsibility are inseparable here. You could say that a response or an answer is demanded that has nothing to do with opinions, ideas, views or moral codes, but rather with a relationship of inter-subjectivity that has developed; with the relationship between people, which takes priority over any discussion of content or issues and, even more so, over any attempt to form a consensus.

Although the figure of the witness has its origins in Greek theatre, where what happened on stage was always enacted for the audience as both target group and witness, it has taken performance art to really emphasize this dimension of the act of bearing witness which is inherent to the theatre. Without wanting to suggest that self-declarations by artists be ascribed any preferential validity as an explanation for their works, I would like to mention Chris Burden in this regard, who described his Shoot performance as failed, where a friend shoots him with a rifle in the upper arm while he is standing in the corner of a gallery with an audience present, and not because the bullet was supposed to graze him and ended up passing through his arm, but because the audience did not intervene. The fact that many a performance artist has been stopped in the act by the audience's concrete intervention, and many performance art participants have taken performers to court for inflicting bodily harm, is also evidence of the fundamentally changed relationship between performer and audience during such violent artistic acts.

Elaine Scarry writes in her book *The Body in Pain* that pain, as an experience of the limitations of language, must be taken seriously. Pain destroys language, since it can not be pinpointed or adequately expressed in words; it undermines the possibility of communication: "Whatever pain achieves, it achieves in part through its unsharability, and it ensures this unsharability through its resistance to language" (Scarry 1985, 4). Now, what we are experiencing in performance art are not, or at least not only, images of pain, nor merely expressions of pain, but the pain that bodies experience in the act of presenting it (cf. Lehmann 1999, 392).

From its very beginnings, theatre was familiar with the notion, and practically established itself as the very mimesis, of pain: torment, suffering, pain and horror were imitated and suggested in a deceptively real way, so that—and the long and effective tradition of catharsis utterly confirms this—painful empathy could and still can be brought to bear on the simulated pain.

Performance art and postdramatic theatre is particularly familiar with

> mimesis *to* pain: when the stage is made to reflect life itself, when real falls and beatings actually occur there, fear about the safety of the *players* arises. The fact that a transition takes place from *presented pain* to *pain experienced during a presentation*—is the new element that, in its moral and aesthetic ambiguity, has become the indicator for the issue of presentation. (Lehmann 1999, 392-3)

These performances of "*pain-bearing bodies*" cause a split to occur in perception, "on the one hand the presented pain; on the other the playful, pleasurable act of its presentation, which itself reveals evidence of the pain" (Lehmann 1999, 392-3). One could say that performance acts demonstrate the rejection of verbal communication. Here it is not in the—frequently real—linguistic-semiotic, symbolic or meaningful levels of representation where pain reveals itself, but rather in the real, actual execution of cutting or injuring oneself, falling over, beating oneself up, bleeding etc.

To have this intense effect, incidentally, it is relatively unimportant whether the performers actually experience pain during the moment of their performance, or whether they are able to minimize or even avoid it by the use of certain techniques—whether that be specific dance and exercise moves, techniques of concentration, or in some cases a shamanistic or mystical sense of self, or whether it be the specific way in which the self-harm is inflicted.

On the other hand, the pain may well be perceived on the receptive side as a thoroughly painful experience; Antonin Artaud's scream and the auditory-vocal experiments of performance art and contemporary theatre that follow in his tradition demonstrate this in a striking way, similar to Luk Perceval's brilliant rendition of Lear, *L. King of Pain* (2002). By means of extreme technical effects applied to voices and sounds, this production breaks the audiovisual contract usually entered into by any watching, listening audience; i.e. that it will always be possible to work out which body is responsible for producing which sounds, and that a particular voice always stands for a distinct personal identity. Instead, the electronically alienated and distorted voices in *L. King of Pain*—voices technically detached from bodies—never prove to be voices of their own, but always the voices of another person, as voices of the special effects team or of the collective imagination, morality, tradition etc. Mediated produced echo and doubling effects, cacophonies and shrill dissonant tones, along with the continual crackling, rustling and piercing whistle of the soundtrack, underline this revocation of the audiovisual pact.

During the performance, the volume increases significantly and the gradually intensifying soundtrack of technical voices, musical notes and electronic effects takes over the role of building dramatic tension from the increasingly redundant literary model. Voices are pushed to their limits and sometimes beyond; for instance in bloodcurdling scream-arias, fits of rage lasting several minutes, concerted-choral battle cries and the already mentioned crackling of electronically induced static and irritating whistling, or unidentified sounds that seem to oscillate between mechanical voices and twittering birds. Microphones periodically handed around the actors amplify and multiply these scarcely intelligible speaking, screaming and bellowing attacks. In the process, the sensory organs of the audience—as well as the vocal chords of the actors—are tested to their physiological limits. The pain of these vocally radical utterances causes pain in the overtaxed ears of the audience, who is pushed to the point of exhaustion by the extreme volumes and the suspension of normal electronic limits on vocal pitch and frequency.

I cannot go into this in any more detail here, but I would ask you to consider whether the sonic and vocal quality of performance art is perhaps an essential medium for conveying and also transferring pain, for the very reason that the hearing and visual senses are each arranged differently. While the eye affords an overview and a distance, the ear assimilates voices, sounds, tones and noises as they penetrate the entire body, and it is frequently impossible to tell where they are coming from, (are these sounds in me, surrounding me, or both?), or to simply evade them.

Yet I would be painting a completely one-sided and indeed false picture, if I were to give the impression in relation to these borderline auditory experiences, that the painful perception of performance art was based solely on physical assaults or intrusions on the audience. No, what is more frequent and significant for performance art, it seems to me, is the rather paradoxical situation, which I would like to briefly illustrate in closing by citing the example of the Brazilian dance company Grupo Cena 11. The aesthetic of Cena 11 is based on falling, or to be more accurate, the dancers allowing themselves to fall onto the hard stage floor. In the process the protagonists frequently take a short run up, before leaping into the air, catapulting themselves for a moment into a fleetingly suspended horizontal position, only to bang their flat, unprotected and unsupported bodies down hard on the floor, always accompanied by the loud noise of the impact of their fall. The reaction of the audience is very telling. Although they are sitting in relative comfort on theatre seats in the auditorium, the room is filled with a continual sense of disquiet, and they can clearly be heard sliding back and forward uneasily in their seats, uttering barely hushed groans or hissing through their teeth, with the occasional "ouch!" clearly audible, along with a general flinching and physical starting when the dancers' bodies hit the stage floor with a loud bang.[1] The totally (physically at least) unharmed members of the audience lose their poise completely at the sight of these plummeting bodies. Their hurt and concern is expressed in strong reactions such as bodily unease, uncontrolled muttering or sharp intakes of breath, along with much flinching and looking away. What happens here, obviously, is a— completely intangible, yet certainly very real—assault on the body of the audience, which is virtually incapable of warding off what is happening.

The mere act of observing something turns into an unexpected physical empathy—not pity—a physically shared and understood sensation, which activates each physical perception and memory of pain in the people witnessing it, as much as it demonstrates their primarily irritating, unpleasant and, in some cases, even painfully felt helplessness about how they should react to what they are seeing and how they could respond in a *responsible* way.

Notes

[1] cf. also Katharina Rost (2007). "Das Leiden anderer spüren. Zur Übertragung von Schmerz" [Sensing the Pain of Others. Communicating Pain] (MA diss., FU Berlin).

Works cited

Lehmann, Hans-Thies. 1999. *Postdramatisches Theater*. Frankfurt am Main: Verlag der Autoren.
Mersch, Dieter. 2002. *Ereignis und Aura. Untersuchungen zu einer Ästhetik des Performativen*. Frankfurt am Main: Suhrkamp.
Scarry, Elaine. 1985. *The Body in Pain. The Making and Unmaking of the World*. New York: Oxford University Press.

Sontag, Susan. 2004. *Regarding the Pain of Others.* New York: Picador.

CHAPTER FIFTEEN

THE SILENT UTOPIA:
AN APPROACH TO LIGHT AND COLOUR
IN THE WORK OF ROBERT WILSON

ANTONIO GARCÍA AND FRANCISCO GUILLÉN

Introduction

This approach to the universe of Robert Wilson seeks to uncover the most significant aspects which contribute to make all his artistic productions, be they installation, theatre, dance opera, video, etc, share a special interest in the treatment of illumination and its chromatism. The way in which the chromatic irradiation invades the whole field of vision of the spectator pursues an autonomous narrative direction. This paper seeks to analyse Robert Wilson's capacity when separating what is purely visual from what is heard to create a type mental image where there is no traditional hierarchy of the word over the image. Finally, we conclude that the peculiarity of Wilson's production, independently of the medium employed, is defined by the pictorial concepts of Cézanne, and premeditatedly connects with the intention to incorporate this pictorial space into other manifestations such as theatre, opera, cinema, installations, etc. He thus manages to inject into his works the necessary conditions for the narration and the script – understood as read theatre – to lead to the most open interpretation of meanings which the spectator finishes building from his own most intimate sensations. In short: the treatment of light and colour in the work of Wilson serves to heighten the spectator's subjectivity by developing a perception involving reflection, which rounds off the meaning of the works.

Any talk of the light and colour dramaturgy in the work of Robert Wilson means taking into account a series of fundamental questions from his life which led him to conceive lighting as an autonomous element in the field of performance. Possibly the first factor that led him towards this search for meaning in the chromatic field was the well known correction of his speech defect, which was brought about thanks to classes given him by the septuagenarian dancer and teacher of dance Mrs. Byrd Hoffman: "After three months of working with her I learnt to relax and to take the time I needed and, finally, to pronounce and to speak" (Brecht 2005)

It is curious that by a phonetic slowing down he overcomes this barrier; but no less curious is the tool which he makes from it to give expression to the different elements which make up the theatre action.

Another nucleus for staging his work comes from the teachers who took part in his academic training. Two figures stand out—the first was his teacher of History of Architecture, Sybil Moholi-Nagy, the widow of the well known artist of the Bauhaus. Wilson recalls her peculiar way of teaching which consisted basically of a series of slide projections in which she used up to three projectors at the same time so as to create a type of three dimensional effect, and while the slides were pushed through at a fair rate she accompanied them with a measured commentary that was not connected to the visual input. Something, in short, that it was impossible to find in any bibliographical source. It is noteworthy how this technique of dislocation between what is seen and heard was key in how he stated his creative process, which was metaphorized in an apple in a glass case, which served as a nucleus: "like a cathedral in medieval times, a centre of studies, a concentration of people of all conditions, a place where the artist had his place" (Morey and Carmen 2003).

Wilson also recalls his period of training with the architect Paolo Soleri, in turn a disciple of Frank Lloyd Wright, as a paradigmatic meeting, in the visionary and dreaming way in which the builder projected his designs. It was to Umberto Eco that he described most abundantly the details of his admiration for Soleri:

> I was fascinated by the scale of his thought. He was a dreamer. He built cities underwater, on water or in the sky …Soleri would draw architectural designs on the sand with a stick. He didn't know what would come out of these, a casino, a show hall, whatever! He just started to draw. And that was how he conceived buildings. It was amazing to see an architect working like that. It really left its mark on me. (Eco 1991)

And no less amazing is the effect produced on us when remembering the concomitances between Soleri's way of working and the pictures on the sand by Joseph Beyus, which are so alike in their action and concept, or when we think of the way of cutting out colour that the late Matisse would give us.

Other elements that make up his concept of light are those which are set in the performing arts which spring from the dance spectacles. In fact,

Wilson captured very well the dramaturgy of the void with which such types of works were equipped, especially the choreographies of Georges Balanchine, Merce Cunningham and Martha Graham. The absence of atrezzo responded to a narrative economy which allowed the dancer an amount of space which the actor could never enjoy, and this was translated into turn into a mental surplus for the spectator to make up the meaning of the work, something which a spectator of opera and theatre mental did not have available.

> I especially liked the abstract ballets of Ballanchine. One immediately realized that the dancers were moving within a virtual space … In the case of Merce Cunningham and John Cage there were two events: one visual and the other musical…Music and dance, conceived separately came together as in a collage. (Guatterini 1991)

Graham was able to choreograph his spectacles as if they were an amniotic cloth, in which dancers, dress, gesture and light formed part of a whole; a gestaltic concept which she expressed through the metaphor of choreography as if planning the graph of her heart.

The final nucleus of elements which make up his stage vision is of an extra-academic and extra-artistic character and it refers to those meetings that would give him an empirical understanding of the perceptive abysms existing between word and deed.

Through his contact with Professor Daniel Stern, head of the department of Psychology at the University of Columbia, Wilson had access to the more than three hundred films the researcher had made in exploring mother-child interrelations. In these he had recorded a simple event in which mothers went to look after their babies when these started to cry. The simplicity of the scene filmed at normal speed illustrated the affective-emotional link when the child cried out for its mother. But when viewing the sequence frame by frame, Wilson observed a series of emotions registering on the faces of the mothers which went from initial anger and aggression, to indifference and finally to serenity and tenderness. In short, a whole landscape of emotions which when viewed at 24 frames per second passed completely unnoticed and one which the mothers in question, when they saw them, justified themselves with a tremulous "but I love my child!" This paradoxical trick that the visual plays on the gestures was one of the effects that Wilson took for his scenic paradigm, illuminating the slow motion gesture, now removed from verbal discourse, and shown to the spectator as an element for reflection and analysis, and not just as a stylistic concept.

> The text is at times related to what can be seen, but at others it is not. The
> visual and the textual parts can be considered as two grids that are
> superimposed. They are also like two masks. They possess a different
> mental space. (Lago 1999)

To understand this staging, there are two other meetings which while
fortuitous are no less important, and which must be taken into account:
Wilson has related on numerous occasions how his relationship with
Raymond Charles, the deaf boy with a peculiar speechless intelligence, has
enabled him to give his spectacles a stage language which is not secondary
through its being silent. This turning point in his conception of staging
works by seeking to observe the world through the eyes of a deaf boy.

Finally, the Wilson's sensitivity in extracting from a limitation material
for a reflective creation is fully embodied after having access to some
recordings of Christopher Knowles, an autistic child with a peculiar metric
sense of understanding the duration and the volume of an utterance.
Underlying the utterances there is a secret desire to bestow meaning on
what is said from the sound itself of what is narrated and not from the
narration. This narrative logic, which is based on a deciphering of the
alphabet so as to disarticulate the words from their appearance, which
reveals their meanings, may well be one of the elements which close the
Wilson's compositive universe, to which later would be added the
contributions of the playwright Heiner Müller, the writer Vicente Molina
Foix and the musician and composer Luigi Nono.

Light as writing on which the subjective gaze is sustained

To understand the particular universe of Robert Wilson it is necessary
to go to his piece *Deafman Glance*. (1971). Here all the elements which
make up his way of performing come together. Louis Aragon—in a letter
to André Breton—realised the transcendence of this work:

> The spectacle is reminiscent of new ways of light and shadow, or
> reinvented machines from before visual Jansenism… All is experiment. All
> the way the game left free to those wich I won't call dancers nor actors,
> because they are all that and something else: experimenters in a science
> still nameless, that of the body and his freedom. (Aragon 1976)

Aragon is without doubt referring to the univocal relationship that the
theatre has established between the word and the look, to that underlining
that the gaze bestows on the logos of performance.

The very theatre device is left dumb in a vessel of subtle yet infinite references which provide a wealth of information to the spectator, but which finally are not concentrated under any linear discourse. All of this contributes to provoking abundant fugues of meaning and, in consequence to a greater participation on the part of the spectator in the final meaning of the work.

Indeed, Wilson forces the gaze towards stages of contemplation through the chromatic transits which accompany the scenes and their changes. Thus does light formalize its temporal and spatial nature. His notebook, like a visual libretto, gives good account of the compositional weight of the lighting design in his works. The gelatinous colour which is characteristic of his chromatic spectrum is directed with the same rigour as the performance of the actors. And this is why light has the same importance as the actors. Moreover, it is on such a luminotechnical design that the spatial concept that leads to the development of the temporal elements, as occurs in dramatic action, truly lies. The resource he uses to drown his spectacles in light is that of transferring to the light the narrative keys that were before the property of the word. The luminotechnical set-up incorporates the movement of the dance and gives rise to atmospheric pigmentation of the scene, which takes place like a fluid that guides our vision. Wilson sets up a distancing game using mechanisms which are similar to those that Buñuel employed in Perro Andaluz, and there is the clear intention to put the spectator on his guard so that he cannot contemplate the spectacle passively, so that he takes an active role. In some way, both take on the skin of the eye of perception as the real writing on which the narration is sustained[1].

The lighting system that Wilson employs allows close-ups and detailed shots within the general scene. This feature is a strong link to the pioneers of the cinema in terms of the formulation of the system of shots and their language. Furthermore, the cuts in light that he practises in the spotlights make the body onto which the light is projected a metonym in itself, while never allowing the whole to disappear from the spectator The actor becomes an object, a fragment, his presence is assured, but not the interpretation of the same. The light bathes the actors and their shadows are yet another presence. From the short waves to the long waves, the light becomes a texture, and at the same time it constitutes itself as the true text of the image.

In Wilson, painting a space is to animate those forms so that they cease to be objects and become actors. Baroque artists from the Spanish School, like Juan Sánchez Cotán or Francisco de Zurbarán, may be seen as clear forerunners of the stage concept of Wilson. This link is highlighted in the huge contrast between light and shadow and in the geometric construction of the space. Unlike the Dutch still lifes, each element of the composition acquires the status of true protagonist, the light reveals and transforms these organ-less actors and focalizes them, so anticipating German expressionist cinema. Like avant-garde cinema, the works of Wilson contain elements which refuse to function simply as objects or as parts of the scenery and which end up being true protagonists of the action.

In *Portrait, Still life, Landscape* (fig. 15-1), Wilson set up an exhibition for the Boymans-Van Beunningen Museum in Rotterdam (1993). The exhibition came from the Museum reserves and the artist adapted aspects that were proper to the tradition of art genres. For the part devoted to *Still life (Room 8)* he made a first drawing which was inspired by the geometric composition and the chromatic treatment of Spanish still life. In the final display he grouped together such varied works belonging to the museum´s reserves as Allan McCollum's *The Dog from Pompey*, a vacuum cleaner designed in the 1950s and a crystal glass from the XVIII century.

Figure 15-1 Robert Wilson, *Portrait, Still life, Landscape*, 1993. Boymans-van Beuningen Museum, Exhibit Room 8, Rotterdam. Photo by Jannes Linders.

On the other hand, the aesthetics of the silent movies, the actors' way of gesturing and in particular the high contrast lightings serve as an inspiration for our author. The artist himself says: "You and the spectators have to listen to each one of the gestures, each one of the movements. Remember Charlie Chaplin or Buster Keaton" (Krauthausen 2002).

The inscriptions of space and light make it possible to form atmospheres, appearance and the movement of objects and actors. The ability of film makers like Fritz Lang to bestow the stage trappings with an absolute leading role, reveal the concern to integrate each and every one of the devices that make up the shot. Lang and Wilson coincide in the distribution and movement of the actors, showing the overwhelming obsession for space and geometric distributions. The opera *Einstein on the Beach*, (R. Wilson/Steve Reich, 1992 version) shows clear similarities with specific scenes from *Metropolis*, (Fritz Lang, 1927). In the same way, he assumes the complex task of representing the dissociation between the perception of physical time and mental time. This concretion of the spatial and the light comes from the normative diagrams used by Cézanne, who took the horizontal as the genesis of space and the vertical as that which leads to the temporal axis. Light occurs in virtue of these two lines, it always has the function of an actor, and as such it is taken into consideration by this North-American author who uses them to make the basis to help us see and listen.

One of the functions to which Wilson subjects light is to make it act as a clamour, and so gesture is converted into light and light becomes understood as a sound. It could be said that these gestural attributions also have a long tradition in the contemporary art of his country, and is materialized in artists like Pollock, W. de Kooning, Cy Twombly and Franz Kline. It is above all with the last two that he shares a metaphorical language with clear subjective references to the passing of time and to the gesture as an inner sound that structures the very identity.

The gesture of the American expressionist artists is a total X-ray of mood. Similarly, the surface of the paintings by Cy Twombly are covered in doodles which are not alien to a type of linear superimposition charged with lyrism and extraordinary musicality. We can find the same characteristic in Franz Kline, who studied at the same university as the musician John Cage, something which may seem at first to be no more than a mere coincidence but which meant that they had many things as regards the spatial-temporal conception of gesture and sound. Without going further, the overture of Ibsen's *Fruen fra Havet* [*The Lady from the Sea*], adapted by Susan Sontag[2] is a magnificent example of how the spatial-temporal relations between light and sound make up an ineffable tale in themselves, while not forgetting the antecedents to be found in the *L'Inhumaine* by the avant-garde Marcel Lerbier (1923)

All these peculiarities in one way or another appear in the "theatre of visuals" which Wilson projects, in which the surface of the senses is at the level of the concentrated look, in the drawing itself, in the hands that mechanically fold the paper to create forms and which clearly link up with the pretensions of abstract Expressionism. Physical incorporation of the fragments of the notebooks, which act like a "visual libretto" enlarged as the staging of the work; projection of the trace as an expressive sense.

All this is especially present in the staging of the version of the opera by Mozart, *The Magic Flute*: the abstract trace takes the information to the same level as the sonorous elements or the actors themselves. Likewise, the high contrast of the light in this same expressionist diagrams appear infinitely in his drawings. In this vein it seems interesting to observe the effect of the curtain of light pursued in a sketch for *King Lear*.

This total concentration in each of the senses operates within the formal structure that Wilson creates, in which the senses are divided into channels. The perceptive division of the senses is the supposition for these channels to be able to operate freely. Thus, the light that makes it possible to sense Wilson's world is only possible by assuming that time and space are composed by looking. This concept is perfectly defined in the author's manifestations: "The mission of the artist is to take decisions with respect to time and space."

His capacity to fuel the observation and the listening of the spectator, despite, at times, giving rise to boredom, means that he has approaches and points in common with artists like Walter de Maria and, very specifically, with works like the permanently exhibited the *Lighting field* which the this artist created in 1977, and which consists of the positioning of lightening rods every 6 metres over 16 kilometres. With this work, de Maria assumed that the wait was obligatory and necessary as an attitude as expressive discourse.

But in the case of our author, the light does not only seek to frighten—assuming the role of the leading actor—it also makes the architectural construction possible. This is a recurring question in all his production and one which appears continually in his visual librettos. An example of this is the staging of The Death of Danton, (1992). Here he constructs a powerful game of light and contrast in the form of vertical windows which establish a dimension of temporal depth such that it perforates the spatial stability. On other occasions the architectural elements created by the projection of light seek a subtle way of paying tribute to his master, Paolo Soleri. The clearest example is in the staging of

The Days Before DDDIII.

The scale of Soleri's thought is breathable in the scene from this work that we are commenting on. The Italian architect was capable of planning cities under the water, on top of the water or in the sky. But what really impressed Wilson, more than the results, was that particular capacity to project ideas. And so it is that we may understand this scene as a true tribute to the mental construction of images and to our ability to be thrilled by their mere pre-existence in our brains.

The various manifestations that we can find in Wilson's creativeness are characterized by the assignation to light of an infinity of functions, which join the expressive and architectural senses already mentioned. We refer to the role of light as a symbolic form, a concept that in Wilson is crystallized in the archetypal image of the light bulb. This is a stylistic hallmark of his work which again links him to contemporary painting and very specifically to the scenes constructed in the pictures of Francis Bacon

The solitude of the model in the face of minimum furnishing, (something which Wilson appreciated so much in the choreographies of Balanchine, Cunningham and Graham), connects with the iconography of Bacon, which specialized in making a situation of the representation of the human figure, and not a position. Both seem to show a special predilection for the disturbing sensations that simple objects like chairs and light bulbs produce in the final meaning of the image. Secret ceremonies dominated by a confusing feeling at times accompanied by brusque changes in the movements of the actors. Well known in this aspect are the influences of the chrono-photographs of Étienne-Jules Marey and Eadweard Muybridge in the sweep effects present in the characters of Francis Bacon. It is a sense of analytical observation that fully connects with the interest shown by Wilson for those films of Dr Stern which he analysed frame by frame. But this symbolic association of light and the disturbing sensation it produces may on occasions reach the levels of oniric nightmare. Thus, those huge eyes that appear in the staging made for POEtry manage to illustrate perfectly the literary world of Edgar Allan Poe, the leitmotiv of this piece made together with Lou Reed. "Those who dream by day are aware of many things that escape those who dream only at night". Specifically, this sentence of Poe's has its equivalent in the spatial conception that breathes in Wilson's version, and which is manifested in the amplitude of the chromatic vibrations of blue light. In general, his stagings maintain an always-extreme visual definition, to the point that they often, as we have mentioned, achieve the character of an optical illusion. Their measured precision is equally famous. We know that each light matrix is for him a number in power. This obsession is equally evident in the use of colour an aspect which takes him back to the pictorial tradition, which is revealed in the admiration Wilson has always professed admiration for the similar obsessive constancy of Cézanne. He coincides with him in the conception of the chromatic study of forms as a way to reach higher levels of spatial and temporal condensation.

Colour as absence and plenitude

At this point of our exposition, and taking as a starting point our training as painters, we can consider that the moment has come to make special mention of the particular way of approaching colour in dramaturgy. We can begin by analysing the ability the author shows to arouse subjective feelings and sensations in the spectators. In some way or another there is a constant in all his works that is harboured in a musical conception of colour in which contrast and duality are always present. There is an exhaustive treatment of colour which allows, as spectators, to feel the evolutions between the chromatic effect of the wall-colour at the limit and the reverberation of the light and colour as a spatial expansion of our look. His chromatic approaches seem also to inherit some concepts from the North-American abstract artists like Barnett Newman. Both dispose of the surrounds and as Newman himself observes: "instead of using forms or making reliefs and spaces, my works claim the space. Instead of working with what is left of the space, I work with the whole space." (The New York School of Abstract Expressionism)

It is a formulation that appears to have become axiomatic in Wilson. But besides the spatial sensations provoked by such a particular chromatic approach, we have also to contemplate the reaction sought from both the actors and the public. We observe that his way of relating actors to the spaces where the scenery is reduced to a minimal expression is in line with that of one of his compatriots, the sculptor George Segal (1924-2000), who remarked:

> I like the smell of paint, the brushstrokes.... But I switched over to three-dimensional creation because all those so intelligent abstract concepts and those so interesting ideas about art are flat when on canvass. (Piquer 2000)

This observation is very clarifying given the posture that both Segal and Wilson adopt to painting. Both profess a love of painting but need the third dimension that space can give them. Yet they never lose sight of the expressive possibilities of continuing to act as a painter despite using the spatial ubiquity as their support. Wilson, Segal... frequently pierce the wall colour of the pictorial plane with a vertical cut of light and colour.

Thus, both reflect that longing to introduce a temporal depth, materialized in a vertical plane, which enriches and transcends the horizontal dimension.

At the same time it is possible to find in the works of Wilson other tasks assigned to the chromatic construction which seem to approach the silent utopia. This creates a filiation with the artistic concept of painters like Mark Rothko or film makers like Michelangelo Antonioni. All three seem obsessed with the same ideas but in different media. So it was that on a certain occasion Antonioni wrote in a letter to Rothko: "You and I do the same thing. You paint nothingness and I film nothingness". It is a sentence that without doubt can be extrapolated and applied to the theatre of Wilson. For when we contemplate the pictures of Rothko, both the colour and the light are submitted to reducing art to the category of silence, expressing certain moods in an inimitable way. This expressive, chromatic conception of silence is an indispensable source if we are to understand the work of Antonioni, and at the same time it has served to construct the Wilson's extraordinary theatrical universe. Antonioni's frequent interrelations between the actors and the abstract spaces of pure colour serve for Wilson to complement other sources (kabuki theatre, among others). The peculiarity of the relation we have established between the two artists radiates from the evolutions and the very breath of the actors, who, especially in the spectacles of Wilson are reinforced by their interconnection with the chromatic treatment of space.

That colour stimulates the senses while at the same time allowing the spectators' feelings to be evoked, feelings that draw the spectator towards the unspoken thoughts of the actors. There is also the quality of an architectural space that has been constructed and which to a large extent is the successor to the architecture of Luis Barragán. This architect of light and colour, like Mark Rothko, was interested in expressing the fundamental emotions of man through architecture and colour. Architectures, which are to be felt, and the refined chromes of Wilson participate in this specific sensorial meaning.

But colour in Wilson also wants to speak out, acting literally as text and as actor. This aspect takes him towards other artists, among whom stand out Joseph Kosuth or Bruce Nauman, who, respectively, in their works like *Four Colors, Four Words* (1965), or *My Name as though It Were on the Surface of the Moon* (1968) anticipated the tautological formulas of colour-text and text-space association that Wilson himself would finally apply in *Woyzeck*, an adaptation of the work of the same name by Georg Büchner.

In concluding this study, we should pay special attention to reverberated chromatic tratment which, in his works, reaches a solid parity with expanded sound. In Wilson, the colour leaps out to meet the spectator, it invades his field of vision and alters his relation with time and space. The chromatics in his works reverberates with the space of the look. It is in this way that the chromatic gradation of the light also brings a sensation of sonorous perspective. The parallelism with the work of José María Yturralde is so graphic that a comment by the painter could close the section exegesis:

> I have finally managed to dilute, to dematerialize geometry. This aspect of the intangible interests me greatly that a form can be perceived without it, but my idea is to transmit it from spatial multiplicity. (Aimeur 2007)

Wilson also highlights this spatial multiplicity, conceiving light and colour as writing which moves the drama. The space and time of his spectacles have been created so that image and sound can live together autonomously on the stage. Thus, in *Lohengrin*, a horizontal bar of light slowly, almost imperceptibly ascends, and acts as a counterpoint to the Wagner's score.

The presence of the luminous bar in *Lohengrin*, in *Orlando*, in *Pelléas and Mélisande*, and in other pieces by Wilson, which slowly moves around the scene, finds its reference point in the works of Dan Flavin which as of 1963 he realized exclusively with fluorescent tubes. In fact, the artist was one of the first to set up a set of static displays, which go beyond the material nature of the place and the object. There is planning behind each one of the elements because, in the end, these actively modify the temporal perception of the work. Such principles which allow changes in the gaze require, as we have said, contemplation; it is not in vain that this game, set in the interrelation between space, natural light, electrical light and the changes produced in the gaze when perceiving these elements, has its compositional matrix in the nominalist proposals of Guillaume d'Occam. Abounding in this sense, the Briton Richard Box through his installations of fluorescent tubes, which are lit just by the electromagnetic fields generated by the high tension pylons, is proposing aspects that are habitually present in Wilson's theatre. Like him, he seeks to make visible that which is usually invisible–Box makes the invisible electromagnetic field perceivable. The artist has declared that the people who come to look at the spectacle produce changes in the light through their mere presence, since the human being is a great conductor of energy. Wilson would sardonically remark in respect to this minutely elaborated finding that "things happen in front of us, but we don't take the time necessary to perceive them".

On the other hand, Wilson, as a conceptual and citationist artist, moves within the current panorama in which fragmentation seems to be the one of the few ways to understand the contemporary world. His facet of fitter and video artist is perfectly constructed from the fragment and the collage as a way of operating. His admiration for artists like Robert Rauschenberg is made patent in the constant irreverence of works like *Video 50*, a work from 1980 which includes as a film-collage fifty short scenes, all separated by a black border, and signed by Wilson, as it were a painting. These scenes imitate the aesthetics, in cliché form, of all the cinema genres imaginable, from melodrama to suspense to science fiction. There are also nods to avant-gardecinema of to Warhol.

Conclusion

Wilson's utopia is realized from a diaphanous silence which stretches beyond that likewise utopian fall of the fourth wall brought in by naturalist theatre. To enter Wilson's project is to enter a *Denkraum*, i.e. a "thinking space." It is a space of light that is filtered through the lens of abstract thought, far from the literary thought, which is so prone to take stage writing as part of the literary field.

While in the theatre of word the spectator follows the traces that the language imposes on him, in the experience that Wilson offers, there arises all the plastic power of visual thought. The eye is granted the freedom to look, and the ear to hear. In the past changes in the way of understanding the space of the stage had already come about, like in Gordon Craig's superpuppet, where identification between the spectator and the human face disappears through the use of a mask, which serves the same function as the actors' make-up in avant-garde cinema. Or there is the idea of Antonin Artaud, who through his theatre de la cruauté, replaces the appeal to the mind of the spectator by the human subconscious approach, materialized in a weighting of plastic elements over the domain of the word. But the scene which Wilson offers us, while built up from Brechtian surprise, is to no lesser extent built up from formal abstraction of art, especially from those postulates of Cézanne, and it gives expression even to tedium, to boredom as an act of freeing which the spectator cannot elude. Yet if Brecht, with his epic theatre, combats the fascination that the word holds over the stage and shows up the conventions through which we distinguish art from life, in Wilson we find a shift of the virtual space of drama, produced by the virtual space of the plastic arts, where light and colour is the inaugural element. This is possible thanks to the leading role that Wilson grants to pictorial concepts and which he bears to the universe of the scene, to his dramaturgy, and which, to us, seem to have been undervalued. In other words, the revolutions and the utopian postulates that until now have been carried out in the scenic sphere never ceased to take this as a literary element. But it is Wilson who scenifies it, treating it like a painter treats his painting, in compositional terms of light and colour, and it is this that has enabled him to dissolve the primacy of the word in the theatre, not so as to reduce it to a merely formal proposal, nor to lead it to its dissolution, but precisely to renew it, to restore it to its norm.

Notes

[1] Luis Buñuel makes the surface of the cinema screen visible, see Talens (1986).
[2] We refer to the Spanish version of 2008, *La dama del mar*.

Works cited

Aimeur, C. 2007. Entrevista a J. María Iturralde. *Revista Valentia* 13 (26): 12-15.

Aragon, Louis. 1976. An open letter to Andre Breton on Robert Wilson's "Deafman Glance". *Performing Arts Journal* 1 (1): 3-7.

Brecht, Stefan. 2005. *The theatre of visions: Robert Wilson*. Part I (Images). New York: The vanishing rotating triangle.

Eco, Umberto. 1993. Robert Wilson and Umberto Eco: A Conversation. *Performing Arts Journal* 15: 87-96.

Guatterini, Marinella. 1991. *Lezioni milanesi: La parola a la danza*. Milano: Ubulibri.

Krauthausen, Ciro. 2002. En el taller de Robert Wilson. *El pais. Cultura,* July 31. http://www.remiendoteatro.com/Notas/Elpais_es%20-%20Robert%20Wilson.htm (accessed December 20, 2008).

*The Nueva York School abstract Expressionism. Barnett Newman (1905-1970).*http://www.campusred.net/straining/Cursos/C3Bignacioargote/Lecciones/newman.htm (accessed December 20, 2008).

Lago, Natalia. 1999. Un viaje mental para acabar un milenio. Entrevista a cerca del estreno en Madrid de The days before death, destruction & Detroit III. *El Mundo*, November 19. http://www.elmundo.es/1999/11/19/cultura/19N0123.html (accessed December 1, 2008).

Morey, Miguel, and Carmen Pardo. 2003. *Robert Wilson*. Barcelona: Polígrafa.

Piquer, Isabel. 2000. George Segal, uno de los grandes del "pop art",

enterrado en la intimidad. *El país*, June 12.
http://www.elpais.com/articulo/cultura/George/Segal/grandes/pop/art/e
nterrado/intimidad/elpepicul/20000612elpepicul_5/Tes/
(accessed December 1, 2008).
Talens, J. 1986. *El ojo tachado. Lectura de un chien andalou de Luis
Buñuel.* Madrid: Cátedra.

CHAPTER SIXTEEN

QUEER SUBJECTIVITIES: PRACTICES OF EMBODIMENT, POLITICS OF EXPERIMENTATION AND CONTACT PEDAGOGIES THROUGH PERFORMANCE

JUDIT VIDIELLA

Introduction

[Seated in a chair reading the introduction in a clear and distant voice. Her hands are on her lap, hiding the six layers of gloves she wears.]

Of all the pieces in the exhibition "Teatre sense teatre" ["Theatre without Theatre"], shown in May 2007 in the Contemporary Art Museum of Barcelona (MACBA), one in particular caught my attention: the film by Ernesto Giménez Caballero, from 1930, entitled *La Mano* [*The Hand*], starring the writer Ramón Gómez de la Serna, which parodies a conference-performance entitled "El orador" ["The Speaker"].

[Having finished the introduction, she stands. Her right hand remains hidden behind, at her back. Soon she shows the Hand, raising it and revealing a mitten, positioned for action. Interpretation-imitation of the voice of Gómez de la Serna in "El orador"[1]]

Ramón: as the basis of my speeches, I have an invaluable element, a thing that brings the masses behind me, because when one has a convincing hand, the multitude will follow that hand... The speaker must have this hand, a swelling of eloquence.... One can use it to say—'there are five reasons you must follow this path'. The whole world before such reasons, lowers their overwhelmed heads... And at last, when the speaker is near the end of his speech, it serves for the preparation of his descent. Because this thing that this speaker-pilot has, that overcomes, seems surely based on his words, until he suddenly breaks his head on one of them. His spiralling fall is signalled by the word that fails him. The speaker who dominates waits for the planned moment and then, with his hand working, descends, signalling the final paragraph.

This tends to be very long in speakers, because they look for an appropriate terrain; as it is for pilots, who also need their paved terrain. The speaker will then see that there is an inkwell and a glass of water on the table. He will be afraid of falling in the inkwell and in the glass of water, and then, very slowly, so as not to fall either onto a quill pen, the speaker, methodically and with concentration, will place his hand on the table.

[Striptease of the first glove: a gardening glove appears, similar to that worn by Gómez de la Serna in "El orador": masculinized voice, neutral and distant]

With this staged oral version of the filmic register of the action by Gómez de la Serna, I have tried to uncover a series of questions that concern me, and which have been heatedly debated in different queer-feminist scenarios: Questions regarding the celebrated visions of the transgressive capabilities of performance in relation to gender subversion; the efficiency of the politics of visibility; or the spaces that we legitimate as producers of knowledge(s) and relational politics.

But also in this drag act that I just represented for you, in the transvestite role of Ramón Gómez de la Serna, I tried to find a way to localize and embody myself in this text-speech-performance, not as a mere transmitter of words and thought, distant and neutral, but also in order to convert the very talk into an event, an act of pleasure, a striptease of gloves and hands, an unfolding of the relations between discourse, power, knowledge, body, desire, representation, sexuality and performance, in what some authors, like Della Pollock(1998), have baptized as performative writing.[2]

With the progressive theatrical turn of the social sciences (Butt 2005) and the interdisciplinary contributions of performance, the relationships between theatre and visual arts contribute new discussions about the role of corporality and discourse, revealing the tensions between representation and power. The speaker exhibits, and exposes his/herself, given that performative speech acts generate an authorized knowledge, where naming not only describes reality but also produces it.

Figure 16-1 Lecture-performance at "The Expression of Subjectivity in the Performing Arts" Conference, November 26th, 2008, Valencia.

Here today, writing from home and making a prediction into the future, or already in the past in this moment of reading, I have the sensation that the social role of that speech hand, parodied by Gómez de la Serna, does not differ much from what I am doing here, before you. The position of academics, theorists and conference-goers in today's society of immaterial production determines, rather excessively, the interaction with their audiences through instructive performances. More and more, the transmitter format makes me uncomfortable, which is why I try to find other tactical spaces for proliferating experiences, like when I went to the event "Coropolíticas/Body politics in the Americas" organized by the Hemispheric Institute for Performance in Buenos Aires (Argentina) in June, 2007.[3] For ten days all the attendees, without hierarchies— performers, academics, activists, students, and the rest—met each morning in work groups in order to discuss performance, body and politics; or like the workshops organized by Arteleku[4] in San Sebastián (Spain) during their many queer-feminist encounters.[5] But it is also true that occasions such as these are for generating future con/tacts, in addition to theoretical exhibitions and curricular requirements…

[Striptease of the second glove: a pink dish glove appears. A well-mannered voice, hyperbolically "feminine" and a tad naïve.]

It is precisely Jon McKenzie (2001) who maintains that performance has become an analytical framework from which one may understand the close relationship between education, technology and work in contemporary postfordist societies. This author distinguishes between "Performance Management", performance management in multinational companies; "Techno-Performance", which studies the operability of technological tools in everyday life or in telecommunications; and finally, "Performance Studies", a field that analyses cultural performance, in concrete rituals, social and artistic practices, or performative-discursive acts, which configure our subjectivities in relation to a series of body regulations. McKenzie finds similarities between these three paradigms and their respective operating systems, built through similar processes of repetition and optimization: facts, output, cultural, economic, political efficacy... Making a futuristic prediction, McKenzie foreshadows that "performance will be to the twentieth and twenty-first centuries what discipline was to the eighteenth and nineteenth, that is, an onto-hysterical,[6] excuse me, onto-historical formation of power and knowledge" (McKenzie 2001, 176) which will produce a new subject of fragmented, decentred and vitural knowledge.

If I may, please allow me—of course with great tact—to confront the name of the encounter for which I rehearsed this article-presentation-performance: "The Expression of Subjectivity in the Performing Arts". We understand the term subjectivity as forms of being in, inhabiting and thinking the world, as the capacity for making sense of ourselves and others, and also as forms of subjection, conscious or unconscious, that run through us' in all dimensions of our lives. When I read the term "expression" I cannot avoid a certain discomfort when linking it to the expressionist genealogies of education, or individualist psychological theories that foster a supposed celebratory manifestation of an essence and interior feeling that blooms into visibility. As I understand it, subjectivities are anchored more to a series of gender technologies and regulations,[7] as I learned from Teresa De Lauretis (2000) or Judith Butler (2001), and less to a resistant expressivity.

Maybe we should speak of experiments instead of expressions, making it clear that there is nothing central or stable to express or reveal about oneself, but rather the existence a juxtapositioning of a series of states, meanings, and fluid changing understandings dependent on a series of conditions that go beyond oneself in contact with alterity. The performative power of language and the regulatory mechanisms of regulations present in the formation of subjectivity have fostered within cultural politics a growing interest in performance, especially in performance art, as a practice that allows for a rethinking of the politics of resistance in relation to the fetishization of the politics of visibility (Phelan 1998) and representation, as well as the creation of representations that disrupt hegemonic identity categories.

[After reading this last phrase the author stops, takes a deep breath and says...]

oofff, what a dense paragraph!

[She continues reading]

From these linguistic contributions, one may come to understand the performative as pertaining more to speech than to artistic performance. According to Taylor, this territorial conquest of the performative means that perhaps now it will be difficult to reclaim once again the use of the performative in the terrain of performance (Taylor 2007, 6). For this reason, Taylor invites us to find a Spanish word, *performático*, to refer to the adjective form which, therefore, is not only discursive but also embodied. The importance of this turn would be fundamental, given that performatic and visual fields, in spite of being associated and connected with discursive forms, also need their own strategies. Thus, if I may be allowed such audacity, I would propose to rephrase the theme of the encounter as "The Formation of Subjectivities (in plural) in the Performative Arts".

It is just that, far from some people's romanticized idea, performance is not only an aesthetic, subversive practice that allows us to challenge the normative formation of subjectivities, exposing, for example, how gender and sexuality are built through a series of repetitive and regulated acts, but also a normative practice, regulating and restrictive, that can perpetuate them.

[Striptease of the third glove: A black satin glove in the style of Rita Hayworth appears, sophisticated voice. The author sits on the corner of one of the tables in the room, legs crossed and leaning in a seductive position]

As a member of the performance group Corpus Deleicti (without auto-identifying myself as a performer), I try to reconcile relational spaces with political experimentation that go beyond discourse and the academy. Inhabiting militant circuits has allowed me to make contributions to the "convivial" (Dubatti 2007) and "liminal" (Turner 1969) relationship that characterizes performance. The closeness and contact between body-action and the agents involved can contribute to individual and collective reflexivity, via distancing strategies, such as self-denomination, disidentification[8] (Muñoz 1999) and self-representation.

As performers, we "dis/cover" ourselves by putting our own selves at risk, and into play, manifesting the power relations between spectators and actors. As spectators, we attend a performance in order to inhabit zones of alternative subjectivities that we put into play in and outside of the act: we intersubjectify (Jones 1998), desubjectify and resubjectify (Dubatti 2007) ourselves. This allows us to confront, in a concrete time and space, macropolitical and micropolitical subjectivities (Guattari y Rolnik 2006).

Still, however, there is no way of guaranteeing ahead of time that a parody or subversive repetition of the norm, even though it may "fail", does not repeat itself, returning to performance the constitutive, executive and reinforcing power of social laws. Escaping the register is a problematic question for minority communities, which have always been defined, regulated and catalogued by an alienated gaze based on the use of the archive, the register, or on normative representations. Therefore, performance will be a fundamental practice of experimentation that will accompany identity and postidentity politics of queer-feminists, transgender, dis/abled, subaltern, and so on, subjects that will problematize the relationship between representation, presentation and representivity, in a series of community practices of experimentation, which will not distinguish between performers and spectators.

[Striptease of the fourth glove: The speaker removes her glove, mimicking Rita Hayworth in 'Gilda', swirls it and tosses it to the floor with a provocative air. A white latex glove appears: Change of voice and tone, now clinical and aseptic. Sits down in a chair, appears distant.]

My interest in reconciling embodied practices and politics of experimentation within the field of pedagogy and in cultural politics has led me to explore what I call "zones of contact", a useful trope for understanding the type of horizontal practices I was referring to, which escape the habitual asepsis and prophylaxis of pedagogical practices. The contributions of "contact dance", a genre of contemporary dance that emerged in the 70s in the United States, initially developed by Steve

Paxton and Yvonne Rainer among others, is useful not only as a metaphor for illustrating ideas, but also as a methodology of action-acting-participation, which allows one to work with and on bodies (social, cultural, embodied).[9] In this practice, at the moment of the action there is no distinction between educator-learner; performer-audience.

Even though dance has always been a privileged practice for contact between bodies and for embodied experimentation, "contact" interests me for how it can become a political strategy, given that it is less of a disciplinary practice and based more on the materiality of bodies and different subjectivities—in contact and in movement. In "contact", each part of the body becomes an articulation that acts as a node and anchor, so that the other body or object is displaced in space and forms a political figuration. It is about finding the points of con/tact to balance forces; the gravity in power relations; balancing oneself on uneasy alliances; the suspension of the marginalisation of the body as gender, sexuality, age, etc.; the lifting of the weight of visibility; the transferences of discourses, the leap of practices of resistance, etc.

Mary Louise Pratt (1999) uses this concept to refer to the interactions between groups of different people, who use non equivalent terms and ideas. She defines this zone as social spaces where cultures encounter, collide and force themselves upon on another (Pratt 1999, 519). Her text con/centrates on the interactions between subjects, institutions and cultural groups with asymmetric powers, especially in the colonial context and the posterior consequences of this system, in which national heritage, the notion of citizenship, community, language and culture continuously collide. Pratt denotes strategies of resistance within marginalized communities like processes of transculturation, through which subordinated or marginalized groups select and reinvent the material transmitted by the dominant, metropolitan culture. She addresses the interaction between two cultures (of learning) where one learns to transform the dominant without losing its own identity.

In a "contact zone" there are both zones of proximity and zones of distancing emerge, as well as tensions and disagreements, differences in positions and political agenda… it is a political practice of risk in an interpersonal confrontation with others, as Adrian Piper (1990) reminds us in her performance *Funk Lessons* and in her text *Indexical Present*. Racism is not a theoretical and abstract problem, but a relationship that begins between you and me, forcing us into an immediate experience of the complexity of the other and our re/actions.

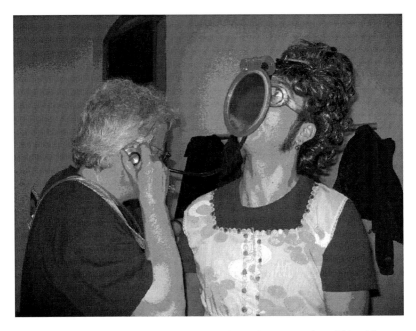

Figure 16-2 Body-crossing workshop on the re-de-construction of identities.
Festival Las Otras Caras del Planeta [The Other Faces of the Planet Festival]
(LOCP), April 21ˢᵗ–29ᵗʰ, 2006, Gijón. Photo by Judit Vidiella.

In a pedagogy of contact there is a tactile and tactic interaction, a
political affiliation, or a putting into play and risk of embodiments, in
addition to the fostering of trust and closeness. But one must permit the
emergence of spaces of reflexivity. This implies:

- Working from positions open to encounters and contact
  between educator and learner, or members of the group.
- Incorporating experiences of all the "actors" involved in the
  educational process.
- Allowing the body to perspirate through performance in
  embodied practices and workshops.
- Opening oneself up to improvisation and interaction of the
  pedagogical relationship, and all the contraindications and
  contradictions that this can have.
- Fostering a sensory and somatic pedagogy that in the area of
  Art and Art Education passes for incorporating
  methodologies of analysis, from Visual Culture, like the

> construction of personal narratives that negotiate the
> meaning of dominant constructs... And, from Performance
> Studies, the contribution of performance as an analytical
> framework and a practice of action and (ad)diction in the
> classroom through workshops, aiming at making the
> performative constructions of gender, race, ethnicity,
> sexuality effective...

Contact can fracture borders and liminal and eccentric positions with the overflowing of bodies. In this moment of friction, a reconsideration of the contributions of queer pedagogy[10] take the stage, with the objective of revising obligatory pedagogies that normalize the corporeal, whether through discipline, invisibilization, practices that control and sterilize desires and corporalities, etc. The practice tries to bestow intelligibility and corporeality on subjects that, until now, had been relegated out of existence, in the margins of the abject: other corporeal topographies...

A transgressive, border pedagogy, as described by Britzman (2002), references liminal spaces as an attempt to deconstruct closed, static and pre-established norms. Speaking of borders and bodies brings us to the tactile dimension of the encounter with the Other. This implies situating oneself in a territory where the regulation, classification and (de)construction of the corporeal Other as subject—unknown, dangerous, exploited, abject, etc.—takes place.

[Striptease of the 5th glove: A black, fishnet glove appears: militant voice, standing, at attention]

Queer pedagogy is structured around hyper-embodied subjects—for their excessive over-representation—and/or by the disembodied—for their invisibility and lack of intelligibility. In the words of Britzman:

> A queer pedagogy resists normal practices and normativity, concerns itself
> with the ethics of its interpretative practices, and acknowledges their
> responsibility in imagining social relations as something more than an
> effect of the dominant conceptual order. (2002:225)[11]

In traditional pedagogy, the focus of attention usually falls more on the supposed inclusion of all the subjects, rather than on acts of exclusion. This inclusion often derives from the disembodiment of some subjects that cannot think themselves within the frames of intelligibility proposed by normative understandings, and often they end up including themselves in normative categories of subjectivity. This occurs, for example, with (dis)abled people, for whom their identity construction often ends up being, albeit redundantly, an excessive objectification of their bodies. With queer identities something similar also occurs: everything centres on their sexuality, such that they end up being constituted as hyper-sexualized subjects, when that element is one more dimension of their own subjectivity.

In order to effect a change in this situation, the next step would be to detour this power relation, which would imply a displacement of the objectification[12] of embodiment, which is to say, to imagine a pedagogy of bodily resistance. From the perspective, one understands that the body is a discursive, political, ideological and pedagogical product, in addition to being somatic, experiential, desiring, phenomenological material. A "pedagogy of contact" that is nourished by feminist practices and queer pedagogies, such as performatic strategies, allows one to think of an educational practice that would help subjects gain an embodied self-consciousness: on the one hand, to show the performative regulatory mechanisms and, on the other hand, to facilitate capacities for action, provoking experimental practices of pleasure and experimentation (Sloterdijk 2003) and the proliferation of subjectivities through performance.

Resistance implies learning to inhabit the body with agency, and also unlearning the categories acquired through repetition. Learning to self-name and self-represent through a series of technologies of the self and embodied practices, which necessarily allow for a margin of agency. As such, it is important to cultivate mechanisms that allow us to symbolize ourselves, textualize ourselves, represent and affirm ourselves, which is to say, to construct our own realities starting at the ability to name and re-present it. In fact, performance is already a way of un/writing the body, of representing and constituting its materiality.

"Contact" also breaks with the traditional conceptualization of more traditional dance and theatre, where narrative, linearity, sequence and the repetition of mechanic movements constitute a spectacular idea (of learning through choreography that is repeated in front of a mirror). On the contrary, "contact" and drag workshops recover bodily sensations as a process and an experiment. There is neither a final product nor a relationship between the stage and the public, in that collective jams are organized for contact dances. It also breaks away from traditional gender roles, so well defined in classical dance—characterized by an excessive sexualisation of bodies.

In "contact", each part of the body can be a lever of support. Perhaps I should object here that this vision of the body can lead to its extreme opposite, diluting entirely desire and eroticism. For example, it may be

useful to recuperate the methodology of the drag workshops by the
performance group La Pocha Nostra[13], formed, among others, by the
Chicano performer Guillermo Gómez Peña (2005), in order to deconstruct
ethnic, cultural and gender stereotypes, or the drag workshops that the
artist Diane Torr has been doing with women for more than 10 years, in
order to deconstruct gender technologies in the learning of both
masculinities and femininities.

Similar to Deleuze and Guattari's "body without organs", the bodies
that emerge from this type of practice are more intensified, magnified
bodies, instituted by forces that configure movements and identity
perceptions with an enormous political potential. A "pedagogy of contact"
would privilege not only the discursive, intellectual dimension that is
representative of the subject, knowledge and learning, but also the bodily,
physical, material dimension of intervention-action. This also implies
seeing practices as open and oblique processes, not only of production, but
also as reception and participation, on behalf of all the agents that are
involved in the diverse dimensions of the process.

As the years pass, we distance ourselves from immediate touch and
close relationships, moving towards a textual excess, in the domain of the
word. Having and maintaining "con/tacts" has been a fundamental
question for the continuity of queer and feminist communities, given that
the support and networks are fundamental to their survival, where
knowledge is lived, embodied and challenged. This lesson is vital in my
uneducational[14] practice, breaking the distant professional relationship,
and collaborating in student projects outside of the academic context, in
tactile and tactic spaces where subjectivities proliferate.

From here, I can do no more than end my role as speaker, lower myself
from this stage and do a final striptease, undressing myself in an act of
surrender.

*[Last striptease: The speaker's hand appears which she extends while
saying the last words]*

I extend my hand out to you, not as a gesture of Christian communion
but as an act of gratitude and an invitation for future contacts and
dialogues.

Thank you for your attention, I hope I have not been an excessively
kamikaze speaker.

Notes

---

[1] http://es.youtube.com/watch?v=RX-FAXxJtSg (accessed December 11, 2008).

[2] Pollock understands performative writing from six possible trajectories: evocative, metonymic, subjective, citational; consequent and inventive; generating and in perpetual movement. Pollock is interested in making writing "perform". This means that with the very act of writing one does not only describe a "reality" but must also be capable of "doing things with the words", or of opening a gap so that possibilities materialize. In this type of writing the body appears and disappears; now it is an image, now it is a "me", an "I", a "we"... It is presented and becomes invisible; it materializes and is diluted; it moves toward the possibility of the subjunctive, of the conditional or the future, and it is concentrated in a practice that displaces instead of produces meaning. Embodied writing reminds us constantly that the historian and theorist have a body, and that this body is involved in the very act of writing, understood as an event. Other theorists have preferred to speak of "occasional writing" (Miller 1991); "anecdotic theory" (Gallop 2002); "writing as event" (Phelan 1997, 1993), etc. For theorist Peggy Phelan 1997, the writing of performance must be conceived as if it was another performance, given how she believes that they are two experiences (versions) that are similar in character but different:

The feminist slogan "the personal is political" fits perfectly into this type of writing conceived as performance, in that it is also a way of breaking with the sedentary meanings, frozen traditions and dominant and neutral narratives. In a certain way, this practice scrutinizes performativity as a self that cites a series of experiences in an act of re-doing and putting discourse into practice, while questioning at the same time the chain of citations.

[3] http://hemi.nyu.edu/esp/seminar/2007/esp/index.html (accessed December 12, 2008).

[4] http://www.arteleku.net/4.1/index.jsp?idioma=ingles (accessed December 12, 2008).

[5] See http://www2.unia.es/artpen/estetica/estetica01/proy_1_art.htm (accessed December 12, 2008).

[6] *Onto-hysterical* does not pertain to the 'script'-citation of McKenzie, for this reason it is not in italics. It was included for humour and is corrected by the following term 'onto-historical'.

[7] Based on the Foucauldian notion of the materiality of discourse, De Lauretis analyses an entire series of devices and declarations that "subject" individuals to a series of subjective bodily dispositions of gender construction. For De Lauretis, gender is a representation, the representation of gender is a construction; gender construction continues today, and gender construction is also affected by its deconstruction.

[8] Identity configuration is only based on the generation of practices of identification and disidentification with a culture. José Esteban Muñoz analyses

those practices that are outside mainstream culture—racial and sexual—in order to
see how they negotiate majority culture and transform it with their own cultural
proposals. Muñoz calls this process *disidentification*, a process of toxic identity
infiltration in the hands of subjects that have been labelled in identity categories
without being able to generate their own identity "brands". Through a study of
practices, performances, movies, ethnographic work, etc., he develops a "minor"
perspective—in Deleuzian terms—through performances of activism and survival.
The process of disidentification is a performance on its own, an attempt to
materialize a queer world against a dominant ideology, detecting the points of
intersection and contact between identities and desires that result in a
discontentment with dominant contemporary culture.

Reformulating Muñoz's term, I speak of "active disidentification", in order to
understand a way of negotiation with the dominant ideology that neither
assimilates with the dominant structure nor totally opposes it, but that moves
between disidentification and dissidence. This concept is useful in that it distances
itself from binary oppositions and understands that throughout all acts of
subjectification there is identification and also disidentification, but especially in
the case of queer communities, there is also bodily dissidence. Thus, it is also a
political stance in the space of visibility and action, in that it does not pretend to be
visible in the mainstream but rather to generate visual-embodied strategies, often
criticized by dominant criteria as "in bad taste", and which depart from a parody or
reappropriation of the canon.

[9] See Broza (2000) "En torno a la definición del Contact Improvisation desde una
triple perspectiva: coreográfica, acrobática y pedagógica," *Revista digital* 22, June.
Buenos Aires. http://www.efdeportes.com/efd22a/ci.htm (accessed December12,
2008).

[10] See Talburt and Steinberg (2005).

[11] My translation from the Spanish version.

[12] Note on the translation: In the original text, this word appears as *cos/ificación*,
which translates as objectification but, when divided as in the original version, also
references the word for body.

[13] http://www.pochanostra.com/ (accessed December12, 2008).

[14] Note on the translation: In the original text, I use the word 'indocente'. This
word is a modification of the word for teacher/faculty member ('docente') and for
Spanish readers, the addition of the prefix communicates the idea of un-teacherly
behaviour, as well as creating an association with the word for indecent
('indecente').

Works cited

Butler, Judith. 1990. *Gender Trouble. Feminism and the Subversion of
    Identity*. London / New York: Routledge.

Britzman, Deborah. 1998. "Queer Pedagogy and its Strange Techniques."
    In *Inside the Academy and out: Lesbian/Gay/Queer Studies and Soul*

Action. eds. Janice L. Ristock and Catherine G. Taylor. Toronto: University of Toronto Press.

Broza, María Paz. 2000. En torno a la definición del Contact Improvisation desde una triple perspectiva: coreográfica, acrobática y pedagógica. *Revista digital* 22.
http://www.efdeportes.com/efd22a/ci.htm.

Butt, Gavin. 2005. *After Criticism. New Responses to Art and Performance*. Oxford: Blackwell Publishing.

Carlson, Marvin. 2004 [1996]. *Performance: a Critical Introduction*. London / New York: Routledge.

De Lauretis, Teresa. 1990. Eccentric Subjects: Feminist Theory and Historical Consciousness. *Feminist Studies* 16: 115-150.

Dubatti, Jorge. 2007. *Filosofía del Teatro I, Convivio, Experiencia, Subjetividad*. Buenos Aires: Atuel.

Gallop, Jane. 2002. *Anecdotal Theory*. Durham and London: Duke University Press.

Gómez-Peña, Guillermo. 2005. *Ethno-techno: Writings on Performance, Activism and Pedagogy*. London and New York: Routledge.

Guattari, Félix, and Suely Rolnik. 2006. *Micropolítica. Cartografías del deseo*. Madrid: Traficantes de Sueños.

Jones, Amelia. 1998. *Body Art: Performing the Subject*. Minneapolis/London: Minnesota University Press.

McKenzie, Jon. 2001. *Perform or Else. From Discipline to Performance*. London/New York: Routledge.

Miller, Nancy. 1991. *Getting personal. Feminist occasions and other autobiographical acts*. London/New York: Routledge.

Muñoz, Esteban José. 1999. *Disidentifications: Queers of Color and the Performance of Politics*. Minneapolis: University of Minnesota Press.

Phelan, Peggy and Jill Lane, eds. 1998. *The Ends of Performance*. New York and London: New York University Press.

—. 1997. *Mourning Sex. Performing Public Memories*. London/New York: Routledge.

—. 1993. *Unmarked. The Politics of Performance*. London/New York: Routledge.

Piper, Adrian. 1990. "Xenophobia and the Indexical Present I: an essay." In *ReImaging America: The Arts of Social Change,* ed. O'Brien Mark. Philadelphia: New Society Press.

Pollock, Della. 1998. "Performing Writing." In *The Ends of Performance*, eds. Phelan Peggy and Jill Lane. New York/London: New York University Press.

Pratt, Mary Louise. 1999. "Arts of the Contact Zone." In *Ways of Reading,* eds. Bartholomae David and Anthony Petroksky. New York: Bedford/St. Martin's.

Romero, Pedro. 2007. "Actors, Situations, Outcomes. Theater Machine and Theater: Subaltern Stages in the Spanish State." In *A Theater without Theater*, eds. Blistene B. and Falguieres Borja-Villel. MACBA Barcelona and Fundaçáo de Arte Moderna e Contemporánea, Lisboa.

Schechner, Richard. 2002. *Performance Studies. An Introduction.* London /New York: Routledge.

Sloterdijk, Peter. 2003. *Experimentos con uno mismo.* Valencia: Pre-textos.

Talburt, Susan, and Shirley Steinberg. 2000. *Thinking Queer: Sexuality, Culture and Education.* Oxford/New York: Peter Lang Pub Inc.

Taylor, Diana. 2003. *The Archive and the Repertoire, Memory in the Americas.* Durham/London: Duke University Press.

Turner, Victor. 1969. *The Ritual Process.* Middlesex: Penguin Books.

CONTRIBUTORS

María J. Alcaraz is a Lecturer in Aesthetics at the University of Murcia, Spain. She has published "The rational justification of aesthetic judgments", in the *Journal of Aesthetics and Art Criticism* 66, (2008), "Art's Historical Nature" *Enrahonar* (2007), and is co-editor of *Significado, emoción y valor. Ensayos sobre Filosofía de la Música* (with Francisca Pérez-Carreño, 2008).

Inma Álvarez is a Lecturer at the Department of Languages, The Open University, United Kingdom. She is also a Visiting Lecturer at the Conservatorio Superior de Danza in Madrid, Spain. She has published "La imagen del movimiento. Danza fotografiada", *La balsa de la Medusa*, 1995; "El tesoro de Cervera", *Por la Danza*, 1996 ; "La temática religiosa en la danza teatral: el caso de Vesalii Icones." *Por la Danza*, 1998.

Alessandro Bertinetto is PhD Researcher at the University of Udine, Italy. He has published L'essenza dell'empiria. Saggio sulla prima «Logica trascendentale» di J. G. Fichte (2001), and Lineamenti di storia dell'estetica. La filosofia dell'arte da Kant al XXI secolo (with F. Vercellone and G. Garelli, 2008).

Noël Carroll is Distinguished Professor of Philosophy at The City University of New York, USA. He is the author of *The Philosophy of Motion Pictures* (2008), *Beyond Aesthetics* (2001), *Comedy Incarnate: Buster Keaton, Physical Humor and Bodily Coping*, (2007); and *Interpreting the Moving Image* (1998).

Miguel Corella is Associate Professor of Audiovisual Communication and Aesthetics at the Universidad Politécnica de Valencia, Spain. He specializes in art and politics, and the figure of the avant-garde artist. He is the author of *El artista y sus otros. Max Aub y la novela de artista* (2003).

Paola Esposito is a PhD Candidate in Social Anthropology in the Department of Anthropology and Geography at the Oxford Brookes University, UK. She has published "Il Film come Danza: la Raprresentazione del Butoh come Destrutturazione del Rapporto SoggettoOggetto", in *Cent'anni di Danza: Omaggio a Kazuo Ohno*, (2007).

Susan L. Feagin is the Editor of *The Journal of Aesthetics and Art Criticism* and visiting research professor of philosophy in the Department of Philosophy at Temple University. She is the author of *Reading with Feeling* (1996), co-editor of *Aesthetics* (1997), and editor of *Global Theories of the Arts and Aesthetics* (2007), as well as numerous articles that deal with issues on the relationships between mind and art.

Antonio García is a Lecturer in the Department of Fine Arts at the Universidad de Murcia, Spain. He is the author of *Diving into the relationships between cinema and painting. Analyzing cinematographic types* (2004), "La inhumana. Cine y pintura de vanguardia. La historia de un flirteo tan inconciliable como provechosos" in Ortiz, A. *et. al. Del cuadro al encuadre: la pintura en el cine* (2007), and "La pintura de Gerhard Richter y sus aproximaciones a la estética del cine negro. El ciclo 18 de octubre, 1977", in Morgado, B. *et. al., En torno al arte* (2008).

Antoni Gomila is Professor of Psychology at the University of the Balearic Islands, Spain. He is the editor, with Paco Calvo, of the *Elsevier Handbook of Cognitive Science: an embodied approach* (2008).

Francisco Guillén is a Lecturer in the Department of Fine Arts at the Universidad de Murcia (Spain). He has written "El rostro en viaje hacia el retrato", in Pérez, F. and E. Santos, *La alteridad vestida. Una experiencia de arte y subjetividad* (2008). Exhibitions: *Donación*, 2009, The Drawing Center, New York; and Terrestral, 2007, at HbK. Kassel.

James R. Hamilton is a member of the Philosophy Department at Kansas State University. He specializes in Aesthetics and has written *The Art of Theater* (2007).

Doris Kolesch is Professor of Theaterwissenschaft at the Freien Universität Berlin, and a member of the Jungen Akademie at the Berlin-Brandenburgischen Akademie der Wissenschaften. She is the author of *Theater der Emotionen. Ästhetik und Politik zur Zeit Ludwigs XIV.* (2006), and *Das Schreiben des Subjekts. Zur Inszenierung ästhetischer Subjektivität bei Charles Baudelaire, Roland Barthes und Theodor W. Adorno,* (1996). She is also editor of *Stimm-Welten. Philosophische, medientheoretische und ästhetische Perspektiven* (with Vito Pinto and Jenny Schrödl, 2009).

Sven Kristersson is a Senior Lecturer in Singing at The Malmö Academy of Music, University of Lund, and a doctoral student at Academy of Music and Drama, University of Gothenburg. His discography includes *Mélodies* by Francis Poulenc and *Chamber Samba*. He has also translated operas like *The Magic Flute* and *Carmen*. Together with three other Swedish singing teachers, he has published a pedagogical work on singing technique, including a DVD: *Fyra sångpedagoger*.

David Levin is Associate Professor of Philosophy in the Department of Germanic Studies, the Committee on Cinema & Media Studies, and the Committee on Theater and Performance Studies at the University of Chicago (USA). Among his main publications are *Unsettling Opera: Staging Mozart, Verdi, Wagner, and Zemlinsky* (Forthcoming), and *Richard Wagner, Fritz Lang, and the Nibelungen: The Dramaturgy of Disavowal* (1998).

Graham McFee is Professor of Philosophy at the University of Brightom, and at California State University Fullerton. He is the author of *Understanding Dance* (1994), *The concept of dance education* (2004); and *Ethics, Knowledge and Truth in Sport Research: An Epistemology of Sport* (forthcoming [2009]).

Héctor J. Pérez is Associate Professor of Audiovisual Communication and Aesthetics at the Department of Audiovisual Communication, Documentation and History of Art and a member of the Technology and Information Group, CALSI, at the Universidad Politécnica de Valencia, Camino de Vera s/n, 46002 Valencia. He is also Director of the Postgraduate Program in Music. His main publications are "Shakespeare jenseits des Dramas", Nietzsche-Studien 27, 1998; El Nacimiento de la tragedia. Un ensayo sobre la metafísica del artista *en el joven Nietzsche* (2001); *La naturaleza en el arte posmoderno* (2004); "Opera Narratives:

From Mythology to Audiovisual Aesthetics", in *The International Journal of Technology, Knowledge and Society*, 2006.

Francisca Pérez-Carreño is Professor of Aesthetics and Theory of the Arts at the University of Murcia. She is the author of *Arte Minimal. Objeto y sentido* (2004), "Looking at metaphors", in *Journal of Aesthetics and Art Criticism* 58(4), 2000; and is the editor of *Significado, emoción y valor. Ensayos sobre Filosofía de la Música* (with María J. Alcaraz, 2010).

Salvador Rubio is a Lecturer in Aesthetics at the University of Murcia. He is the author of *Comprender en arte* (1995) / *Comprendre en art* (2006) y *Como si lo estuviera viendo* (forthcoming 2010).

Rosella Simonari is a PhD student at the Univesity of Essex, with a research project on Martha Graham's *Letter to the World*. She is member of the SDR (Society for Dance Research), SDHS (Society of Dance History Scholars) and AIRDanza (Associazione Italiana per la Ricerca sulla Danza). She has presented papers and published essays on Martha Graham, Carmen and Alberto Spadolini.

Judit Vidiella is a Lecturer of Visual Arts Education and Visual Culture Studies at the University of Barcelona (Spain), and a member of the performance group *Corpus Deleicti*. Her main publications are "Posicions desubicades?, espais deslocalitzats? Geografies del performance", in *Papers d'Art* 88, (2005); "Beyond Lucian Freud: Exploring Body Representations in Children's Culture", with Fernando Hernández, in *International Journal of Education Through Art* 2 (2) (2006), and "Performatividad y poder. Políticas de representación e identidad: corporización y performance", *DCO, danzacuerpobsesión* 7 (2007).

INDEX

Abbate, Carolyn, 60, 61
Acín, Ramón, 208
actor(s), 3-4, 6-7, 11, 16, 17, 18, 20, 21, 28, 30-31, 35, 80, 105, 111, 112, 120, 207, 219, 232n, 237, 238, 240, 244, 249-257, 259, 267, 269
Acts of Light, 159
Adorno, Theodor, 104
Aeschylus, 63n
aesthetic ambiguity, 243
aesthetic distance, 12, 218, 219, 231, 239, 240, 242
aesthetic experience, 2, 3, 98, 103, 107, 218, 226, 228-229, 231, 235
aesthetic phenomena, 240
aesthetic properties, 6
aesthetic reception, 73
aesthetic revolution, 54
aesthetic value, 6, 66, 67, 68, 71, 94, 99
aesthetics, 95, 102, 103, 133, 146n, 157, 203, 214, 242, 253, 259
    contemporary aesthetics, 67, 104
    formalist aesthetics, 68, 82
Alfons, Sven, 43
Algulin, Ingemar, 43, 45
Alison's House, 157
American Document, 160
ancient Greece, 44, 161
Animal Farm, 28
Anscombe, Elizabeth, 131
Antonioni, Michelangelo, 257
Appalachian Spring, 160
Appiah, Anthony, 105, 106
appreciation, 2, 12, 33, 86, 87, 92, 96, 99, 100, 119, 124, 131, 135, 136, 138, 140, 142, 143n, 145n, 226
Aragon, Louis, 250
Argonautica, 45

Aristotle, 52
Armida, 108, 110
art, 2-3, 9, 12, 28, 38, 46, 50, 55, 58, 66, 67, 81, 95, 99, 102, 103, 104, 105, 107, 113, 114n, 119, 120, 123, 127, 132, 142n, 144n, 191, 195, 218, 219, 226, 228-231, 232n, 237, 240-241, 257, 259 *See* also performance art, performing arts, visual arts
    abstract art, 10, 92, 96, 97
    body art, 236
    Bourgeois art, 10
    contemporary art, 235, 240, 253
    narrative art, 5, 74, 87, 94, 96, 98
    representational art, 10, 67, 75, 88, 93, 99
Artaud, Antonin, 239, 243, 259
artist(s), 1-3, 5, 7, 36, 38-39, 46, 64, 81, 92, 93, 97, 103-104, 106-107, 114n, 126-131, 137, 139, 142, 144n, 171, 218, 220-223, 225, 227, 230, 237, 238, 242, 248, 252-254, 257, 258-259 *See* also performance artist
    abstract artists, 256
    Baroque artists, 251
    artistic methods, 11, 39
    artistic nature, 4, 228
artistic practices, 4, 102, 238, 265
    artistic research, 10, 35, 36, 38, 39, 46
    artistic traditions, 2, 36
artwork(s), 1, 2, 5, 38, 67, 82, 118, 119, 120, 127-132, 136, 143n, 218, 219, 228, 229, 242
Ashton, Dore, 106
Atkins, Malcolm, 170
atonalism, 69, 81, 82, 83
audience, 1, 3, 6-12, 20, 26, 29, 30-31,

33-38, 44-45, 60-61, 66, 68-70, 72-73, 75, 77, 78, 80, 81, 82, 90-91, 93, 100, 131-133, 142, 144n, 152, 153, 158, 162n, 172, 185, 187-189, 192-194, 196-198, 218-225, 227-230, 231n, 232n, 236-245, 264, 268 *See* also public, spectator
Austin, James, 122, 129
avant-garde, 7, 8, 22, 102, 103, 113, 185, 222, 238, 252, 254, 259
Bacon, Francis, 42, 255
Bakhtin, Mikhail, 61
Balzac, Honoré de, 106
Bar Mitzvah Boy, 132
Barthes, Roland, 104, 105
Baryshnikov, Mikhail, 126, 128
Bataille, Georges, 104
Bauhaus, 248
Becque, Catherine, 122
Beethoven, Ludwig, 69, 111, 112, 114
Benjamin, Walter, 4, 104, 105
Berg, Alan, 51
Best, David, 131
Birth of a Nation, 199
Black Angels, 122
body, 4, 5, 12, 33, 41, 94, 111, 155, 162, 169, 172, 184, 236, 240, 241, 243, 244, 245, 250, 251, 263, 264, 265, 267, 268, 269, 271, 273n, 274n
Bordwell, David, 188
Borgdorff, Henk, 36, 38
Borges, Jorge Luis, 108
Bourne, Matthew, 129
Box, Richard, 258
Brahms, Johannes, 71, 111, 207
Brecht, Bertolt, 31, 207, 248, 259
Breton, André, 250
Breuer, Joseph, 51, 52
Breugel, Pieter, 133
Brittle Heaven, 157
Brook, Peter, 10, 35
Bruce, Christopher, 121, 122
Büchner, Georg, 257
Buñuel, Luis, 12, 203, 204, 207, 208, 209, 210, 211, 212, 213, 214, 251, 260n

Burge, Lucy, 122
Cage, John, 103, 249, 253
Camus, Marcel, 40, 170
Castiglione, Baldassare, 44
Cèzanne, Paul, 106, 247, 253, 256, 259
Chaplin, Charlie, 253
character(s), 6-8, 10, 16-21, 24, 26, 28, 31, 33, 50, 52-54, 60-62, 74-75, 77, 88, 92, 94, 96, 105, 107-113, 120, 125, 152-153, 155, 157-158, 160-161, 172, 174, 183-185, 189, 193, 196-197, 208, 238, 239, 240, 255
character types, 31
choreography, 126-128, 138, 144n, 161, 170, 249, 271
choreology, 161
choreosophy, 152, 156, 159, 161
choreutics, 161
chorus, 57, 60
cinema, 4-5, 9-10, 60, 77, 83, 98, 158, 175, 182-183, 185, 188-189, 195, 197, 199, 204, 247, 251, 252, 259, *See* also film, documentary
cinema studies, 7, 182, 200
cinematic image, 184, 186, 187
cinematic laws, 79
cinematographic, 8, 212, 213
Cocteau, Jean, 40, 170
cognitivist, 7, 19, 20, 25, 27n, 72, 124, 182-183, 187-189, 194-195, 200-201, 203-205
composer, 5-6, 12, 36, 40, 43, 61, 68, 69, 70, 72-74, 78, 81, 93, 97-100, 108-113, 120, 170, 220, 222, 250
conductor, 1, 7, 111-113
consciousness, 24, 227
self-consciousness, 18, 271
conventions, 2, 5, 13, 22, 72, 159, 168, 222, 259
corporeality, 8, 270
costumes, 5, 18, 25, 53, 153, 162, 172
Craig, Gordon, 259
creativity, 1, 81, 110, 131, 152, 154, 159, 160
criterial prefocusing, 8, 192, 194, 196, 201

critical reflection, 17
critics, 42, 62, 152, 160, 236
Cubist, 102, 119
culture, 22, 54, 64n, 123, 183, 200,
    220, 235, 237, 268, 269, 273n, 274n
    American culture, 160
    German culture, 81
    Hellenic culture, 161
    Japanese culture, 168
    popular culture, 167, 170
    Western culture, 43, 197
    cultural exchange, 39
    cultural life, 36
    cultural norms, 106
    cultural politics, 266, 267
Cunningham, Merce, 120, 121, 142,
    249, 255
d'Occam, Guillaume, 258
da Milano, Francesco, 44
Dahl, Roald, 111, 112
dance, 2, 6, 7, 10, 12, 52, 56, 59, 60,
    94, 113, 118, 120-135, 137, 138,
    140-142, 151-154, 156, 158, 159,
    161, 168, 169-171, 175, 178n, 219,
    222, 232, 238, 243, 247-249, 251,
    268, 271
    abstract dance, 94
    American dance, 160
    butoh dance, 4, 12, 167-170, 178n
    classical dance, 271
    contact dance, 267, 271
    Western dance, 168
    dance studies, 161
dancer(s), 2, 5, 12, 79, 120-131, 133,
    134, 138-142, 143n, 144n, 145n,
    151, 159, 162n, 168, 173, 175,
    232n, 244, 248, 249, 250
    butoh dancer, 167
danceworks, 12, 120, 121, 124-127,
    131, 142
dancing, 4, 6, 7, 62, 130, 133, 151,
    154, 155, 159, 167, 168, 232n
Deafman Glance, 275
decoro, 44
Deeper than Reason, 68, 74
Deleuze, Gilles, 155, 272

Der Blaue Reiter, 82
Der Rosenkavalier, 63n
Derrida, Jacques, 105
Dickinson, Emily, 6, 151-161
Die Sonette an Orpheus, 40
Die Welt des Tänzers, 161
Diener, Melanie, 53
director, 10, 27n, 30-31, 35, 37, 39, 40,
    53, 54, 62n, 134, 162n, 193, 197,
    238
disindividualisation, 7, 107
documentaries, 8, 9, 12, 203-209, 213-
    215
Don Giovanni, 54, 110
Doolittle, Hilda, 157
Dowland, John, 36-40, 43
drama, 4, 35, 170, 171, 232n, 258
    melodrama, 189, 197, 259
dramatic, 39, 52, 60, 62n, 96, 103, 155,
    171, 209, 244, 251
dramaturgy, 55, 58, 60, 247, 249, 256,
    259
DVD, 38, 53, 54, 63n
Einstein on the Beach, 253
Eisenstein, Sergei, 197
Ek, Mats, 129
Elektra, 11, 50, 51, 52, 53, 54, 55, 60,
    62, 63n, 64n, 65n
embodiment, 10, 45, 46, 53, 59, 152,
    238, 262, 269, 271
emotion, 7-12, 16, 17, 18, 21, 51, 66-
    75, 78, 80, 86-100, 112, 167, 173,
    174, 183, 187-201, 203-209, 212-
    214, 220, 223, 225, 226, 232n, 249,
    257
    moral emotions, 8, 183, 194, 195,
    196, 198-199, 201, 207
emotional address, 188, 189
emotional appraisal, 198
emotional character, 94, 207
emotional content, 69, 75, 95, 220
emotional effect, 211
emotional engagement, 99
emotional events, 67
emotional experience, 10, 66, 69, 75,
    78, 79, 204

emotional impact, 189, 213
emotional involvement, 77, 82, 203
emotional life, 80
emotional meanings, 220
emotional mousetrap, 208
emotional nature., 207
emotional property, 98
emotional puzzle, 167
emotional quality, 26
emotional response, 8, 9, 10, 11, 66,
    73, 74, 75, 87, 88, 90, 91, 92, 93,
    95, 96, 97, 98, 99, 100, 193, 197,
    205, 224
emotional state, 7, 67, 69, 70, 75, 77,
    86, 87, 89, 91, 92, 93, 94, 95, 97,
    98, 99, 100, 135, 192, 193, 194
emotionally expressive, 73, 79
empathy, 76, 82, 134, 189, 207, 243,
    245
Emperor Concerto, 112
Erdman, Jane, 151
evaluation, 19, 40, 118, 189, 191, 192
    self-evaluation, 45
experientialist, 19
experimentation, 104, 105, 106, 262,
    267, 268, 271
expression, 3, 5, 6, 7, 9, 11, 12, 16, 17,
    18, 29, 37, 42, 43, 45, 46, 50-55, 58,
    67-75, 77, 78, 80, 81, 82, 86, 90, 91,
    102-108, 112, 113, 118, 140, 159,
    170, 176, 177, 223, 225, 232n, 235,
    243, 248, 256, 259, 265
    aesthetic expression, 70
    experience of expression, 9, 67
    expression of emotion, 11, 16, 17,
    68, 71
    expression of pain, 235
    expression of sadness, 71, 87, 88,
    89, 93, 94, 99, 214
    expression of subjectivity, 7, 11, 50,
    54-55, 58, 102-105, 107, 112-113,
    118
    means of expression, 37, 223, 225
    methods of expression, 177
    musical expression, 9, 50, 70, 75,
    80, 86

theory of expression, 69, 75
Expressionism, 7, 74, 81, 102-104,
    254, 256
    expressionist, 10, 57, 60, 68, 81, 82,
    102-104, 252, 253, 254, 265
    neo-expressionist, 102
expressive aspects, 75
expressive attitudes, 10
expressive behaviour, 135
expressive character, 10, 90
expressive codes, 69, 72, 81
expressive conception, 6, 76
expressive content, 2, 67, 69, 73, 74,
    80, 81, 82, 90, 95, 93, 100, 106
expressive dimension, 67, 77
expressive discourse, 254
expressive elements, 71, 72
expressive features, 71, 76, 78, 89,
    232n
expressive force, 168
expressive gesture, 7, 70, 113
expressive intention, 1, 6, 9, 72 80
expressive means, 58
expressive origins, 58
expressive perception, 67-70, 71, 73,
    75, 79, 80, 81
expressive possibilities, 256
expressive power, 82
expressive properties, 1, 2, 10, 90, 93,
    94, 95, 231
expressive qualities, 67, 68, 94
expressive resources, 73, 74, 81
expressiveness, 12, 29, 67, 68, 80, 86,
    95, 144n
expressivity, 6, 10, 68, 72, 225, 265
feelings, 7, 11, 16-21, 24, 25, 26, 70,
    71, 135, 138, 156, 174, 187, 188,
    190, 195, 199, 204, 206, 208, 213,
    232n, 256, 257
    ambiguous feeling, 78
    feeling of discomfort, 12, 209
    feeling state, 87
    qualitative feeling, 73
    spectators' feelings, 257
    subjective feelings, 188, 256
fiction, 3, 8, 96, 98, 188, 191, 192,

193, 201, 203, 205, 206, 216, 220
fiction author, 205
fiction paradox, 8, 12, 205, 206
theory of fiction, 205
fictionality, xii, 24
film, xi, 4, 8, 9, 60, 146, 166, 170, 178,
    182, 183, 185, 207-209, 211-213,
    216, 237, 241, 249, 255, 257, 262,
    278 *See* also cinema
    essay film, 204
    film making, 4
    film theorists, 182,184, 187, 188,
    200
    film theory, 188, 201, 216
film producer, 60
filming, 215, 205
filmmaker, 4, 40, 185, 253, 257
Firebird, 126
Fischer-Lichte, Erika, 3, 219ff, 231n
Flaherty, Robert, 204, 214
Flavin, Dan, 258
Fo, Dario, 35
formalist, 10, 68, 79, 83
    formalist atonalism, 82
    formalist purity, 9
    non-formalist account, 74
    non-formalist aesthetics, 68
Foucault, Michel, 104, 105
Four Colors, Four Words, 257
Frege, Gottlob, 124, 135, 136, 148
Freud, Sigmund, 51, 52, 105, 108, 114,
    186, 280
Frontier, 160, 165
Futurist, 102,
Georg Friedrich Händel's
    Resurrection, 109
gesture(s), 7, 21, 27n, 31, 63n, 67, 70,
    74, 93, 94, 96, 102, 112, 113, 135,
    197, 249, 253, 274, 277, 278
Ghost Dances, 121,
Gilfond, Edythe, 153
Gilgamesh, 10, 20, 21, 26, 37, 38, 39,
    40, 47
Giménez Caballero, Ernesto, 262
Glaspell, Susan, 157
Glittenberg, Rolf, 53, 57

Gluck, Christoph Williband, 170
Gómez de la Serna, Ramón, 262, 263,
    264
Gómez Peña, Guillermo, 272, 275
Gould, Glenn, 128
Graham, Martha, vi, 6, 12, 122, 151-
    153, 155, 156, 159-166, 249, 255,
    280
    Graham technique, 162
Gravity's Rainbow, 40
grazia, 44, 45
Guattari, Félix, 155, 163, 267, 272,
    275
Hackl, Heidi, 53
Hall, Jesper, 35
Hamilton, James, v, 2, 6, 7, 11, 13, 16,
    21, 22, 23, 27, 30, 34, 126, 143n,
    148, 232n, 278
happening(s), 126, 129, 145n, 219,
    220, 221, 223, 226, 231n
harmony, 46, 75, 81, 82, 231
    classical harmony, 51
Hayworth, Rita, 266
Hoffmann, E.T.A., 108, 110, 114n, 115
Holborn, Mark, 168
Homer, 37
Horst, Louis, 153
Ibarz, Mercè, 207
Ibsen, Henrik, 253
identity, 1, 46, 51, 62n, 104-107, 111,
    114n, 128, 129, 144n, 149, 154,
    172, 174, 238, 244, 253, 266, 267,
    268, 271-272, 273n, 274n
Iliad, 45
imagination, 3, 5, 9, 26, 57, 106, 107,
    150, 206, 228, 244
improvisation, 3, 5, 6, 44, 127, 167,
    171, 222, 224-225, 231n, 269, 274n
interaction(s), 78, 167, 172, 174, 175,
    177, 209, 220-222, 224-226, 229,
    230, 233, 239, 264, 268
    emotional interaction, 76
    intersubjective interaction, 68, 75
intuition(s), 7, 17, 70, 197
Ion, 28
irony, 107, 111, 154, 160

Ivanov, Sergei, 128
James, William, 195
Jay, Martin, 104, 105, 115
jazz, 38, 223, 230, 231, 233, 234
Johansson, Eva, 53, 55
Johnson, Hunter, 153
judgment(s), 2, 8, 72, 118, 124, 126,
    128, 133, 136, 140, 143n
Jung, Carl, 64
Kandinsky, Vaslav, 82
Keaton, Buster, 253, 276
Kierkegaard, Søren, 110
kineaesthetic sense, 133
King Lear, 254
Kivy, Peter, 3, 4, 10, 28, 29, 30, 32, 34,
    71, 81, 82, 84, 86ff, 101, 143n,
    145n, 148, 222, 233
Kline, Franz, 253
Kolesch, Doris, vii, 8, 12, 20, 27, 235,
    279
Koran, 37
Kosuth, Joseph, 257
Kramer, Lawrence, 52, 53, 64
Krauss, Rosalind, 113
Kusej, Martin, 11, 53, 54, 56, 57, 59ff
Kvalbein, Astrid, 38
L'Inhumaine, 254
La Clemenza di Tito, 54
Laban, Rudolf, 161, 163
Labanotation, 121
Lacan, Jacques, 64, 184, 187
Lang, Fritz, 253
Lang, Pearl, 151, 156, 165
language, 4, 41ff, 60, 61, 65, 67, 81,
    83, 105, 121, 148, 156, 158, 161,
    177, 186, 200, 242, 250, 253, 259,
    266, 268
    artistic languages, 81
Las Hurdes. Tierra sin pan, 12, 203,
    207ff
Laureter, Arch, 153, 165, 166
Legnani, Pierina, 122, 144n
Lerbier, Marcel, 254
Letter to the World, 151, 152, 153,
    154, 155, 163, 164, 165
libretto, 55, 56, 61, 62, 64, 251, 254

lieder, 35, 36, 39
lighting, 18, 25, 55, 193, 248, 251, 253
Lighting field, 254
Lipovsek, Marjana, 53
literature, 3, 5, 10, 28, 36, 39, 40, 74,
    84, 95, 108, 111, 119, 159, 164
Lohengrin, 258
Longfellow, Henry Wadsworth, 157
Lulu, 51
Lyotard, Jean-François, 104, 105, 114
Marey, Jules, 255
McCollum, Allan, 252
medium, 11, 67, 69, 146, 239, 241,
    244, 247
Midnight's Children, 31
Miller, Cristanne, 157
Milloss, Aurel, 161
mimesis, 62, 67, 246
mimetic, 57, 61
mirror neurons, 133, 135, 137, 145,
    146
mise-en-scene, 61
Molina Foix, Vicente, 250
Monet, Claude, 113
mood(s), 6, 7, 11, 16-26, 27n, 73, 153-
    154, 158, 174, 224, 253, 257
    mood changes, 7
Moore, Michael, 214
moral actions, 198
moral affect, 196
moral assessment, 196
moral codes, 202, 242
moral concern, 196
moral domains, 199-200
moral interests, 197-198
moral judgments, 195-196, 202
moral reasoning, 195
moral systems, 200
moral viewpoint, 161
Moses und Aron, 51
motion, 18
motion pictures, 7, 12, 148, 182-183,
    188, 192-196, 2902, 277. See also
    movies
movement, 29-30, 41, 59, 68, 71, 74,
    78-81, 92-97, 109, 113, 120-127,

127, 132-139, 147, 148, 149, 151, 154, 156-161, 162n, 167-171, 192, 215n, 219, 236, 251, 253, 255, 268-272, 273n

movies, 5, 12, 182-183, 185, 187-190-201, 253, 274n,

Mozart, Wolfgang Amadeus, 54, 108, 110, 254, 279

Muff, Alfred, 53

Müller, Heiner, 250

music, v-vi, xi, 4, 6-11, 26n, 35-41, 44, 47, 49, 52-53, 56, 58, 61-62, 63n, 65-85, 86-99, 100n, 101, 103, 106-114, 120, 125, 131, 136, 138, 143n, 145n, 148-149, 153, 155, 158, 162, 165, 166, 171, 174, 178, 179, 207, 209, 213, 219, 222, 224, 231n, 235, 238, 249, 279

absolute music, 10, 88, 92, 93, 97-100

atonal music, 82

expressive music, 80, 87, 90, 91, 98

Turkish music, 38

musical experience, 66-67, 69, 71, 78, 83, 86

musical expression, 5, 9, 11, 50, 66, 70, 75, 77, 80, 84, 86

musical expressiveness, 86, 101

musical work, 1, 11, 32, 72, 88, 95, 120, 124, 142

musician(s), 1, 9, 10, 12, 32, 36, 40, 82, 107, 113,'120, 127, 174, 175-176

Muybridge, Eadweard, 255

My Name as though It Were on the Surface of the Moon, 257

narrative, 5, 7, 10, 16-22, 26, 33-34, 40, 52, 60, 68, 74, 83, 100, 119, 158, 167, 170, 183, 185, 187, 193, 194, 206, 270, 271, 273n, 279

collective narrative, 52

narrative architecture, 40

narrative structure, 105, 186

narrative temporality, 107

narrative voice, 74

non-fictional narratives, 21, 26

theatrical narrative, 7

narrativization, 51

Nauman, Bruce, 257

New Science, 45, 47

Nietzsche, Friedrich, 104, 107, 279

Nikolais, Alwin, 143n

Ninth Symphony, 69

Nono, Luigi, 250

normativity, 124, 136, 270

Novalis, 42

novel, 3, 7 28, 30-34, 95, 96, 99, 105, 107, 110, 171, 218

artist novel, 7, 11, 102, 16-108

realist novel, 104

romantic novel, 111

novelist(s), 40

Nureyev, Rudolf, 126, 128

Nye, Edward, 156

Odyssey, 45,

Offenbach, Jacques, 110

One Thousand and One Nights, 37

opera, xi, 11, 40, 60-54, 58, 60,61, 62n, 63n, 64n, 108, 110, 113, 125, 128, 143n, 167, 170, 247, 249, 253, 254, 279

opera composers, 40

opera house, 53

orchestra, 1, 6, 56, 64n, 111, 113, 131, 235

Orfeu Negro, 40, 170

Origin of Species, 139

originality, 81, 113, 115, 224, 231

Orlando, 259

Orphée, 170

Orpheus, 4, 11, 12, 40-47, 167, 169-178

Orpheus myth, 40, 45, 169

Orwell, George, 28

Ovid, 40, 45

painter(s), 1, 40, 82, 106, 123, 256, 257, 258, 260

impressionist painters, 82

painting, 2, 5, 82, 113, 119, 130, 143n, 144n, 150, 221, 230, 238, 241, 251, 253, 255, 256, 259, 260, 278

abstract painting, 92

avant-garde painting, 113
contemporary painting, 255
cubist painting, 119
pantomime, 80
Parrot, Karin, 36
Paxton, Steve, 268
Pelléas and Mélisande, 258
perception, 50, 67, 77, 82, 83, 84, 90,
    93-98, 107, 104, 120, 133, 134,
    143n, 167, 190, 192, 221, 235, 238,
    239-240, 244, 247, 251, 253, 258,
    272
    expressive perception 67-81
    sensory perception, 240
performance, v, vi, vii, xi, xii, 1-13,
    16-26, 27, 28-34, 35-47, 53, 66, 73,
    80, 83, 108-113, 120-132, 141,
    144n, 149-152, 157, 168-169, 171-
    178, 192, 218-229, 231, 232n, 236-
    237, 239, 244, 247, 250, 264, 265-
    267, 270, 272, 273n, 274n, 275, 280
    dance performance, 121, 126, 128,
    129
    expressive performance, 139
    narrative performance, 7, 16, 17
    performance art, vii, 3, 8, 12, 129,
    168, 177, 219, 222, 235-244, 266,
    267, 268, 292
    performance artists, 236, 238, 240,
    242
    theatrical performance, v, 2, 7, 11,
    12, 16, 17, 20-25, 26, 29, 34, 111,
    172, 238
*Performance—Revealing the Orpheus
    Within,* 43
performative, vi, xi, 1, 4-8, 11, 12, 107,
    113, 167, 172, 178, 204, 220, 223-
    228, 263, 265, 266, 270, 271, 273n,
performer(s), v, 1, 3, 4, 6-9, 11, 16-22,
    25, 27n, 34, 30, 32-34, 35, 43-45,
    66, 109-114, 119, 120, 122, 123,
    126-133, 142, 145n, 172, 219-223,
    228, 230, 231n, 232n, 238-243, 264,
    267, 268, 272,
    performers' intentions, 25
    physicality of performers, 11, 225

performing arts, vi, xi, 1, 2, 11, 12, 44,
    107, 109, 111, 112, 118, 120, 125,
    127, 129, 131, 149, 218-224, 230,
    248, 260, 264-265, 279
Petipa, Marius, 122, 126, 128, 144n,
    145n
photographs, 154, 164, 236, 241
photography, 238, 239, 241,
physicality, 7, 11, 16, 17, 20, 21, 25,
    26, 120, 123, 175, 221, 225
Picasso, Pablo, 106
Piper, Adrian, 268
Plato, 7, 28, 33, 184, 189,
pleasure, 59, 101, 107, 143n, 148, 227,
    231, 239, 263, 271
Poe, Edgar Allan, 255
poem(s), 42, 43, 71, 144n, 153-157,
    160, 162n, 163
poet(s), 40, 42, 43, 45, 46, 157
poetry, 6, 11, 29, 36, 39, 41-45, 83,
    144n, 151, 152, 156, 157, 159, 163,
    164, 170, 233, 255,
    epic poetry, 37
Pohl, Frederick, 157
Pollini, Maurizio, 128
Portrait, Still life, Landscape, 252
Poulenc, Francis, 35, 279
prejudice, 17, 19
production, 4, 5, 6, 11, 12, 19, 28, 30,
    31, 33, 39, 40, 50-62, 64n, 144n,
    160, 162, 167, 169, 176-178, 193,
    220, 230, 243, 254
    production process, 4, 5, 12
proprioception, 133, 149
props, 10, 18, 25, 29, 143n
psychoanalysis, 50, 51, 63n, 164, 182,
    186, 187, 188
psychological states, 67, 74
public, 1, 3, 5, 8, 51, 70, 112, *See* also
    audience, spectator
Puccini, Giacomo, 51
puppets, 3, 17
    superpuppet, 259
    Pyncheon, Thomas, 40
Pythagoras, 161
Quignard, Pascal, 115

Rashed, Karim, 37
Rauschenberg, Robert, 259
Raymonda, 125, 126
reactions, 12, 16, 23-26, 88, 94, 188, 189, 207, 221, 222, 225
  emotional reactions, 88
reading, 3, 4, 28-32, 34, 60-61, 65, 100, 106, 114n, 144n, 149, 158, 168, 218, 219, 262, 264, 266
  reading practices, 29
  silent reading, 3, 28, 29, 32, 34
Rear Window, 185
reception, 1, 19, 24, 25, 55, 73, 164, 205, 215, 272
recognition, 6, 7, 17, 18, 19, 20, 24, 32, 70, 74, 77, 78, 113, 123, 126, 132, 136, 143n, 156, 168, 187, 189, 195, 200
  misrecognition, 183, 186
  pattern recognition, 77, 189, 195
  pictorial recognition, 187
Reed, Lou, 255
rehearsal(s), 3-4, 11, 18, 28-34, 36, 54, 60, 65n, 129, 141, 169, 170, 171-172, 175
  theatrical rehearsal, 3
Renaissance, 40, 43, 45
representation, 4-5, 8, 16, 21, 26, 74, 84, 103, 199, 223, 225, 232n, 238, 243, 255, 263, 266-267, 273n, 280
  normative representations, 267
  representation of pain, 8
  self-representation, 267
  theatrical representation, 267
representational aesthetic, 242
representational content, 10, 67, 88, 93, 100
representational devices, 88
representational qualities, 97
resemblance, 68, 71, 72, 75, 78-100
  resemblance theories, 75
response, 1, 3, 6-9, 11, 17, 23, 25, 66, 70, 73-74, 76, 84, 86-88, 90-93, 95-100, 136, 140, 143n, 174, 187, 190, 193-195, 197, 199, 205, 221-224, 227, 242, 275

affective responses, 1, 6, 190, 195
appreciative responses, 7, 17, 95
bodily responses, 194
emotional responses, 8-11, 66, 73-75, 84, 87, 88, 90, 91, 92, 93, 95-100, 193, 197, 205, 224
empathic responses, 76
moral responses, 195
psychophysiological responses, 66
Rhodios, Apollonios, 45, 47
rhythm, 33, 113, 158, 206, 232n
  rhythmical speech, 38
Rilke, Rainer Maria, 40, 106
ritual, 44, 64n, 74, 136, 171-173, 176-177, 226, 232, 240, 265
  ritualization, 78, 81
Robinson, Jenefer, 68-69, 74-75, 84, 195, 201n
Romanticism, 67, 81, 107,
  Romantic aesthetics, 102
Rooley, Anthony, 43-47
Rosenthal, Jack, 144n
Rothko, Mark, 92, 142, 143n, 257
Rushdie, Salman, 32
Sánchez Cotán, Juan, 251
Schasching, Rudolf, 53
Schechner, Richard, 178, 276
Schönberg, Arnold, 38, 51, 82, 83, 106,122, 128
Schopenhauer, Arthur, 104
Schubert, Franz, 35
score, 5, 32, 56, 106, 108, 109, 121, 127, 258
screenwriters, 60
script, 1, 12, 31, 33, 35, 247
sculpture, 92, 103, 119, 238
  Minimalist sculpture, 103
Segal, George, 256, 260, 261
self-consciousness, 18, 233
sense of discomfort, 18
sense of self, 241, 243
senses, 70, 173, 240, 244, 254, 255, 257
setting, 55, 57, 73, 168, 174
Sewell, Elizabeth, 41, 42, 43, 45, 47
singer(s), 3, 10, 35, 38, 40, 45, 128

singing, 7, 35, 37, 39, 40, 43, 45, 51
  classical singing, 35, 39
  lieder singing, 39
Skriabin, 83
song(s), 11, 35, 37-41, 63n, 66, 73,
  115, 170, 171
  historical songs, 11
Sontag, Susan, 239, 241, 246, 253
Sophocles, 63n, 65
sound(s), 2, 5, 10, 17, 18, 21, 31, 41,
  44, 56, 84, 92-94, 100, 103-104,
  109, 111, 120, 122, 124, 141, 142,
  145n, 156-158, 163, 164, 173, 175,
  207, 211, 213, 219, 244, 250, 253,
  258
  sound montage, 207
  sound qualities, 44
  sound structure, 93
  soundtrack, 244
space, 9, 11, 19-20, 29, 35, 36, 37, 44,
  53, 55, 57, 64n, 103, 131, 143n,
  158, 172, 174, 175, 183, 230, 239,
  240, 247, 250, 251, 253, 256-259,
  263, 267-270, 272
  abstract spaces, 257
  expressive space, 53
  liminal spaces, 270
  mental space, 250
  performance space, 121
  performing space, 44
  pictorial space, 248
  rehearsal space, 175
  sacred space, 44
  social spaces, 268
  thinking space, 259
  virtual space, 249, 250
spatial sensations, 256
spectator, 1, 4, 6-9, 11, 17-25, 27n, 36,
  68, 71, 77, 82, 107, 112-113, 124,
  126, 144n, 183, 184, 185, 186, 187,
  201n, 218, 221, 222, 226, 227,
  232n, 239, 247, 249, 251, 254, 258,
  259, 267 See also audience, public
spectatorial engagement, 52
Sprechgesang, 38
sprezzatura, 44

stage, 1, 5, 10, 21, 28, 35-36, 38, 44,
  45, 51-53, 55, 57, 59, 62n, 64, 111,
  151, 154, 157-159, 219-220, 224,
  229, 235, 237-240, 242-245, 249,
  250, 251, 258, 259, 270-272, 276
  backstage, 157, 167, 171, 177
  downstage, 157
  stage directions, 56, 59
  stage director, 53
Stella Dallas, 197
Stepanov, Vladimir Ivanovich, 121
Still life (Room 8), 252
Stockhausen, Karl Heinz, 103
storytelling, 35-36
Strauss, Richard, 50-52, 55, 59-65
Studies in Hysteria, 52
style, 18, 22, 26, 63n, 74, 105, 108-109
  free style, 105, 108, 109
  regional styles, 200
subject, 9, 18, 41, 68, 73, 75, 77, 79,
  103-106, 108-112, 133, 138, 182-
  184, 186-188, 200, 201, 205, 227,
  235, 236, 239, 253, 265, 267, 268,
  270, 271, 272, 274n
subjective character, 68
subjective experience, 30, 74, 80, 174
subjective forms, 7, 108
subjective interiority, 58
subjective quality, 92, 227
subjective states, 50
subjective world, 82
subjectivity, 6-8, 10-12, 21, 50, 52, 54,
  55, 57-59, 63n, 75, 102-104, 107,
  109-114, 118-119, 123, 131, 142,
  167, 182-187, 194, 200, 201, 203,
  215, 235, 242, 247, 265, 266, 269,
  271
  alternative subjectivities, 267
  experience of subjectivity, 111, 235
  inter-subjectivity, 242
  objective subjectivities, 80
subjectivization, 52
Swan Lake, 121-122, 125, 128-129,
  144n
taboo(s), 199, 236-237, 240
technique(s), 138, 162, 235

television, 238, 241, 245
The Battleship Potemkin, 196
The Cabinet of Doctor Caligari, 60
The Dog from Pompey, 252
The Enchantress of Florence, 31
The Kreutzer Sonata, 110, 115
The Lady from the Sea, 253
The Magic Flute, 254, 279
The Magnificent Seven, 185
The Orphic Retreat, 43, 45
The Orphic Voice, 41, 45, 47
The Tales of Hoffmann, 110
The Unknown Masterpiece, 106
theatre, 4, 6-8, 11, 36, 39, 80, 120, 126,
    143n, 148, 163, 165-168, 171, 178,
    219, 222, 236-240, 242, 243, 245,
    248, 249, 250, 254, 257-261, 263,
    271
  ancient theatre, 8
  contemporary theatre, 243
  Greek theatre, 242
  postdramatic theatre, 243
  puppet theatre, 28
  theatre company, 4, 167
theatrical understanding, 23
Todd, John Emerson, 160, 161, 164
token, 1, 5, 74, 127, 128, 129, 144n,
    221
Tolstoy, Leo, 110
Tomassini, Stefano, 161, 164
tonality, 72, 79
Torr, Diane, 272
Toscanini, Arturo, 112
tradition, 2, 7, 10, 35, 36, 38-39, 44,
    107-108, 110, 119, 143n, 155, 167,
    170, 198, 200, 204, 241, 243-244,
    252-253, 256, 272,
  artistic traditions, 2, 36
  Shakespearean tradition, 10, 36
  theatrical and literary traditions, 11,
    39
tragedy, 35, 51, 52, 63n, 89
  Greek tragedy, 52
Turandot, 51

Turner, Victor, 171, 172, 179
Unanimist, 103
Val del Omar, José, 208
  moral values, 94
Vertigo, 191
Vertov, Dziga, 214
Vico, Giambattista, 45, 47
video, 113, 124, 133, 138, 139, 151,
    168, 173, 174, 247, 259
  video artist, 259
Video 50, 259
Vigo, Jean, 204, 214
Virgil, 40, 45
virtuosity, 32
visual arts, 74, 92, 170, 263, 280
voice, 20-21, 44, 51, 61, 67, 74, 102,
    105, 107, 111, 153, 157, 158, 159,
    207, 209, 213, 243, 244, 264, 265,
    266, 267, 270,
von Dohnányi, Christoph, 53
von Hofmannsthal, Hugo, 50-52, 55-
    59, 61, 62, 65
Vorticist, 102
Wagner, Richard, 65, 81, 258, 279
Warhol, Andy, 259
Westman, Lars, 38
Wiene, Robert, 60
Williams, Tennessee, 40
Williams, William Carlos, 157
Wilson, Robert, 12, 247, 248-260
Winterreise, 35
Wittgenstein, Ludwig, 76, 85, 125,
    127, 146-147, 149
Wolf, Hugo, 35
Wollheim, Richard, 1, 2, 13, 69, 85,
    100, 101, 120, 142, 144n, 150, 205,
    206, 207, 212, 216
  Work of art, 143n,
Woyzeck, 257
Wright, Frank Lloyd, 248
York, Vincent, 157
Yturralde, José María, 258
Zurbarán, Francisco de, 251
Zweig, Stefan, 109-110, 112, 115